SENECA

SENECA

The Life of a Stoic

Paul Veyne

*Translated from the French
by David Sullivan*

ROUTLEDGE
NEW YORK AND LONDON

Published in 2003 by
Routledge
29 West 35ᵗʰ Street
New York, NY 10001
www.routledge-ny.com

Published in Great Britain by
Routledge
11 New Fetter Lane
London EC4P 4EE
www.routledge.co.uk

Routledge is an imprint of the Taylor & Francis Group.

Originally published as *Sénèque: Entretiens Lettres a Lucilius*. Copyright © Editions Robert Laffont, S.A., 1993.

The publishers wish to record their thanks to the French Ministry of Culture for a grant towards the cost of translation.

Printed in the United States of America on acid-free paper.

10 9 8 7 6 5 4 3 2 1

Cataloging-in-Publication Data is available from the Library of Congress

ISBN 0–415–91125–7

CONTENTS

PREFACE

Born roughly at the beginning of the present era, Seneca committed suicide at the age of sixty-four, in 65 C.E., on Nero's orders, whose mentor he had been, and whose "friend" (an official title: in their palaces, the emperors did not hold court, but had appointed companions) he remained. For fifteen years, Seneca's destiny had been bound with those of Nero and his mother, Agrippina; his life and death are a sort of nonfiction novel of the Neronian period.

Seneca played other roles as well. To the French, at least since the Revolution, the ideal destiny of an author consists of three chapters, one consecrated to each of three noble endeavors: literature, women, and politics (thus Chenier and Shelley in the past, Malraux and Sartre today). In Rome, a century before Seneca, Cicero invented another model of the complete man: he should be at once senator, man of letters, and philosopher. Seneca had been Cicero's great successor in this triple role, and his contemporaries saluted him as such. Because of his abundant production of essays, and the tragedies that made him the Roman rival of the Greek dramatists in the eyes of his compatriots, he was their preeminent writer. He entered the Senate and belonged to the establishment governing the empire; he embodied its grandeur and its traditions; and he did more: he created one of the great investment banks of the century. Finally, he was, as we anticipated, a philosopher.

In the Greco-Roman world, philosophy was practiced by sects, much as in Asia. A philosopher was not concerned with philosophy in general, but was a Platonist, a Pythogorean, an Epicurean, or like Seneca, a Stoic. Philosophy was not part of a university curriculum, but an advanced study that attracted rich amateurs like Seneca and gave meaning to the lives of private citizens. Many took an interest in it out of cultural curiosity (a cultivated person needed at least a veneer of philosophy), but to truly be a philosopher was to live out the sect's doctrine, conform one's conduct (and even one's attire), to it, and if need be, to die for it. As disciplines of living and as the spirituality of the elite, the philosophical sects occupied the position filled in other societies by religion. Philosophers formed a kind of lay clergy, and like every clergy, they at once aroused respect, surly mockery, and occasionally the distrust of the imperial power. Seneca afforded proof of this, dying for his philosophy after spending his life attempting to reconcile it with his other professions as a politician and as an extraordinarily wealthy court favorite.

Sectarian knowledge versus academic instruction, spirituality and a discipline of living rather than cultural object, a lay clergy—all these traits are mutually self-explanatory. Certainly, an ancient philosophy, just as a modern one, was a system of generalization about the world, mankind, or knowledge; it implied a metaphysics, a philosophy of nature, a logic, and so forth. But it was also, and perhaps above all, an art of living, a wisdom. For Seneca, Stoic doctrine is almost exclusively reduced to these.

We cannot stress enough that this was an art of living, not a "morality." Despite its false reputation as a moralistic and voluntaristic system, Stoicism was rather an affair of the intellect and had nothing whatever to do with any "morality." Again, a comparison to Asia is in order. Like more than one philosophical Asian sect, Stoicism was, in the fullest meaning of the term, a recipe for individual happiness, although not in the way of Montaigne's art of living: it was rather a method of self-transformation. We shall see that at the end of his life, Seneca had almost completed his transformation into a sage, and from that drew the strength to die a brilliant death.

Seneca's philosophical opus, at least the part that survives to us, consists of two parts: the *Dialogues*, which are not genuine dialogues but might instead be called "Conversations about . . . "; and the famous *Letters to Lucilius*, which form the masterpiece of the dramatic final three years of his life. For a number of reasons, these offer the best introduction to his work.

One of these reasons is the modernity of their style: short, clear, penetrating, telling sentences that can make difficult questions accessible by means of a sudden metaphor. This has been the style of French intellectual prose since Montesquieu, and of our best journalism, but in antiquity it was considered the antithesis of what was viewed as high style, or eloquence: those ample Ciceronian periods in which, at times, the reader forgets the beginning before reaching the end. This was beside the point: ancient eloquence was in general a sort of bel canto, and like it, attracted innumerable fans. There were, indeed, exceptions such as Demosthenes, whose method was not to charm, to lull, or to seduce, but rather to project a nervous impulse to a captivated audience. Seneca's style follows in his path.

Despite his clarity, Seneca still must be taken seriously as a philosopher. The time is past when he was regarded as a belletrist lightly brushed with philosophy, studied only by specialists in Latin literature. His clarity reveals a firm conceptual foundation, that of Greek Stoicism in its authentic form: Seneca practiced neither a debased nor a vulgarized philosophy aimed at the supposed "practical spirit" of the Romans.

There is another reason to begin with the *Letters to Lucilius*: their exposition of Stoicism starts from the self, the *I* of the neophyte Lucilius, to whom they offer a knowingly graduated course in Stoicism and a series of exercises in self-persuasion. They start from the interest the *I* has in becoming a Stoic, and create the perception that the *I* is all-powerful, that only it matters, and that it can be sufficient unto itself. In order for unhappiness and death not to matter, it is enough to consider them as nothing; if the world is hostile, it is enough to ignore it; the *I* can do this, and the only thing that matters to it will remain, itself. This is so attractive that one wishes to believe it, and it is the reason the *Letters* are captivating reading from their opening pages.

There is, then, a contemporary application of Stoicism, precisely that suggested by the *Letters*, directed as they are to the person of a disciple: an egocentric Stoicism. It is no coincidence that the revival of Seneca began, in France at least, in the early 1980s, in a certain publishing circle connected with Michel Foucault, living under the threat of AIDS. In the face of death, the *I*, with its capacity for denial, is the only weapon remaining to us.

Stoicism has thus become, for our use, a philosophy of the active turning in on itself of the *I*, and of a determined denial of a menacing or absurd world. It was nothing of the kind in its own day, but the *Letters* permit us to view it as such. It has become an archaic, quaint, moving philosophy we dream of in a contemporary world where being has become unbearably light because no prescriptive authority remains; not nature, not god, not tradition, not Kant's imperative. Only the *I* can lay down its own laws, and it remains our only secure base. "Everything has gone, but *I* remain for myself," as Corneille's Medea says. *I*, face to face with the death that denies me, which is nothing if *I* decide that to me, death is nothing.

The role of this reinterpretation of Stoicism in Michel Foucault's interior life as he was writing his last book, in which he hoped to sketch a morality for the Nietzschean, post-Christian age, is well known.[1]

We certainly are not claiming that every possible reading of a system of thought is valid, or that Stoicism is whatever one chooses to make of it. It is, moreover, easy to state the gap between authentic Stoicism (as we will attempt to present it) and the modern or postmodern use we make of it. Indeed, we are quite conscious that this exploitation is abusive, but it is true that we have the right to model our dreams on ancient thoughts, reemploying them just as the men of the Renaissance reused columns taken from a pagan temple in a church. The paradox is this: Stoicism, the most incredible of philosophies for a modern person (because it was an intellectualized, optimistic naturalism, convinced of the unity of the *I*), has become for us moderns an object of reverie and exaltation, thanks to a decisive detail of its doctrine: the *I* as active subject, without god (because the Stoic god is man's equal) and without master. By the same token, because the *I* is the fulcrum on which to apply the lever, Stoicism has become the means to survive in a world where there is no longer god, nature (everything is a cultural construct), tradition, or moral imperative (the categorical imperative is merely the sublimation of social obligation). Where Stoicism affirms the fullness of the world and the certainty of a happy ending for the human condition, we see the void and a reshuffling of the eternally returning cards of the human game. The paradox is that a point of detail within Stoic doctrine, the autonomy of the *I* and the possibility of a transformative work of the self on the self, has become a means of survival for us despite the disappearance of everything whose existence Stoicism affirmed: nature, god, the unity of the self. For us, Stoicism is an "immune system" in the biological sense of the word: the individual can rely only on the self for support in defense against a world (contrary to that seen by Stoic optimism) not made for him.[2] All that is left to think or believe is that, despite Freud, denial is not an illusion and that it is enough to say "Unhappiness is nothing to me" for it to be just so.

CHAPTER 1

Prologue: Seneca from Birth to Final Disillusion (1–65 C.E.)

Seneca's social trajectory was quite exceptional: a rich citizen from the imperial province of Andalusia, he rose to the Senate and indeed to the rank of consul. As far as we know, he was among the first four or five provincials to rise to this supreme honor, one generally reserved for native Italians.[1] His career reminds us of the upstart Cicero's a century earlier. In both cases, literary celebrity played a major role: the Roman Empire prided itself on its culture.

"I, a simple Roman knight from the provinces, find myself among the greatest figures of the state!" he is supposed to have said one day.[2] He could apparently poke fun at his petty nobility and his non-Italian origin, but in return, no one dreamed of questioning whether he was a descendant of Italian colonists who had emigrated to Spain rather than of native Spaniards, nor whether Roman rather than Hispanic blood flowed in his veins—ancient racism was different from ours. The odds slightly favor Spanish descent, for in the imperial provinces, most Roman citizens were members of powerful local families made political allies by the Romans through the granting of citizenship.[3] Whether he was the descendant of an Italian veteran or of an Iberian princeling, the distinction was moot, and no one inquired further. Seneca was quite simply a Roman.

The Guadalquivir Valley and southern Spain had been the earliest territories to be Romanized under the empire, a good fifty years prior to southern France. Romanization was not planned: the native elite spontaneously adopted what we call Roman civilization. This was simply the universal culture of the time: Hellenistic civilization translated into Latin. Italy, civilized, had become the conduit of Greek civilization to the

Western barbarians. Seneca's father (known as Seneca the Elder) was a member of Corduba's municipal elite; his mother came from a distinguished family from a nearby village.[4] Around 1 C.E., Seneca was born in Corduba itself, the chief town of the region, residence of the governor, and a Roman city for a century and a half. If there was no lack of cultural life in Corduba, there was equally no lack in Rome, fifty years before Seneca's birth, of ironic smiles for Corduba's Latin poets, Iberians who had become Roman citizens.[5] To be regarded as a Roman, it was enough to live as one. Seneca the Elder was passionately fond of culture, and went to live in Rome, apparently leaving his wife in Corduba. He wrote a history of his times and became enamored of the fashionable literary genre of the day, oratory, which had become a kind of witty cultural parlor game. The highest reaches of Rome's governing nobility, with its obligatory infatuation with culture, opened their doors to him. Culture, more than manners, was the mark of social distinction, just as a Roman way of life and the adoption of its civilization constituted, in themselves, nationality.

Culture could also open the gates to a public career and to membership in the governing nobility of the empire. For such an exceptional ascent, it was necessary to have ample ambition and to be rich, but above all, it was necessary to be taken under the protection of leading social figures because everything was accomplished through the system of client-patron relations called in Latin *clientela*. *Clientela* was as much a mode of selection as it was simple favoritism. One young man or another might be favored over twenty equally deserving others, but the choice was not made at random. Along with political abilities, a client had to demonstrate patriotism and a sense of clan solidarity that were both blameless and recognized by his peers, as well as the monarchic loyalty owed to the emperor. It was a necessary, but scarcely sufficient, condition that his family be wealthy. Certainly Seneca the Elder was. He had been admitted on the basis of wealth to the lesser nobility as a Roman knight, and could afford to live in Rome and maintain his status there; his sister-in-law had married, if not a senator, at least a very high imperial official, the governor of Egypt.[6]

Seneca the Elder wanted a great public career—he frankly admits as much in one of his books—but there is no doubt that, deep down, he preferred literature. He also feared the hazards that were part of public office under Caesarism, as he himself states.[7] His sons were less cautious, and all three went on to brilliant careers; the *clientela* system and nepotism benefited entire families. The eldest, Gallio, known from the *Acts of the Apostles*, became a senator and the governor of Greece, where, one day, Saint Paul appeared before his tribunal. For political reasons, Gallio committed suicide under Nero in 65. The youngest, Mela, never reached senatorial rank, but became a high official, also committing suicide in 65. Our Seneca, the middle brother, rose even higher and also killed himself in 65, followed in death by his nephew, Lucan—a senator, a great poet, and for a long time, Nero's intimate friend.

Thus did this Andalusian dynasty, richly endowed with talent, indeed with genius, die out. They added glory to Latin literature and Greek philosophy, even if their grandmothers probably wore the barbarian coif of the Dama de Elche.[8]

Seneca the Elder did not have the highest regard for the intellectual gifts of the Younger. He viewed his son as a social climber, less intelligent and less literarily inclined than his older brother Gallio.[9] It is easy to guess why: by culture, Seneca's father understood playing the parlor game declamation or eloquence had become. He failed to see, or chose not to see, that his middle son's character and talents inclined him rather toward philosophy. For four centuries, since Socrates' days, the debate existed between rhetoric and philosophy, and four centuries later, some Christians would again make the question an issue of conscience. On one side were the charm of eloquence and the songful beauty of the skillfully modulated human voice; on the other, seriousness of thought and the internalization of a commanding message.[10] Seneca wrote a dutiful biography of his father, lauding his talent as an historian, but his own character and style extended beyond the superficialities of rhetoric.

The art of declamation was the final pinnacle of every noble, or as it was called, "liberal" education. Seneca the Elder sent his three sons to Rome, where they could hear the best orators and study with the best teachers. Although Seneca attended the classes of a declaimer admired by his father, he was fascinated to discover that, with age, the teacher had become a convert to philosophy and had set his conduct in accord with its strict convictions. Seneca had other teachers as well; let us hear him in his own voice:

When I used to listen to my teacher Attalos stigmatize the evil, the follies
and the errors of our existence, I would take pity on humankind and conclude that my teacher was sublime and mightier than kings. If he praised
poverty, when I left the class I would want to be poor or to forbid myself
gluttony and sensuality. I still retain from this certain habits, never
indulging in oysters or mushrooms or perfumes or steam baths. I still
sleep on a hard mattress. Likewise, enthusiastic about Pythagoras and
reincarnation, I had become a vegetarian. But just at that time, the police
had been swept by a wave of suspicion against alien superstitions contrary
to Roman mores. My father wasn't afraid of the police, but he despised
philosophy, so he dissuaded me from vegetarianism. I have told you this
story to show you how enthusiastically adolescence embraces virtue.[11]

Thus, my paraphrase of Seneca's *Letter* 108. To his dying day,
Seneca kept his respect for the purity and idealism of his youth between
the ages of fifteen and twenty.

His teachers did both less and much more than instruct Seneca in
philosophy—they converted him to it. One of them would talk to him
about Pythagoras; another passed on a different tradition of moral
absolutism originating with a certain Sextius, founder of the only
philosophical sect that was not Greek (and which died out quickly in
Rome). Seneca claimed that Sextius had basically been a Stoic,
although the latter denied this in his books. Finally, he had a genuinely
Stoic teacher named Attalos, a Greek from Alexandria who in all likelihood taught in that language. (Like all nobles of his time, Seneca was
perfectly bilingual.) Attalos inspired his young student deeply. Seneca
arrived first to class, was the last to leave, and sought private conversations with the teacher. In old age, Seneca often spoke of Attalos and
faithfully quoted scraps of his teaching, which seems especially to have
dealt with ethics, intentionally ignoring Stoicism's formidable metaphysical and logical framework,[12] with good reason. The adolescent
Seneca was too young for that, and besides, the point was not to imbibe
doctrines but to change one's life. Fiery with the ethical zeal Attalos
had instilled in him, as a youth Seneca underwent a conversion to philosophy as a quasi-religion; people in those day seven spoke of initia-
tion into the holy mysteries of wisdom.[13]

Seneca was probably about twenty when this happened; then there
is nothing written about him for the next fifteen years. His public

career began after he turned thirty-five. Did he write during the intervening years? We do not know when he composed his tragedies, which the French are only beginning to discover, and which are held in even higher regard by Shakespeare's countrymen, but during these fifteen years he certainly must have independently learned the arcana of Stoicism as he read their Greek texts. (Greek was the language of philosophy and Marcus Aurelius wrote his *Meditations* in Greek.) Reading the classic authors was one of the spiritual exercises of Stoicism, and Seneca practiced it to the end of his days. Whatever the details, Seneca became what was known as a philosopher during these fifteen years: he formally "professed," as they said, Stoic philosophy as his faith. His oldest surviving work, the *Consolation to Marcia*, was addressed to a great lady. In it, Seneca, who at the time was almost forty, takes the tone of one speaking with the authority of philosophy. It was granted that philosophers had the right and the duty to advise individuals and cities (in this period, taking advice was seen in no way as humiliating). The *Consolation* concludes with an allusion to the cycles of the eternal return, separated periodically by the destruction of the cosmos, a specifically Stoic doctrine that is stated without a trace of hesitation. Seneca is speaking in the name of his sect.

What was a philosopher? A person who lived his inner life and bore his outward mien philosophically,[14] even if he wrote nothing and did not teach. He did not need a personal system of thought: he had that of his sect. By sect, we do not mean an organized group. It was simply the collectivity of individuals who, across the globe, in their inmost conscience, had professed Stoicism, Epicureanism, and so on. This common conviction united them, and they paraded it; public opinion acknowledged this personal "trademark" as one that, in principle, brought them high regard. They were granted the honorable title of philosophers: one of them was named "consul and philosopher," and the profession of philosophy was assimilated into what we still refer to as the "liberal professions." My justification for using the word sect is that every such affiliation was exclusive of any other, and that the sects conducted vigorous polemics among themselves, much to the satisfaction of their detractors, of whom there were many.

Seneca possessed a rich and multifarious personality. Being a philosopher alone did not suffice. He eventually conducted a public career in which he gained a reputation for hypocrisy and duplicity that is the customary reward for multiplicity. He wished to act politically as a philosopher; this was, in his eyes, acting simply as a conventionally honorable man: speculative, utopian, and ideological politics were not the Romans' strong point. Stoicism had no political doctrine: certain adherents were partisans of Caesarism, while others, in the senate, made up what has been called the "Stoic opposition." Today we can ask of any thinker, "But how does this bear on politics? Is he Left or Right?" It was not so in antiquity. On the other hand, a Roman was little inclined to worry about the contradiction between his words and his political actions. He readily admitted that politics was the art of the possible and that it was necessary to sacrifice certain means to certain ends. The philosopher Seneca admitted it calmly, and had the ability to carry on several more or less incompatible activities simultaneously. Public opinion, essentially indifferent to philosophy but still envious of entertaining an idealized image of philosophers, could never forgive him this. It must be said in Seneca's defense that this parvenu, this *homo novus*, with all the resulting resentments (he has harsh words for the arrogance of the ancient nobility), did not make his career by the flattery, delation, or judicial murder of his peers, as was the normal practice of his age.[15]

If his career was late in starting, it progressed rapidly, and was soon interrupted by catastrophe. Shortly before his fortieth birthday, Seneca entered the Senate. (He tells us himself that he owed this to his aunt, the wife of the governor of Egypt.) In addition, he attracted attention through his talent as an orator, which he had exhibited in the quasi-theatrical realm of the Roman courts, stages no less literary than judicial, where he played the benevolent role of the lawyer, according to the custom of those seeking fame.

Seneca became a celebrity, bound with the reigning family. The ancient historians say his conversation was witty and sharp, but suave, elevated, and courteous. Ronald Syme summed it up nicely:[16] he pleased the princesses and especially the three sisters of the emperor Caligula, bold and forward women, as many were among the Roman aristocracy. It is pleasant to imagine a philosopher surrounded by women intrigued by his force of expression and his virtuosic talent for the internal life: a kind of Stoic Saint Jerome or Francis de Sales, with the same kind of circle of noble penitents.

He had already become and would always remain an intimate of the closed world of the women of the imperial court. He loved and profoundly respected the great figure Passienus Crispus, of whom he wrote, "a spiritual and well-educated mind, an upright character, and the least likely to be fooled by the appearance of virtue." Passienus was a hereditary friend of Seneca's: despite their unequal rank, their fathers were united by a literary friendship. Passienus's wives were, successively, the aunt of the future emperor Nero and Nero's own mother, princess Agrippina, who was herself the sister of the reigning emperor, Caligula. Thus a career was made and a destiny knotted.

Caligula had plenty of blood on his hands, and the death penalty for each senator was only a matter of time. The emperor's excuse was that he had had become raving mad. When his despotic reign was amended, and ended, by his assassination, everyone breathed free, except for Seneca. One of the first cares of the new emperor, Claudius, was to condemn Seneca to death for adultery with a princess, Agrippina's sister. The death penalty was commuted to a sentence of exile. At forty, Seneca was relegated to Corsica, a semi-barbaric island. He stayed there for eight long years, and could have remained there forever. He read widely, published, and developed an interest in the natural history and ethnography of the island (the Stoics traditionally cultivated the sciences), but he was slowly dying of solitude, and his career had been shattered. I presume that the most likely reason for his sentence was the prominent role he assumed among the women of the court, which troubled the new master. As for his highly promising debut in public life, it depended on the fact (among others) that, as a Stoic, far from aligning himself to the Stoic senatorial opposition, he was a sincerely convinced monarchist.

If Seneca's political biography is not to be lost either to detail or anachronism, we must form a picture of the sort of despotism known as Caesarism and of the pathological relations among successive Caesars and their senatorial advisors.

Seneca's life unrolled under four emperors, Tiberius, Caligula, Claudius, and Nero. The second was a madman, the fourth, an original megalomaniac, and all four eventually succumbed to the psychosis of "purifying" the senate through judicial murder. They aimed to eliminate from it the offspring of the old nobility, suspected of harboring nostalgia for the old republic, when an oligarchy prevailed and no single family possessed all power for its own ends. The imperial regime was anything but liberal: it was not even a lawful state (despite Roman law). It was a despotism uncertain of its own legitimacy. Although the Julio-Claudian family seized control of the state, those of its members who became emperors were considered simply the preeminent magistrates of Rome, and the first among their equals, the senators. They were kings without the title, to whom the sincere monarchist sentiment of the people was directed; they were the objects of a genuine cult, just like the potentates of the ancient Middle East (for example, the portraits of the emperors were, like icons, sacred). Caesar's own role was so ambiguous it provoked his own madness. Stalin, too, went mad, from being at the same time a brilliant chief whose personality was the object of cult, and comrade Stalin, first among comrades, and the legitimate head of the proletarian state. Comrade Stalin and the first magistrate of Rome developed the same psychosis of blame and suspicion against their peers, whom they had effectively ousted while maintaining them in their posts. Hence the purges in the ranks of the old Bolsheviks and in those of Rome's senatorial families. That drama had been going on for one-third century when Seneca, at the beginning of the young Nero's reign, believed he had discovered the prince who would put an end to the infernal cycle. The senators had their own psychoses, which depended entirely on nuances: they were resigned to let the prince enjoy the reality of power and to pay homage to him, but only if the prince did not demand adoration and feigned, at first, to reject it and then treated the senators as his equals. This nuance distinguished good from bad emperors.

Faced with a power whose legitimacy was suspect, the only remedy was to bid up the expressions of loyalty. This resulted in the cult of personality or flattery. It was both a simple matter of a style appropriate to empire, but also a strict obligation, under pain of suspicion of high treason or, at the least, of forfeiting the offices and profits of a brilliant career. Even the proudest members of the Stoic opposition could speak only in this language. Forgetful of this, we might find certain of Seneca's attitudes servile, and might see mere platitude in his *Consolation to Polybius*, a kind of supplication in which he indirectly solicited pardon and his return from exile; he had to wait longer, and only returned to Rome when he was nearly fifty. In 49 C.E., Agrippina, who had meanwhile become the emperor's wife, secured his pardon. Tacitus writes

> She had become convinced that public opinion would favor this measure because of Seneca's literary celebrity. She wished to entrust the education of her son Nero to this prestigious master; she thought that Seneca, by his advice, would aid both mother and son to gain supreme influence; and that Seneca would become attached to her, as much through gratitude as through hatred of Claudius.

The empress hoped to advance the interests of Nero, son by her previous marriage, against those of young Britannicus, born of the emperor's prior marriage and the heir apparent.

Claudius had only another five years to live. On his return to Rome, Seneca became the most renowned citizen of his time: the greatest living writer in prose and verse, the greatest name in literature since the golden age at the beginning of the century, and the favorite of the imperious empress. Like Voltaire, he simultaneously engaged in a variety of activities in the next ten years under Claudius, and then during the early years of Nero's reign, publishing an immense body of work, making himself the apostle of his philosophical sect, and amassing an enormous fortune, less by greed than by exercising his innate business sense, all the while playing the role of old-fashioned farmer, like Voltaire signing himself "the peasant of Ferney." During this time he also married (at an unknown date) a sweet-tempered and wealthy provincial from Arles, Paulina, who would elect to follow him in death.

He made literary headlines: in the Via Argileta, where the booksellers set out the latest publications,[17] one could buy *On the Steadfastness of the Sage* and, later, *On the Tranquillity of the Soul*, in which he traced the evolution of his relations with a senior official attracted by Stoicism, whose spiritual mentor he had become. Finally, Rome had a thinker of a scope to rival those of Greece; sometimes, to soothe the Roman inferiority complex, Seneca would drop a xenophobic phrase, granting that the Greeks were not perfect and could even be childish, so laying claim to intellectual independence from the founders of his own sect.[18]

Meanwhile, our philosopher was becoming wealthy, and would

later become colossally rich when Nero, ascending the throne, heaped real estate and other royal gifts on his former teacher. He had one of the greatest fortunes of his age, seventy-five million denarii (Judas's thirty denarii represented a good monthly salary), a sum equivalent to one-tenth, or even one-fifth, of the annual revenues of the Roman state.[19] The scandal of a philosopher whose Stoic heart was unaware of the purse he held in his right hand buzzes on today. Under Nero, Seneca was besmirched for this in a public trial. We do not intend to act as Seneca's advocate under the pretext of being his editor (nineteen centuries have passed since the reach of the courts was eluded by the death of the accused), but aim simply to illustrate certain points of economic history:

1. Far from fearing to stoop, the Roman nobility had perfectly bourgeois ideas: it was highly praiseworthy, to be able to enrich oneself and increase one's patrimony. Those who lacked business sense were scorned.

2. Social classes were not differentiated by their relationship to the means of production, and there was no specialized bourgeois business class. Nobles did just as much business as those plebeians who had capital. Both employed teams of professionals composed of their slaves and freedmen for this.

3. Superiority was general, not specific: whoever was socially elevated was rich, expected to be involved in public affairs, presumed to be cultivated, and so on. A person promoted to a high public office was expected to profit by it: once Seneca's disciple, Lucilius, became a high financial official, he immediately became active in business and arranged in advance to acquire an inheritance suitable to his rank.

4. The emperor owed it to himself to live magnificently and was expected to surround himself with "friends" of equal grandeur, and so naturally showered them with riches. To refuse the gifts of Caesar would have been an offense and a political miscalculation, one Seneca was well aware of, and repeated.

5. In business matters, a Seneca or a Lucilius used and abused their credit, their social authority and their connections to seize occasions for enriching themselves. Once England had been conquered, Seneca made himself its creditor, advancing ten million denarii. He could be sure that his debtors would repay the friend of the emperor.

6. As in all of Europe until the 19th century, it was normal for a person in office to profit from it. Cicero provided a rare example of virtue, pocketing only two million denarii in his year as governor, and boasting of it to his friends.

7. Legacies were another source of enrichment. Among the nobility, custom demanded that a significant amount of one's patrimony be distributed to one's peers, including the emperor. Prominent people were the most favored, and prominent writers were not forgotten. The two great orators of the following generation, Tacitus and Pliny, measured their celebrity by the sum of the bequests their peers made to each of them. Seneca similarly pocketed considerable bequests.

8. Whoever disposed of capital followed the evangelical principle of lending it at interest rather than letting it lie dormant. In Roman society, banking was not the exclusive specialty of professionals: everybody was everybody else's banker. The most significant lenders, obviously, were the nobility. "I have the revenue from my lands and I also lend a bit at interest," declared Pliny, without any embarrassment. (He was also disinterested; he allowed his mother-in-law interest-free loans.) Seneca was know to be the biggest lender of his time, because he was the richest.

9. Lending at interest was not considered a trade, but a private, individual action. It was also a matter for tact: Pliny lent "a bit." The Romans said that Seneca was a shameless usurer; we would say that he created one of the most important investment banks of his time. It goes without saying that he put a team of specialist slaves in charge of his bank. His only duty was to supervise them.

10. Seneca had a good head for business and sided with those involved in it, without any noble snobbery. His *Letter* 101, to a rich entrepreneur, whose banker he may have been, seems quite up-to-date.

11. When Seneca wanted to amuse his readers with a glimpse of his private life, he avoided talk of banking, preferring to display himself in the ancestral, patriarchal role of farmer and expert in viticulture: "It's my job" as he put it in *Letter* 111, among more philosophical considerations. François Mauriac, when he was not talking about his yellowed copy of Pascal, spoke willingly of his vines, and the vineyard that Seneca owned at Mentana, in the Roman suburbs, was famous.

The long and the short of all this is that the social importance of capital and credit for the entire community and for economic growth and

the rise in standard of living is an idea that did not develop until the
nineteenth century under the name of capitalism. Before then, the
amassing of capital and credit were ascribed to individual egotism, to
greed, or to a love of money. The direct sale of a material object from
the producer to the consumer passed muster: the law of exchange is
strict, but at least the thing exchanged is palpable and the parties are
face to face. What was unjustifiable and ascribed only to the thirst for
profit was the trade of the intermediary or retailer, of the merchant
who insinuated himself between producer and buyer, making prices
rise; this intermediary, whether courtier (Seneca himself refers to *prox-
enetai* and *pariarii*), trader, or banker, sells nothing except (as we would
put it) commercial information as a courtier, space, as a trader of
imported goods, or time, as a lender at interest. But information, space
and time are not things: like air, they belong, or ought to belong, to
every one; a passerby asking for directions is not charged. Therefore, the
intermediary, the retailer, and the lender abuse their power, indeed they
are extortionists. Among the vices, avarice alone could provoke them to
such abuse.

Viewed differently, from the point of morality, wealth was judged
in two distinctly different ways, or rather, it arose simultaneously from
two moral bases. If one understands morality to be the attitude of an
individual conscious of what should and should not be done, then possession of a great fortune gave proof of a conscience with weak scruples
and potent greed. However, if morality is understood as the tacit code
of behavior implied by conduct normally held to be normal, then
wealth was an object of prestige and its possession was, for a senator, a
kind of duty. Every great figure had the obligation to be wealthy
because wealth is fortunate, and good fortune is admirable: authority
necessarily must command admiration.

Finally, to understand what Seneca's contemporaries thought of
the philosopher's enormous fortune, we may reflect on the bishops of
the *Ancien régime*. They were the lords of rich dioceses and were obliged
to maintain their status, which was also that of the church; at the same
time, they were Christians and, as pastors, had to set an example of
poverty. If they were only lords, their wealth, far from offending, would
have been legitimate, but their pastoral function gave occasion to their
adversaries to stigmatize them as false Christians swimming in luxury.
Similarly, in Rome, a senator had the right and duty to display his

grandeur, but if he was also a philosopher, he opened himself to malicious attacks.

This said, Seneca obviously found it quite pleasant to be both Stoic and rich, and developed many arguments that it was possible to be both rich and a philosopher. There was nothing of the ascetic about him, aside from a few symbolic gestures, just as more than one bishop in the early days of Christianity preferred to take a vow of celibacy rather than renounce his fortune. For both pagan philosophers and the later bishops, two paths were available: a middle-of-the-road morality and a maximalist one. For Christians, the maximalists were the ascetics; for the Stoics, they were the Cynics, who formed Stoicism's left wing, as it were. Professed Cynics expressly refuted wealth, at least insofar as they were faithful to their dogmas (and there was no lack of mockers who claimed that they were not always so; Seneca insinuates this himself in *On Benefits*, II, 17). Cynics stripped themselves of their wealth or, more likely, were born poor and had never gained wealth. When they were faithful to their vows, they refused valuable presents from the mighty, as one Demetrius, a close friend of Seneca did, daring to turn down a gift from Caligula, and lived in extraordinary destitution. He did, however, have the tact not to insult Seneca for his riches (and insult was the Cynic's Ur-gesture); Seneca rewarded his discretion with unbounded admiration and praise for his poverty. Cynics did not renounce wealth so that the poor might share in it: rather, they considered it superfluous and foreign to nature stripped to its essence. Seneca took a maximalist position only with regard to suicide, not to politics or to money. Only a maximalist morality gives the impression of sincerity because the individual has sacrificed every other conviction to it, becoming the champion of his vocation and so leaving an imperishable souvenir of himself or, we might say, establishing a moral record. Maximalist morality, the morality of a champion, sincere morality: these three are one, all aiming at a unification and simplification of the *I*.

Because of philosophy's self-proclaimed authority and its lofty promises, public opinion expected a sage to be a disinterested ascetic and, in politics, to be willing to defy the powerful at the risk of life. But there also existed a middle-of-the-road morality of wealth requiring no more of the philosopher than of anyone else, a morality of charity. Seneca was an old man when the reputation of the Stoic preacher Musonius was established at Rome. Although Musonius was a Roman

knight and a native of Tuscany, he wrote in Greek and this is what he
had to say about luxuries:

> These are superfluous, unnecessary things that cause a host of troubles.
> With so much money, it would be possible to do good to many people,
> collectively or individually. Is it not nobler to spend money on human
> beings than on marble and wooden sculptures? Isn't it more worthwhile
> to acquire numerous friends than a grand palace? For it is zealous char-
> ity that procures friends.[20]

Seneca thought on the same lines (his treatise *On Benefits* develops
these ideas) and, as far as we can tell, conducted himself accordingly.
The charity in question was not a matter of giving to the poor or the
needy, but rather to those who begged a favor and who could return
one to people in the same social circle as their benefactor.[21] Charity and
gratitude went hand in hand. Those obligated to the benefactor became
his "friends," his faithful allies: charity and *clientela* went hand in hand.
Charity was nonetheless the virtue of an elite: few could extend an
obliging, nonpatronizing generosity to their supplicants. Seneca must
have practiced this virtue in his sponsorship of poor writers and
philosophers,[22] and in his activities as a banker not motivated by greed.

Indeed, Seneca was a banker, but also a senator and philosopher. A
senator *because* he was a philosopher, and more the latter than the former: he did not have the senatorial tone (in the sense of what we would
call a statesmanlike tone); he was an intellectual in the seat of power.
He set himself the difficult task—or the insoluble and sterile problem—
of philosophizing his politics, as we will see. He made practical concessions to the compromises (or worse) of politics, but he never made
intellectual concessions. He wrote as a philosopher, never as a senator.
He never spoke down to his readers, while normal senatorial arrogance
secretly laughed at the religious or moral convictions paraded to convince the Roman people of their validity. Cicero, like the two augurs of
whom he speaks, smiled askance at the state religion, and thought that
if the gods did not exist (and for him, they certainly did not), it would
have been necessary to invent them. The future emperor Augustus
smirked at the pious beliefs of the people in an edict in which he deftly
defends them.[23] The grave senator Tacitus was never as happy as when
he spoke of a colleague whose politics were as strenuous as his private
life was licentious. The paradox of the "energetic effeminate," running

contrary to all accepted and acceptable ideas, deliciously raised the senate above the common herd: it was good for the mass of citizens to subscribe to a well-ordered morality and to believe that it would be impossible to be a great public figure without also obeying the strictest moral standard in private life. But it was part of the dignity of a senator to be above the morality he professed: an energetic effeminate sitting in the Senate was flattered by all his colleagues. Seneca the intellectual never wrote of such things, and did not amuse himself at the expense of ethics or of philosophical theology.

As compared to the other great Latin philosophical writer, his predecessor and rival, Cicero, Seneca functioned primarily as an intellectual; for Cicero, philosophy was simply a mouthpiece for convictions and attitudes acquired elsewhere. I am not making the claim that Cicero was no more than an ideologue, while Seneca's thought escaped from social prejudices, nor that Seneca's ideas were more true because they were more pure. Very simply, if you read the two of them, you realize that their minds were compartmentalized in different ways, whether for better or worse. For Seneca, philosophical considerations took precedence over personal convictions, or rather they were inseparable, while with Cicero you sense a subtle rift where philosophy is used to enhance his underlying convictions like a varnish.

Finally, Seneca the philosopher was, like Cicero, a writer. This is recognizable from a single fact: although they were philosophers, they both wrote in Latin and not in Greek. In Rome, Greek was the technical language of philosophy, just as it was of medicine. Marcus Aurelius kept his journal of meditations in Greek; a generation before Seneca, the only Roman who dared to compete with the priority of the Greeks and founded a philosophical sect, Sextius, whose very Roman rigor Seneca admired, wrote in Greek. Whenever a Roman physician or philosopher wrote in Latin, it was because he was "less a philosopher or a physician than a philosophical or medical writer."[24] The physician Celsus, for instance, wrote a medical encyclopedia (with rare elegance), which is anything but a technical publication. Cicero and Seneca must have chosen Latin because they sensed within themselves authorial talent, and, because they wanted to enrich their national literature, not restricting themselves to the milieu of specialists. They took aim at the broad, cultivated public.

As a writer enjoying literary, worldly, and political success, Seneca came to view himself as a great writer, at least at the end of his life, when he wrote the *Letters to Lucilius*. "I have my personal stamp: everything I write is imprinted with my identity." Still, he did not imagine that he was original, any more than anybody did in his period (and, doubtless, in any period prior to the Romantics). "I impress my mark on everything I've filched from here and there, so well that no one recognizes my models," he writes. Thus he suggests, rather indiscreetly, to his readers the good opinion he hopes they will form of him. To do this, he advised Lucilius (himself an author) to be "personal" in this manner and, very characteristically for the arts in the Greco-Roman world, he imagines (*Letter* 84) his disciple crying out against this advice: "What? Then no one will know whose style I am imitating, whose arguments I have borrowed, whose ideas I am reproducing!" This fear strikes us as paradoxical, but it would have been shared, for instance, by all our classical painters. They would scarcely have been pleased if a connoisseur did not recognize that they had joined the draftsmanship of Michelangelo with the coloring of Titian, the softness of Correggio and the harmony of Raphael, according to the approved recipe.[25] To be a great artist was to set one's own mark on a judicious selection of models. If Seneca had been less sure of his genius, he would not have prided himself on making his models unrecognizable, and would have only hoped to have imitated Cicero's philosophical works satisfactorily.

We have gotten a bit ahead of ourselves, and it is time to return to Seneca as the preceptor of young Nero during Claudius's reign. Because his own son by a previous marriage was too young, Claudius adopted Nero, who took his name, becoming his eldest son and heir apparent. The Roman family system was quite different from ours: names counted for more than blood, and legal bonds were equivalent to so-called natural relations. Seneca's pupil had become the future emperor. In a monarchy, ambition swirls around the heir to the throne, whose supposed character is the object of political speculation. Subsequent events seem to indicate that Seneca perceived the originality and talent of his student and imagined in him a person of culture to whom politics and its conflicts were of no interest. Such an imagined disinterest in politics was a good omen: an intellectual wearing the crown would likely remain uninterested in the unholy marriage of imperial distrust and senatorial pride of position that had bathed the three previous reigns in blood.

When Claudius died in 54 and Nero mounted the throne at the age of seventeen, Seneca thought it was his chance to change the course of history. He was widely believed to be all-powerful, and whatever issued from his pen passed for official doctrine. In 56 he published the treatise *On Clemency*, addressed to Nero himself, in which he suggested a new political compact, one dissolving the misunderstandings and errors of the past, a reconstitution of Caesarism on a sound footing. Over the course of the nine years left to him, Seneca saw a potentially lasting realization of his hopes, then the first signs of trouble, the first doubts and compromises, and at last the unfolding of a political calamity as unforeseen as it was unprecedented.

On Clemency purports to be advice given to Nero under the authority of Stoicism, but it was intended to make known to the broad public that Nero was, indeed, a clement prince; the law of this genre was to give advice only to those ready to accept it. As we shall see, clemency had broad implications: it sufficiently established the difference between tyranny and an ideal form of government, valid a priori, that of the Good King. Not hesitating to use the word "king," anathema in Rome, Seneca wanted to push public opinion toward breaking the old taboos and accepting the reality of the monarchy, which would not be offensive to civic pride because Nero would rule as a clement king; this was seen as an unassailable argument.

To us, the political philosophy of earlier ages is as baffling as anything can be. *On Clemency* exists in a sphere as abstract as that of Rousseau's *On the Social Contract*, to name one example, but not the *same* sphere. In ancient thought, the unstated guiding principle was not popular sovereignty, the rights of the people, or social justice. It was rather this conviction: free people can accept as their master only a person who has achieved self-mastery, capable of restraining passion and, in brief, morally respectable.[26] In sum, what was essentially at stake in politics was the mental attitude of the master. Seneca was announcing that a new era had arrived: since the earliest years of Tiberius, the first successor of Augustus, there had never been such a good government, nor a prince as clement as Nero.

Kingship and tyranny, Seneca continues, have the same constitutional content and derive from the same word; only clemency distinguishes them. Seneca used clemency in its customary sense: not going beyond the necessary rigors of the law, not desiring to punish. He seems not to have imagined anything further, and makes no mention of taxation, wars of conquest, public institutions, or the senate.[27] The reason for this is simple: the arbitrary power of the emperor was limited not by a government of law, but only by his respect for the dignity and lives of his equals. The word "clemency" rolled as satisfyingly off the tongue then as "democracy" or "human rights" do now.

We must remember that imperial policy was a simple matter of routine, a kind of housekeeping: subdue a revolt here, a barbarian invasion there, answer petitions. There was no talk of economic development, income redistribution, or other problems with ethical overtones. If Seneca seems to place exaggerated weight on clemency, that is because it was situated within the ruler's only margin for free action, where he could give proof of his character and his moderation. In how he treated those guilty of attacks against his person or one of his subjects, clemency provided the revealing detail. An inclement king would reveal his tyrannical soul; his subjects would find obedience to such a soul insufferable, and Seneca warns Nero that tyrants end up toppled—or assassinated.

The underlying message of *On Clemency* is this: Rome had to accept the monarchic regime that had been a reality for almost a century. In fact, "Kingship is an invention of Nature." In return, the emperor would behave as a good king, would practice self-restraint, and would consider himself the servant of the governed, not their master. For two years, at least, Nero gave ample proof of this new spirit of Caesarism.

He would, in fact, continue to exhibit such spirit. The unanimous ancient tradition regards the first five years of Nero's reign, until he murdered his mother, Agrippina, as a blissful period—with one gory exception, the murder of Nero's half-brother Britannicus who, thrust from the throne, was poisoned three months after Nero ascended it.

Plutarch writes, "In almost all dynasties, the murders of children, mothers, and spouses are frequent; as for the execution of brothers, it has always been a general custom on a par with the axioms of geometry, freely granted to kings for their security."[28] In Persia, in the time of François Bernier, all the brothers of the new shah were blinded on his succession. Some have been shocked that Seneca could write of Nero, "You have no blood on your hands," but he was not in a position to contradict the official account, that Britannicus had succumbed to a fulminant fever. Some are also shocked that he had the effrontery to write a work called *On Clemency*, but contemporaries greeted the murder of Britannicus with a mixture of horror, fatalism, and relief. According to Tacitus, "The great majority of the public excused the murder. Such fratricidal hatred had always existed, people said, and the kingdom could not be divided." In old monarchies, births in the royal family are greeted with rejoicing, while the prospect of a regency arouses fear. An unstable succession and quarrels among princes raise the specter of civil war. Rome must have experienced a mean-spirited relief on Britannicus's death. To begin a reign with the murder of a potential rival had become a dynastic tradition.[29]

The bulwark of Caesarism was the loyalty of the powerful praetorian guard; its foundation was the fatigue following thirty years of civil war and the monarchist sentiment of a populace devoted to the ruling family. It functioned using the ancient institutions of the republic, distorting them to its own ends, and negotiated the hypocritical relations of deference and servility between the throne and the six hundred families of senatorial rank from whom 120 governors, generals, and high officials were chosen annually. Joining these were sixty high financial officials chosen by the emperor from the lesser, equestrian nobility. (Lucilius, Seneca's correspondent, was one of them.) This was Seneca's social universe; he would not have known anyone outside it, except for his own domestic slaves and freedmen,[30] and those philosophers whose selfless poverty he admired and whose company he allowed.

When the imperial regime sought legitimation (or a rational gloss), it amounted to a reduction of politics to the relations between free ethical consciousnesses and to a moral attitude toward the governed. We have seen how Seneca gave Nero this legitimation in *On Clemency*. He had already written Nero's address on assuming the throne; he was, as M. T. Griffin said, Nero's "public relations man,"[31] so much so that public opinion would ascribe to him the imperial speech justifying the murder of Agrippina. Did he play a more consistent political role, at least during the five "good years" at the beginning of Nero's reign?

Seneca, as senator and former mentor of the prince, was honored with the titles of "friend" (*amicus*) and suffect consul in 55, though he held no official post. Whatever his political influence may have been, our knowledge of it boils down to two or three generalities. At the beginning of *On Clemency*, we see him participating with Burrus in a council of state. To these, the emperor invited, at his discretion, men of affairs or, more generally, whomever he wished. We learn from Tacitus that Seneca and Burrus, the praetorian prefect, were closely linked (Seneca composed a vivid eulogy for him). Tacitus adds that the two of them held sway over the young prince, and also tells us that Burrus's death in 62 destroyed Seneca's influence in the palace. From all this, we may safely conclude the following. Burrus, originally from Vaison, was not the veteran soldier imagined by Racine (he never rose above the rank of tribune, equivalent to a colonel). He was, above all, a financial administrator[32] and as chief of the praetorian guard, he occupied a position of more than strategic importance: the praetorian prefect was the emperor's factotum, effectively his substitute, his grand vizier.[33] Seneca, with his juridical and financial skills, must have joined the councils whenever Nero summoned him to them, supporting Burrus and receiving his support in return.

We must not misunderstand the nature of the influence he could have wielded. Our sources do not attribute any precise decision, any political initiative to Seneca. There is likewise no hint of the slightest intervention on his part during the Senate's deliberations. The famous five good years were spent forwarding current affairs and naming civil servants. It is scarcely an exaggeration to say that imperial policy consisted, above all, of maintaining or re-establishing the status quo.[34] There was no pretense of perpetual adaptation to a perpetually changing situation. The five years saw no wave of reform; they were years of good administration, "good" meaning no more than abstinence from abuse and crime—in this sense, these were excellent years. It would be the purest rhetoric to give credit to a Stoic policy put in place by Seneca for everything that happened in those years. As Maurach has said, we hear nothing of Seneca's political initiatives because no one had knowledge of any, and no one had knowledge of any because, in fact, he made none of note.[35] Moreover, he had none to make: Stoic politics had no content other than to forbid the emperor from tyrannizing his subjects; it was devoid of any reformist program. Searching for originality in Marcus Aurelius's politics would be just as futile.

Possibly the greatest service that Seneca rendered lay in his superior ability to rein in the eighteen-year-old prince. From time to time, Nero proposed initiatives as generous as they were ridiculous, for instance, abolishing indirect taxes.[36] His flabbergasted council praised his magnanimity to the skies and in the end avoided catastrophe, but there were more worrisome concerns. Nero was sowing his wild oats and, according to the habits of the gilded youth, would make nocturnal expeditions to harass passersby and assault ladies and their attendants. Youth must have its day, and the Roman aristocracy smilingly granted that such scrapes were a traditional right,[37] but Nero was sowing his oats a little too widely. Beyond his apparent lack of interest in politics (which conveniently left the field free for his entourage), people noticed something odd and unsettling about him. If we are to believe Tacitus, Seneca tried to keep Nero in check by means of his concubine, a freedwoman named Acte. In the future, Seneca would write that the wise man despises sexual license, but should employ it as a means, if the end is praiseworthy.[38]

One day in 59, around Seneca's sixtieth birthday, he and Burrus were urgently summoned by a panicky Nero. They correctly feared the worst: Agrippina was daring to raise the people and the Senate against him, to call the praetorian guard to join in the revolt, or to arm her own faithful slaves to launch an assassination attempt against the emperor. They also learned—or guessed—that Nero had tried to assassinate his mother, and that the attempt had failed. It would be necessary to anticipate her revenge. Burrus replied that the guard would never agree to put a princess of the blood to death, but in the end, Nero found a more flexible accomplice, and Agrippina was slaughtered. Burrus, obviously overwhelmed, had no other recourse than to try to patch up the palace's enormous hidden scandal and to explain to the guard that Agrippina had plotted her son's death—thanks to the gods, he was safe and sound. Public opinion, because of credulity or another reason, docilely accepted the official version. Throngs came to congratulate Nero and to render thanks to the gods in their temples. The master was the master, believable in his every word, his every desire to be anticipated.

The most disturbing thing about this murder was its uselessness. Agrippina had been removed from a position of power five years before, in the first days of her son's reign. Rome, having scarcely put the purges of the senate behind her, had fallen victim to another more exotic plague, one all too familiar to the well-read: the tragedies of the seraglio which, two centuries earlier, embellished the annals of the Greek dynasties of the East and which would henceforth furnish an endless supply of bloody tales of intrigue to historians.

With the murder of his mother, Nero came into his own; he would, bit by bit, reveal that he concealed within himself more political ideas than had been thought. He was twenty-one years old: deemed a ham actor sporting a crown, he would soon show that no emperor, past or future, would be as infatuated with his power as he.

During ages when kings outweighed the masses, utopias were the creations of crowned heads rather than of the collective imagination. With Agrippina's death, Nero's revolution was underway. Public spectacles and food distributions burgeoned, while contests on the Greek model were founded in Italy; baths (equivalent to Greek-style gymnasia) began to be built in Rome. Nero put himself on exhibition as a singer, a musician, and as a charioteer (though not yet in full public view.)

Norodom Sihanouk, in the history of our own time, considering himself as much a movie star as a head of state, founded an annual festival of film at Phnom Penh, whose grand prize he received annually. His films were imposed on his subjects like a tax, and he was greeted in the newspapers as the best film artist, the best writer, and the best journalist in Cambodia. He wrote songs for his subjects, and had them sung to the peasants during campaigns. No one supposed that Sihanouk had no lust for power.

Nero, as emperor, had three main ideas. The emperor, in his own being, was even more immense than his empire, which was only an appendage and mirror of his personality. (Just as for Malebranche, God had created and arranged the universe solely for his own glory.) Second, the emperor did not draw his legitimacy from the political function he fulfilled, nor did he impose his power by force: he reigned because he was who he was as an individual, and so rightfully imposed his individual gifts as musician and charioteer on the public. Nero was not a cheap crooner, forgetful that he was emperor; quite the contrary. Everyone understood, if dimly, the implications of his earliest semipublic exhibitions: this was power not vested simply in a person, but in an individual who regarded himself as the center of the universe. Far from degrading the royal dignity, he entered the public space as a sovereign, under the pretext of creating a friendly conviviality, based in music, between himself and his subjects. As luck would have it, Nero's tastes and talents inclined him toward the arts, and an inversion of traditional Roman values resulted.

This was not an "esthetic conception of power." (It is easy to understand that power can have a hand in esthetic activities, but it is hard to see how it can be exercised esthetically.) Nor was it legitimation by talent. Nero believed he was already legitimated by being himself, and was not neglectful of nonartistic grandeurs: he was planning for the conquests of Ethiopia and the Transcaucasus, and sent reconnaissance missions and mapmakers there. He hoped to add to the Empire these fabled lands bordering on the sources of the Nile and the endless steppes of the Don and the Volga. Nor was Nero a philhellene on principle (self-sufficient, he fought for no values); with a personal taste for the visual and musical arts, he was philhellene as a simple matter of consequence.[39] He was not interested in cultural revolution. The "people's Emperor?" Not at all: his people, who were not Greek lovers, got a Greek gymnasium; he preferred the pantomime (a sort of opera) to the gladiators. A plebeian might have said of him what Malebranche said of God: "He loves us only by reason of the love he has for himself and his diverse perfections." Nonetheless, the people embraced him and piously preserved his memory for centuries. After all, Nero had given them spectacles and favored popular taste over serious values, humiliated the grandees and put the people above the Senate. Beyond the narrow bounds of politics, he had opened the gates to millenarian longings. At the very least, he reduced the importance of politics, and thus of the aristocracy. No sovereign had ever displayed such extravagant magnificence, or erected so many buildings, but this extravagance was not that of a Ceaucescu; it bore no trace of official pomp. It was, rather, the tasteful luxury of an individual—megalomaniacal, to be sure—not an ideological monument.

An ordinary tyrant, satisfied with the trappings of power, would not have failed to have himself adored as a living god. Indeed, this was how tyrants were recognized as such. Having himself deified or worshipped as a "Sun King" was exactly what Nero did *not* do.[40] His claim was not to put a sacred gloss on power, but to render those aspects of his personality most foreign to the realm of politics and of power rela-

tions, public. This upset every notion of what was serious about existence. Nero's only tastes were for the arts and pleasure. A ruler could
cultivate oratory or philosophy, arts addressed to all and revealing
truth, but he might not be an artist because art was a personal pleasure.
Nero was no lover of philosophy, and the Stoics detested everything
dear to him. In his letters, Seneca could scarcely touch on such current
topics as the games or the baths without seeming to pen epigrams
against Nero. The emperor had none of the cruelty of the classical
tyrant, and on this one point Seneca proved correct: it seemed that the
purges of the Senate would not begin anew. Nero harbored no suspi-
cions of the Senate for the simple reason that he was too much a nar-
cissist to notice what was going on around him. Looking into his
mirror, he saw someone likeable, and could only imagine that the
Senate adored him. In 65, when a conspiracy involving a score of senators aimed at his assassination was discovered, Nero awoke, astounded,
from a long dream. Seneca was only one of many senatorial victims of
the ensuing repression.

He had failed: *On Clemency* had made plain the great hopes he had
placed in the new regime, hopes he had wanted to arouse in all.
Caesarism left no room for a balance of power, and the Senate was no
counterweight to the emperor: its only role was whatever the current
emperor chose to allot it. Proof of this abounds in the panegyrical style
they were obligated to adopt even toward "good" emperors. At least
Seneca, in writing *On Clemency*, had not deceived himself by pinning all
his hopes on the self-restraint of a virtuous king; Nero was far from
self-restrained. Contemporary historians report that Nero consulted
less and less frequently with his philosopher-mentor, who was a sort of
clergyman in his eyes, and that he envied his reputation as the greatest
living writer.

Seneca's position was made worse by the unusual division of public opinion into two camps: Nero had enthusiastic and combative partisans in all classes of society, not only among the people but among
the literati and the Senate, while his opponents were, naturally, reduced
to silence—as happened even under so-called "good" emperors. A poem
of the day displays the bitterness of these one-way polemics, of which
Seneca was a target, being accused of slandering the artistic talents of

his pupil.[41] While the Stoics were not (or were not yet) persecuted, they were regarded in a dim light. Because there was an official, imperial vision of the universe, all other philosophical visions became oppositional. Those who were young in this age would come to remember it as one in which any studies aiming above mere erudition became suspicious because they paid little heed to Nero.[42]

Enthusiasm for Nero became an emotion required to be expressed—as though irresistibly—on every occasion, although normally flattery of the prince was confined to ritual circumstances such as public offerings of thanks, the conclusion of an audience, or the Senate's response to the emperor, whose canonical virtues were praised. For Nero, these rules had to be broken or surpassed: he was no ordinary prince. By and large, this enthusiasm was sincere, and literary circles in particular waxed warm for a ruler who was a fellow artist. Such was the case of Lucan, Seneca's nephew, who at twenty-three (a few months younger than Nero) thrilled for his friend on the throne.[43] From our perspective, this might appear to be youthful rebellion and intergenerational conflict: in Rome, where public careers began before the age of twenty, this was not unusual.

Seneca's writings are the proof of the new climate that had settled in. Before these years, around 63, Seneca had never deigned to publish even a line in praise of the ruling emperor, although this was practically a loyal duty payable even under "good" emperors. The reign of terror had not yet begun. While Nero was showering him with riches during the early years of his reign, Seneca could write without a hint of irony in *On Benefits* that a tyrant was owed no gratitude for his gifts, without seeming to pen an epigram. Surely he scarcely dreamed of making one: under other rulers, that would have bought him the death penalty for lèse-majesté. In 63 or 64, despite his very real standing, Seneca was forced to relent: publishing his *Natural Questions*, he quotes four times over a precocious verse of Nero, lauds his love of knowledge and his other outstanding traits, and celebrates the comet whose appearance bestowed heavenly sanction on the new Golden Age. There was no such flattery in his next book, the *Letters to Lucilius*, which he had already begun when the *Questions* appeared.[44] It is reasonable to conclude that something happened around 63: Seneca chose an interior exile, as we shall see.

Things got worse in 64. For the first time, Nero displayed his talents as a singer on a truly public stage and the fearsome law of lèse-majesté was revived in all its rigor: the blood of senators had begun to flow again. For two years Seneca sought to avoid his duties as a high official, and we are tempted to believe that this was the least he could do; after the assassination of Agrippina, he should have had the self-respect to resign. Unfortunately, this was not an easy matter. Certainly, in an ideal world, we would like to imagine Seneca creating an opposition party to overthrow Nero by obtaining a majority in the Senate—but this was not at all how things were done in Rome. As it happened, Seneca stepped down from the Senate around 61—retirement was permitted at the age of sixty[45]—but he remained a friend of the emperor, an honor that could not be renounced without the approval of his patron.[46] This posed both a political problem and a question of civic morality.

Seneca was a realist, and a deft one, but he did not lack self-respect, nor did he have any illusions about the career of "friends of the king and of those who emulate them." In *On Benefits* he had already asserted that even Augustus, the best of emperors, bore hearing the truth from his friends only grudgingly.

Just as there was a career as a senator, there was one as a friend of Caesar: once embarked upon, there was no exit. One did not normally lay down one's seat in the Senate, and to indulge in absenteeism by skipping sessions was to declare oneself suspect. Attacking Caesar directly amounted to suicide. A Roman senator was not a modern parliamentarian, always able to resign or withdraw: he was pledged to public affairs and to the endorsement of imperial edicts as though to a priesthood.

In all likelihood, Seneca considered himself in no way compromised by the murder of Agrippina or by Nero's tyranny. Like all his compatriots, he had fallen victim to a tyrant who alone was responsible for the whole state. The timeworn response to this was to wait out the season of discontent and to hope that Nero's successor would be better. The only alternative to despotism was that the tyrant might succumb to his guards' rebellion, to a plot of his ministers, to a pronunciamento from one of the armies defending the frontiers, or to the daggers of a group of senators, a risky venture whose very mention raised moral concerns—possibly sincere—among many, including the historian Tacitus. As for futile heroism testifying, however impotently, to the power of human conscience to register protest, it was an attitude expected of philosophers (as those who still take the Catholic Church seriously might expect of the pope), but uncommon among the senators.

Rereading Tacitus is enough to allow us to imagine the dramas of conscience and resentment through which the senators of Seneca's era lived. They could not abstain from the oaths given in the emperor's honor or their pledge to respect his decisions. When one of them was accused of lèse-majesté, it was his colleagues, summoned as the High Court, who condemned him to death while the emperor protested— after the suicide—that he had been about to pardon the victim. How can one live under such a regime? Be absent as often as possible under the pretext of caring for one's estate, so that one was not betrayed to his colleagues or the emperor. Even the proudest senators, the leaders of the Stoic opposition, did as all the rest: they protested as much as they could without putting their lives in danger. One of them protested at the death of Agrippina, but as despotism grew worse, they saved their honor by approving the most scandalous decisions without explaining their votes or by shrouding them in flattery—or they simply voted in silence. In desperation, their leader took significant action: starting in 63, he ceased attending the senate and participating in the annual wishes for the emperor's well-being. However, when Nero took offense, the senator multiplied his flattery to regain favor. He counseled a younger, ardent senator to refrain from any interference—it would not save the accused colleague, but it would cost him his life. He was resigned ahead of time to his destiny, and his suicide followed Seneca's after a year.

How was it possible to escape from dishonor and the suspicion of lèse-majesté at the same time? On one occasion, a senator managed to do so with a witticism.[47] Tacitus evokes the black years when he and his colleagues were compelled to vote for the death of one of their own. This only increased his disdain for the useless heroism of the Stoic opposition, which he treated as pretentious posturing. Reading his account of the ill-fated conspiracy of 65, it is hard to avoid the impression that even the slightest phrase is treacherous, ironical, or denigrating. Killing the tyrant who, after all, was the sovereign, was an illicit act according to him.[48] Under a despotic prince, it was possible to achieve greatness, he writes, if one was able to put one's moderation and deference to the test. He believed the Stoic suicides amounted to so much pretentiousness (*mors ambitiosa*). His resentment was fueled by the fact that only servility to the emperor enabled a successful career, or at least permitted entry to the ranks of the Senate and participation as one of the six hundred pillars of the empire. Tacitus, of course, deplores the humbling of the Senate because of his extremely high opinion of it— Seneca's was no lower.[49]

Caught in an ineluctable tragedy (as Seneca and Tacitus were) and not knowing which way to turn, individuals often set an uncrossable limit where politics and a purely moral imperative stand in opposition. For recent examples, we might think of the use of torture in colonial wars or the Jewish laws imposed by Marshal Pétain. We derive our limits from the rights of man; the ancients took theirs from religion. Counter to all humanity, if political necessity demanded it, they thought it allowable to destroy a conquered city, so long as sanctuaries were respected.[50] We learn from Tacitus that Nero, having exhausted the public treasury for his extravagances, had begun to pillage the empire and to despoil sanctuaries of their riches. It was only then that Seneca asked to be permitted to resign "in order not to be involved in so odious a sacrilege." Was this the philosopher's real motive? Whatever the case, it was not the first time Seneca asked to be relieved of his obligations as a friend of the prince, and his main justification was, as always, to devote himself solely to philosophy.[51]

Starting in 62 (shortly after he had earned the right to retire from the Senate, we believe), Seneca asked Nero to dismiss him from his duties as a friend and to take back all the riches the prince had heaped on him. We are necessarily in the dark about what was said in this interview, held without witnesses, and Tacitus, who reports it, was equally ignorant. His reconstruction of Nero's reply, however, has the ring of truth. "If you return these riches and if you prefer retirement to my friendship, rumor will blame my greed and your fear of my cruelty." Seneca himself would shortly write that keeping distance from a tyrant is impossible without seeming to accuse him; Nero did not accept the withdrawal of his "friend," who remained at his disposal. Not long before the great conflagration of Rome (which malice falsely attributed to him), Nero presented himself in the public theater in the Italian Greek city of Naples; Seneca's letters are dated from Naples, where he had obviously followed his emperor.[52]

Even if Seneca was obliged to follow Nero everywhere, however, Nero was not obliged to consult with him, and he doubtless had little further to say to him. On hearing the news of the fire, Nero returned in haste to a capital in ashes. Seneca, deprived of the right to retire to his country estate far from Rome, moved into a villa he owned close to the city gates and set about living as a man withdrawn from society. Giving his studies and his poor health as pretext, he remained at home. On the rare occasions when he paid a visit or discharged some social obligation, he was not followed by the gaudy train of domestic servants that signaled a man of quality to passersby. He stopped acting like a man whose social aura proved his high position, and declined from this point to be saluted each morning by his throng of protégés. If he had continued to do so, it would have appeared that he continued to have a hand in the government of the empire. The real mechanism of the state was not the few hundred high officials and bureaucrats as much as it was the network of friends, acquaintances, and clients of each member of the governing nobility.[53] To settle an affair of state or to execute a political decision from afar, one went through a client or a patron on the spot. In the common parlance of the times, which was also that of Seneca, power was exercised by alternating "benefits," the exchange of services.

A year or two before the fire of 64, Seneca began writing the *Letters to Lucilius*, which clearly demonstrate the reasons for his retirement.[54] With politics far removed, he could immerse himself in leisurely study and find in this the mental security to prepare him for the worst. He found in the practice of wisdom a way of serving his fellows and of continuing to practice politics by other means; he also found the way to end his days in a state of magnanimity and in the presence of the sublime. Philosophy, he wrote in the spring of 64, sets a great gulf between us and the mass of men, raising us above human stature and making us scarcely less than the gods. "I pass hours on end simply wondering at the nature of wisdom; contemplating it, I experience the same awestruck admiration as when contemplating the cosmos, which I constantly regard with fresh eyes."[55] From this point forward, Seneca is his philosophy's devoted lover, which destroys him. We shall see how.

CHAPTER 2

Seneca as a Stoic

To gain an overview of the landscape of Stoicism, we may simply read the first chapter of Book VII of the treatise *On Benefits*. Nature herself, Seneca affirms, reveals to us the most important lesson we could ever learn:

> If our spirit has only scorn for whatever happens to us, good or bad; if it has risen above fears; if, even in its eagerness, it ceases to imagine limitless prospects, and wisely seeks riches only in itself; if it no longer dreads anything from man or god, knowing that it has little to fear from man, and nothing from god; if it despises everything that is at once the splendor and the torment of our existence; if it has come to see clearly that death in itself is not an evil, and that it rather puts an end to our many misfortunes; if it has devoted itself solely to excellence and finds every path leading to it smooth; if, as a social animal born for the good of all, it considers the whole world as a single, self-same family—then it has escaped from tempests and set foot on firm ground under a clear sky. It knows everything that is useful and indispensable to know. It has retreated into its fortress.

The final sentence says it all: obeying nature in order to pursue excellence is the only way for an individual to reach the haven of security and to escape from the storms of existence. Duty to others and morality are not forgotten: each individual must consider all people as members of his own family. But what always prevails is care for oneself. Stoicism is not so much an ethic as it is a paradoxical recipe for happiness. It never loses sight of the fact that when our situation seems desperate, we always have a sovereign remedy at hand, suicide. Seneca (who would in fact die by his own hand a year or two after writing these lines) faces suicide with visible complacency.

All of this, suicide included, is nature's lesson to us. The reader will no doubt be stunned: can such artificial attitudes really be natural? If this is the beautiful doctrine of nature herself, why is it that only the Stoics have heard it? To exclude good fortune and bad from consideration is surely chimerical, going against the most ardent wish of every living being, which always both desires and suffers. This was not the Stoics' opinion: according to them, far from being a chimera, "it was very easy, it amounted to living according to nature. What makes it difficult is mankind's universal madness. Each of us pushes the other out of the right path." Everyone, each a victim of the other, lives far from nature, in error and illusion. Not that the Stoics thought they were evil: their doctrine was a cure, not a morality. They asserted that mankind was literally mentally ill. If we could be returned to sanity, we would be happy and would be deserving of the proud name, "human." When all seems lost, the only thing that really counts and acts, the *I*, remains. It may seem strange that so egotistical an aim as security could have been celebrated as sublime, and that searching for it could have been identified with honesty or morality, but it is not really so strange: anything requiring effort can be understood as morality. On a more vulgar level, asceticism is often confused with hygiene and a hypochondriacal fear of disease, as in those sects promoting abstinence from alcohol and tobacco.

Stoic philosophy was established three centuries before Seneca, from around 300 B.C.E., one hundred years after the death of Socrates, during the period following the death of Alexander the Great. Seneca frequently mentions the names of the successive founders, Zeno,[1] Cleanthes, and Chrysippus. He intensively read and meditated on them, even though the spontaneity of his writing conceals its technically precise underpinnings. We may find fidelity to a three-hundred-year-old doctrine surprising, habituated as we are to seeing philosophies succeeding each other much more rapidly on the contemporary scene. The life spans of ancient philosophical doctrines were more like those of religions than of contemporary philosophies. Still, if ancient philosophies occupied the position elsewhere held by religion, they were not equivalent to religions either in their content and goals or in their effectiveness, which was confined to a cultivated elite.

Stoicism continued two traditional quests of Greek thought, the problem of happiness and the ideal of the sage, or wise man. Some years before the creation of Stoicism, Epicurus founded another sect that was simply another version of the same two traditions. For him as for Zeno, what mattered was to find the formula, guaranteed by nature, for living happily. The Epicurean sage fears neither death nor the gods nor suffering, and has learned to despise riches and grandeur in order to live on friendship, cool water, and a crust of bread. Thus he too became the mortal equal of the gods. The main difference between the sects was that Epicureanism sought above all to liberate men from their false needs and illusory anxieties, while Stoicism taught them to engage in a patient effort to scrape away, bit by bit, the bad habits of thought that had imprisoned them from birth. Individualism was reduced to the effort of each individual to become what nature intended every person to be: free and happy.

"Happiness amounts to unshakable security"—*summa vitae beatae est solida securitas*—but what is this happiness? Sweet quiet and forgetfulness? An expansion, a blossoming? No, it is a state of security, even of absolute security, although we shall see the cost of such total assurance. One attains such security by imbuing oneself with the conviction that misfortune, humiliation, and death are nothing, and by confining oneself uniquely to natural necessities, a bit of food and water—or at least, for one as rich as Seneca, by preparing mentally for such restraint in case of catastrophe. Is it really enough that our intellect understand this for us to see clearly and for our will to follow reason? Yes, understanding is enough, and reason will follow. The price, it is true, is continuous training every day and every minute. It is a question of time. Self-training (*askesai* in Greek) and self-restraint: Stoic happiness is ascetic happiness.

As this training gradually progresses, a feeling is added to our growing sense of security: joy, the exaltation of our spirit, ever more assured of being able to count on the highest human happiness, the same as that of the gods, all-encompassing and unassailable. Thus arises the sublime figure of the sage, the name given to those individuals who become, literally, mortal gods. Stoicism is a method of self-transformation. Mortal gods, in all events, are extraordinarily rare, but approaching that status is enough to make one feel quite fortunate and (no less satisfactory) almost excellent. It amounts to reaching an absolute security, the only one acceptable to a Stoic because (as Seneca writes in *Letter* 92), "the only happiness worthy of the name is that which nothing can impair." We shall attempt to place Seneca's "morality" in this perspective of absolute security: in any other, the details may be true, but the overall picture is false—the photograph is badly framed.[2]

THE HAPPINESS OF BEING A GOOD MAN

Let us imagine that the reader has been seduced by the doctrine just summarized. Or let us imagine that he has not believed a word of it, but that something in the doctrine has intrigued or stirred a willing imagination. In either case, both danger and privilege await the reader: he will agree to be soothed by such grand words as "happiness" and "excellence," found on every page in Seneca, but will not see how loosely or even abusively they have been used.

Let us begin with Seneca. He does not preach morality to his disciple: he incites him to guarantee for himself his own personal "happiness." Yet he repeats, with the greatest insistence, that if the sage is tortured and bears it stoically, he should be regarded just as "happy" as if he had not undergone the test because excellence, or virtue, is the sufficient and only capable cause of happiness. Is this preferable or happy? Isn't Seneca splitting hairs? Isn't he playing on the word "happiness?"

Seneca gives us other grounds for amazement: from time to time (rarely, it is true), he does not center happiness on excellence and personal security, but says that morality is part of happiness. The sage must be a good son, a good spouse, a good citizen; these duties are as important as the search for personal security by means of a mental attitude of disdain for death and for either good or bad fortune. Seneca seems not even to distinguish between morality and happiness. Perhaps we are dealing with a vulgar sermonizer of virtue under the guise of a theoretician of happiness. Morality is one thing, happiness another. The latter is an internal state dependent on circumstances, luck, or mood. Often it is impalpable, coming and going without apparent reason. Sometimes, people do have "everything needed to be happy," yet are not.

Ancient thinking did not probe so deeply: it simply inquired who had everything needed for happiness, and what that was. This was reasonable: the happiness of which ancients spoke was not an internal sentiment to be judged only by the party concerned. Others, the community or the wisdom of nations were the ones who decided whether a man was declared happy. Because the praise givers were not paying for it, they were more exacting for third parties than for themselves. It was not enough that you lived happily amidst your family for them to proclaim you a happy man.

This must be accepted as simple historic fact. Ancient happiness was not the same as that of which we moderns speak. How could anyone be happy while being tortured? Because everyone else would announce unanimously: "Happy are those who suffer for a noble cause!" and each of them would interiorize this ideal of the *I*. In what sense was morality (virtue or justice, for instance) a component of happiness? In ancient philosophy, the search for happiness was presumed to be the motive of every human action; philosophy had not yet suspected the existence of other motivations. Therefore, virtuous actions could only be attributed to this search. A few examples will illustrate these historical assumptions.

A modern poet, inspired to celebrate the happy and lyrical existence of the grasshopper, might write: "How happy you are, grasshopper!" A tiny Greek poem celebrating the same insect begins: "We declare you very happy, grasshopper!" There is more here than a simple difference of vocabulary: to declare someone happy, or for that matter very happy, is a deliberate act and a traditional subject for discussion. It was called *eudaimonismos* or *makarismos* in Greek. The usual translation, "congratulations," downplays the significance of the word. Aristotle writes, "We declare the gods happy, and those men most similar to the gods." We can easily imagine the elders of a Greek city, gathered in the evening on their public benches, having conversations that freely rose to formulation of wisdom. They would repeat that destiny included so much uncertainty that a man could never be proclaimed happy before his dying day. They would argue whether one of their compatriots could be declared happy, and wonder if riches caused happiness, or whether personal worth—particularly military valor, the virtue par excellence—did so. Happiness became a public problem for philosophy.

The sages, the famous Seven Sages of Greece, were the benchmarks for this. Three centuries before the birth of Stoicism, the sage Solon went to visit the rich king Croesus, who, showing him all his treasure, took the occasion to ask him the ultimate question: "Must I not be declared the happiest of men?" The sage replied that the happiest man in his eyes was a certain Tellos, who had a modest fortune, had seen his sons grow up both handsome and virtuous, and had the glory of dying in the defense of his homeland, which on this account had decreed him public honors.[3] A happy fate was one that might be envied by an honorable man—this was the Greek position on the problem. We would shrink from declaring a villain happy and would be disgusted to stand in his shoes. Rather than wake up in Eichmann's shoes, we would prefer to go to the gas chamber; a noble sentiment, but one that dodges the point because Eichmann did not disgust himself. We have made the judgment for him.

The very Greek sense of glory, the taste for excellence and for contests of all kinds, was added to the universal notion of morality. It was considered praiseworthy to seek praise and to be declared an object of envy. One of Socrates's disciples retells the exemplary life of the Spartan adventurer Agesilaus (called the best knight of his times in the Middle Ages), concluding thusly: "This man may very justly be declared happy: from his infancy, he loved glory, was ever most eager to distinguish himself, and never knew defeat." The same disciple (Plutarch) knew that it was necessary to train oneself to attain glory, happiness, and excellence, just as athletes did for Olympic championships: "You must train for piety, for justice, for temperance."

At this point we make two claims: within the narrow group of militant citizens that each Greek city was, or wished to be, the sway of public opinion sought to persuade individuals that their personal happiness was entangled with the well-being of the city, with military courage, and with moral values in general. The taste for glory was itself affected by this: instead of seeking to raise oneself above others and to become a tyrant, this taste was sublimated by some into a competitive asceticism of high morality. Here a decisive event occurred; the intervention of philosophy, at least from the days of Socrates. Philosophy took up this heritage for its benefit, systematized it, and established it as dogma for several centuries.

Philosophy was a fixture of high culture, adhered to by an elite well aware of its own distinction. It had the intensity that devout religious convictions in other societies. Its dogma can be summarized in the following four points. Asceticism, alone, makes for happiness—a fact commonly ignored. Far from being the unique property of the Stoics, practically all the sects—Platonists, Aristotelians, Cynics, and even Epicureans—adopted the Socratic dogma. For his trenchant language, we cite the oldest, Plato. First, "Vanquishing pleasure means living happily; being vanquished, the opposite." Second, after asceticism, morality: even if rich, healthy, brave, miraculously protected against every evil, indeed, even if immortal, one will be unhappy if unjust or intemperate. Third, virtue truly brings about happiness in the usual sense of the word:

> The fairest life is to be recommended, first because it wins the best reputation, but also because, if one is content to enjoy it instead of being sidetracked from it in youth, it wins too what every one seeks: more pleasure and less suffering for the whole of one's life. One has only to have a true taste of it for this to be instantly evident.

Fourth, this truth is commonly ignored and indeed, thought incredible. Vulgarly, it is admitted that a debauched tyrant leads a shameful life, but it is admitted with much more difficulty that such a shameful life does not have its pleasant side. Common opinion refuses absolutely to believe that morality and happiness form an indivisible whole.[4]

Philosophical sects maintained this doctrine with great zeal. The taste for competition was anything but foreign to them, and it had long been understood that a sage, a philosopher, was a different and superior kind of being as compared to the common man. The ancient sage was a sort of lay saint, the pagan world's ideal of human superiority.

Nothing seems more arbitrary or more dated to us than this ancient idea of happiness. It has only the term in common with what we understand today, assuming that we do indeed understand anything precise and palpable with respect to happiness. A Greek citizen was happy if his compatriots so declared him, in the interests of the community. For their part, the philosophers declared happy the person who conformed to their ideas of human destiny. To them, happiness began in satisfying the imperatives of a common morality, which meant also being a good person in the normal sense. It is, after all, rare that a philosophy dares not incorporate the social imperatives of its time, just as in the Christian world it is rare for a philosophy to dare not positing, before anything else, the existence of God. Only then would the happy man set before himself the lofty, prestigious ideal of the sage. We must not be too hasty in accusing the ancient philosophical systems of morality of making ethics dependent on so self-interested an end as happiness. It was a sort of mental timidity that caused them to make morality one of the conditions of happiness.

The truly elevated, prestigious element of happiness, as it was defined by the philosophers, has little to do with happiness as we understand it. Ancient wisdom (even Spinoza) imagined the possibility of a state of bliss that placed the sage above such contingencies as health, security, and material well-being, in which most people and cultures see the very condition of happiness, in its banal sense. The inhabitants of the Third World can never be happy, lacking basic human rights and a decent standard of living. Obviously, happiness can take on any and every meaning, depending on the period under consideration. It is one of the many terms defined by society with a completely unphilosophical view: they serve only to describe the values of a particular epoch.

At other times, especially since the eighteenth century, and still in Stendhal, happiness is conceived less socially than individually: Stendhal's "mad happiness," which was aroused by countrysides, by love, even unhappy love, by the brotherhood of Romantic souls, even when they are rivals. Such happiness takes leave of objective conditions, of standards of living, and of political freedom. It is only a question of mood: a famous actress, abundantly rich and well-regarded, may not find happiness and put an end to her life. Happiness is imperceptible; private wisdom tells us that it exists only in memory, or that it is at most the absence of unhappiness, thus removing any right to complain. We will only know afterwards if, at this or that time, we were, unknowingly, happy. Happiness has no palpable, precise, positive, lived reality in the moment, except for during those ecstatic states revelatory of a potent, unknown bliss which, after all, occupy only a few hours in the entire lifetimes of a few rare, lucky individuals.

Happiness, viewed through a kaleidoscope or as a mirage, oscillates between the whims of the maladjusted and the decrees of philosophy or society, between the "as you like it" of individual preferences (which totaled would result in the complete enumeration of the potentially desirable), and an ideal, more or less arbitrary and more or less heroic.

If we must imagine a supreme happiness—as the ancient wisdoms did—and push this idea of felicity to the limit, in order to make it more perceptible, how would we picture such a "sovereign good?" Ancient wisdom believed that an individual's destiny was subtly traced, a path at whose end happiness and an end to anguish would be found. Such philosophies seem as odd as the socialist utopias of the nineteenth century. Both share the basic assumption that happiness exists. Is that assumption coherent?

To be honest, the problem of perfect happiness or, as it was called, the "sovereign good," conceals an ambiguity (revealed by Kant in the *Critique of Practical Reason*). At times, happiness is a supreme goal, and whoever achieves it will be viewed as admirable, enviable, but not necessarily very happy, practically speaking; at others, happiness is a condition satisfying to the individual as a whole, that is, ideally, but also bodily and emotionally in day-to-day life. Ancient discussions of happiness consider the former sense, or avoid distinguishing the two.

The problem of happiness (i.e., of the human ideal most to be envied), thus became the central problem of what is called Greco-Roman moral philosophy, which in turn is actually an undisguised philosophy of happiness, a eudaemonism, as we have called it since Kant. It is not, however, a morality, but rather a general theory of human action, a psychology, an explication of what people do.[5] Why is this philosophy of happiness also a philosophy of conduct in general? Because it starts from a premise whose narrowness is never put into question: everything people do, whether moral, immoral, or indifferent, is motivated by the quest for happiness. It never considered other motives like the pressure of the collective conscience, pure respect for moral law, altruism, masochism, will to power, love, admiration, disinterested zeal for an abstract principle, or the like. We shall see how Seneca, in his subtlety, created a more complex idea of human conduct, but we shall also see how he translated that into the single vocabulary of happiness, in which all cats are gray in the dark. Nietzsche was thinking of ancient eudaemonism when he wrote, "Men do not seek happiness, but power; that is, for the most part, unhappiness."

Did these philosophies actually teach the secret of happiness in the ordinary sense of the word? They claimed to: Aristotle concludes on the basis of his own experience that the satisfactions of the mind are far superior to those of the senses, even if the latter are good for the common people and for tyrants. The Stoics fought the Epicureans because pleasure is no sure guide to happiness—there are delicious drinks that sicken, and Seneca exhibited the greatest distrust of those fatal delicacies, mushrooms. The happiest mode of life is the most elevated because it secures joy (*gaudium*) for those who adopt it and an unequaled satisfaction, along with the praise of upright people who will proclaim them happy, even if such praises are hard-won. We have slipped from the idea of happiness to what we may call an ideal of the self.

It is along the same rift that morality is introduced into the concept of happiness. A good man obviously may not cling stubbornly to his personal happiness while laughing at the rest of the world. Indeed, many would maintain that happiness and duty are two different and frequently incompatible things. Aristotle, however, responds that we must not take only the advice of upright people on this point. We admit that if the electoral body were chosen from them, the result of the polling would be in no doubt, and virtue and happiness would be elected jointly. That would not, however, mean that they are one and the same thing. Ancient thought was caught between a rock and a hard place in this matter: on one hand, it never ceased feeling the demands exerted on it by moral sensibility; on the other, it had only the word "happiness" to explain the varieties of human conduct. It was therefore necessary to enlarge—unconsciously—the meaning of the word, even to the point where it embraced the attitude of a man disposed to sacrifice his individual happiness to a higher ideal should the occasion demand.

A higher ideal was indeed what was at stake, and the language of the Stoics proves it. In a single sentence, for instance, they teach that because disease is nothing, we can feel secure, and that on the other hand we must practice the virtue of justice. It remains true that because the security promised by the Stoics comes at the cost of such asceticism, it resembles a quixotic ideal more than an insurance policy.

To the ideal of the self was added, with no real connection, communal morality, whether under the influence of a moral imperative or of social obligation, making a kind of mish-mash. (Ideas are, in a way, material, and can mingle like water and wine; in other times, morality mixes with religion.) However, Seneca rarely stresses common morality, taking it as a given and less interesting than the divine security of the sage. When he speaks of remaining steadfast under torture, he is not thinking about a patriot who would keep silent in order not to deliver his companions in arms to the enemy and the scaffold; he is thinking of someone tortured by a tyrant out of sheer cruelty, who succeeds not in concealing the names of his comrades, but in remaining steadfast as a way of making his contempt of suffering plain.

Common morality is humbler, demanding that one die for one's country at any cost, not that one soar serenely above the instinct for self-preservation. No more does religion demand that every adherent become a saint. The Stoic sage is a saint of security. We might be tempted to consider such a quest for security as egotism or as an obsessional state. How, exactly, would the term "morality" be expanded to include it? How can security be made an ideal? According to the Stoics, the search for security consisted of imitating, even reproducing, a supreme model, nature and God. The Stoic is a person who places himself "in accordance with Nature" in an era when that word counted for infinitely more than "history" or "society." This is the next historic given that we must now unravel.

NATURE CREATED EVERYTHING FOR MAN

"Nature" is a tricky term in Seneca. When our author repeatedly says that it is necessary to follow nature, his words awake little resonance in our modern ears. They seem to mean only "Do what is good to do—it's so natural! It's normal, it's reasonable." This is not at all what Seneca means. Nature, as invoked by the Stoics, is the divine, providential power that organized the earth, with its seasons, its fertility, its living creatures (plants, animals, mankind, and the minor gods) into an immense garden. It causes living species to be born viable and gives them the coverings and teeth that allow them to survive cold and hunger—to live (in which all their happiness lies). As for man, nature gave him reason in order to procure what he lacks, and teaches him the proper happiness and how to attain, thanks to the very same reason, felicity. A practical method for happiness, ancient Stoicism had nothing in common with the crushed resignation of Alfred de Vigny:

> Toil vigorously at the long and heavy task
> In the path where chance chose to call you.
> Then, done, suffer, as I do, and die without a word.

Stoicism has nothing in common with this view because it believes that Nature guarantees our happiness. It was created, and well created, for us. Ancient Stoicism could never have spoken the words Vigny attributes to nature:

> She said to me: I am the impassible theater
> Never to be moved by the feet of its actors;
> I hear neither your shouts nor your sighs; barely
> Do I sense the human comedy as it plays out on me,
> Looking in vain to heaven for its silent spectators.

Both the Socratic and Stoic visions of a providential nature are diametrically opposed to this, and in our eyes surprising, as we shall see.

A disciple of Socrates or the Stoics casting his gaze on nature sees in it, or more precisely strives to see in it, not a jungle, but a well-designed garden. As Socrates would say, nature resembles not shapeless boulders, but a masterpiece of sculpture. Nature is intentional. Indeed, it is usable—it works: crops sprout, sexual reproduction performs its office, eye and light are mutually adapted to each other as are smells and the sense of smell. Grass can be transformed to milk by cows, and milk into cheese, as Epictetus remarks. The seasons follow on each other so that crops will grow, and night follows on day because nature knew that we would require rest. The moon serves as a calendar, marking the months. The regularity of celestial motions, with the ordered course of the stars, by itself would be enough to prove the universe is organized, just as when we observe that traffic in a city is governed by rules and not left to chance, we infer the existence of an organizing intention.

The same nature that makes animal species viable gave mankind a superior status as a reasonable animal. By this we gain the privilege of attaining the same happiness granted to the gods, for nature has prepared a port for us where we will live in security, far from our tempest-tossed wanderings. What must we do to let nature and reason be our guides? We must grant that a simple shelter, that any reasonable animal could build, is all that is needed to live, along with a little water, provided by nature, the creator of springs, and bread, however coarse—nature made the earth fit for farming and arranged the harvest season. If we train ourselves to believe all this firmly, we shall be happy.[6] Nature has given us a stencil, as it were, of the path to happiness; it is up to us to follow it.

Combining the art of living with a metaphysics or, rather, a philosophy of nature, was the founding stroke of genius of Stoicism. It was a double stroke: instead of limiting itself to a wisdom in the manner of Montaigne, Stoicism became a real philosophy. To ancient and modern technicians of this discipline, the logical nuts and bolts came to seem admirably well-adjusted, and the coherence of the system was saluted. It was as monolithic, as any philosophical system is expected to be. To those not inspired by philosophical technique came the comfort of sensing that Stoicism was not a simple illusion born of our existential need for security, but an objective truth. The need for security was supported and fulfilled by the reality of nature. All this would earn Stoicism a half-millennium of success. The history of Marxism helps us to understand this, through an analogy that could not be more distant, but which is not absurd structurally. To a workers' movement that laid claim to a share of happiness in life, Marxism brought three things: (1) the objective certainty that the effort was not futile and that the direction of history (if the workers contributed to it) would lead it to victory; (2) the excitement of participating in a gigantic historical movement, as necessary and determinate as the laws of nature; and (3) knowledge that the movement, by a miraculous coincidence, would end in a result as fortunate for mankind as it was historically predestined. The analogy is all the more justified, as we shall see, because Stoics were as much fatalists as they were optimists.

Nature does her work well; it is well-organized and intends our happiness. Therefore it must be intelligent, and is nothing other than the activity of a providential god. This is the kernel of Stoicism. It was not a naïve vision of reality, a peasant or primitive belief in spirits seen in the material world. It was a pious doctrine and a highly cultured theory that required all one's efforts to penetrate. Many were incredulous or indifferent: when Socrates tries to prove to someone indifferent to religion that Providence exists because nature does her work well, the individual replies that he had never noticed that things were so well arranged and that no matter how hard he looked, he had never been able to find the Great Artisan who had arranged them. For their part, the Stoics devoted themselves to educating their vision (as we do in museums), seeking the traces of nature's providence elsewhere. One day a Roman emperor belonging to the Stoic sect, Marcus Aurelius, looked at the piece of bread he was eating and observed that the fine crackling of the crust increased the pleasure to be had in consuming this humble food. In this he fully recognized nature's providence.

We must not see the ancients as naïve: such edifying views met just as much skepticism as Marxism did during the Cold War. In addition to those who simply did not care (the silent majority), the sect of the Skeptics, admittedly confined to the few, was amused by them: "Hunger will never convince the hungry that it is not an ordeal; and a suffering Skeptic will never hesitate to blame nature and its injustice."[7] At this time, politics was far from being the main topic of conversation it is for us today. If only out of prudence, it was little discussed, but elevated subjects were, and often. Thus one day the physician Galen (who, as his profession demanded, believed in nature's providence) came across an awful person, an atheist—in a word, an Epicurean—who claimed that nature had not done a very good job: it would have been better if nature had put the anus and the urethra at the end of the foot, which would have been more convenient and more esthetic than where they were put. He was badly mistaken: Socrates, according to Xenophon, had explained to Aristodemos that nature had put them in the best place, far from the sense organs. Choking with indignation, Galen put the atheist in his place, and was still choking when he transcribed the encounter for posterity in black and white. We seem to be in a world as excitable as that of Monsieur Homais or of *Bouvard and Pecuchet*.[8]

The idea that nature has internal imperfections and could do better eventually led John Stuart Mill and William James to the conviction that God, if he existed, was not omnipotent or infinite. Carneades objected to the Stoics that nature is not made for mankind, citing the snake's venom and the numberless other evils nature breeds on land and sea as proof.[9] What was the point of inflicting mice, scorpions, and mosquitoes on us? Stoic optimism had an answer for everything: Nature cannot grant us a good without its obverse evil. For example, in thinning the walls of the skull so that we might raise our heads toward the noble firmament, the cranial case was made more fragile. The existence of mice and bugs is owed to pedagogical concerns: the first teach us not leave anything lying around, and the second teach us to bear the loss of sleep with courage. Stoic optimism had decided in advance to find explanations justifying nature everywhere. Do storms swallow up ships? Yes, but if there were no wind, nothing would sweep the sky and purify the climate, resulting in murderous epidemics far worse than a few shipwrecks. Nature acts so that every living species can maintain itself and not be absorbed by potentially destructive external forces. It has done the same for the human species. Our interest, properly understood, invites us to take nature as our guide.

A possible retort would be: "But what if I don't want to follow this interest? Under the term 'security' you seek a total security. But I may not want to maximize my security, preferring a mixture, given that to my eyes, pleasures and passions have a certain measure of good in them, even at the price of some risk." Such a response highlights one facet of Stoicism: the system is replete, as full as an egg, and everything is at its maximum. In a sort of forward retreat, Stoicism reasons by all or nothing. It is easier to renounce everything and enjoy nothing, than to enjoy moderately; it is easier never to put down one's load than to put it down for a moment and then take it up again. The audience for Stoicism is made of anguished voluntarists.

A second trait of Stoicism appears when we ask why it should be necessary to follow nature absolutely. The answer must be one or the other of these: either nature has worked in such a way that it is impossible not to follow its dictates, just as we are unable to exempt ourselves from gravity or prevent our hearts from beating; or nature would *prefer* us to obey. In that case, disobedience is possible, and it is up to us to decide if that suits us. There is a difference between a fact and an imperative, and nature is a fact. Similarly, Marxism states both that the flow of history leads automatically to the emancipation of the proletariat, and that the proletariat *ought* to embark on this historic current. But what if the proletariat has no desire to follow its own interest, so that the supposed direction of history is never realized? In that case, nothing will ever prove that that direction exists and is not just a product of our imagination. In the same way, how can nature's intention for a thing to happen be recognized if there is a risk of it not occurring?

In fact, the Marxist and the Stoic utopias anticipate this objection in the same way, saying, as we might have expected, that the person whose interests are at stake will surely not fail to pursue them. They issue no imperative—what right would they have to do so? They can, however, exhort taking the path of well-understood self-interest: Marxists propagandize, and Seneca's work is one long exhortation.

The idea of a providential nature, created for mankind, did not die out until the nineteenth century, along with the spread of disbelief in God. Shelley was a declared atheist, while Schopenhauer believed only in a blind cosmic will and Leopardi believed neither in providence nor in the immortality of the soul.[10] But the great discontinuity with the past is owed to Spinoza who, a century and a half earlier, denied human liberty along with the immortality of the soul, anthropocentrism, the personhood of God/nature, and good as a human goal. (Mankind does not seek the good, but applies the name to whatever psychological causality makes it seek or desire.) How could storms, earthquakes, and disease be explained as the work of a providential God? Nature was created neither good nor evil, and "everything in Nature is natural." Nature does not seek what mankind calls good or beautiful. With this, modernity had begun, although Spinoza's doctrines would not emerge from a quasi-clandestinity until shortly before 1800.

As for Stoicism itself, it had its own particular difficulty, which determined all its other doctrines. Natural providence aims at the good of the species and the cosmos, not at that of individuals. As we shall see, this meant that Stoicism exhorted its followers to place their individual happiness in the common good and to sacrifice themselves for the good of the cosmos, which they were to love as their true homeland. The individual's true interest, then, is the cosmic common good.

For every person, then, there is the same right way to live which, while integrating moral obligations, secures a utopian state of positive happiness. Nature exists and is indeed good, having prepared this path for mankind because all was done for them. Unlike the child or the primitive who believes either from animism or the argument from design that nature has intentions and creates all things in accord with them, the Stoic idea of nature stems from a sense of morality. Nature does not so much act as it wishes but rather does what it must do in order to be good.[11]

THE EMPTY FORTRESS

People were urged to follow their interests and obtain for themselves complete security by profiting from a strategic opening arranged for them by nature. This opening was the best and only possible one, according to the Stoics, and it was revolutionary in the sense that self-transformation was required to attain it; any other path would be only a pallid and uncertain reformism. In any event, this escape route was real, and mankind was not doomed to a kind of dead end, the possibility of which no one would dare to imagine before around 1820, when a new sort of reflection began—that of philosophies without happy endings.

What was this escape route to a happy life? Internal liberty: no one can force me to think what I do not think, wrote Epictetus. I can set aside everything else and fall back on my power to say "yes" or "no." Thus I can say "no" to the false joys of good fortune, to misfortune, to emotions, and to suffering. Conversely, I can say "yes" to the fate that drags me toward the abyss. "By accepting voluntarily the orders of destiny, we escape from the most painful aspect of our slavery: having to do what we would prefer not to," writes Seneca. Epictetus systematized these ideas a bit academically into the classic distinction between "things that are ours" (the power to say "yes" or "no") and "things that are not ours." What is ours are reason and the power to say "yes" or "no." Everything depends on this central "government," this internal fortress. An impregnable fortress, obviously, but an empty one. Everything that makes up existence in the eyes of non-Stoics—desires, moods, a good or bad moment to get through, distractions, passions, hopes and fears, interests, political opinions, ambitions, the desire for comfort—none of these are "us."

The search for secure happiness is in line with the plan of nature itself. Even today we speak of an "instinct for preservation." We are inclined to assume that because nature has created living beings, it has also given them the means of survival. From this, everything else follows.

Every living being—plant, animal, or human—wants to live, to perpetuate itself in being, and to protect itself from the hostile forces surrounding it and from an environment indifferent to it. It is self-interested, it cares for itself, feels close to itself, loves itself as it does its infant babies, and is its own closest relative. Indeed, nature, in its goodness, never thought to create a living being without making it viable and interested in its own survival. It gives creatures coats, feathers, claws, and instincts of all kinds. In a more general way, nature has assigned to every living being a constitution, a program to fulfill, a series of natural functions to carry out. We still speak of the nutritional and reproductive functions. The primary function is to preserve oneself in good condition: people eat and wash themselves by virtue of this function.[12] Because nature's intentions are good and the program assigned to each species is surely well thought out, every being that functions according to the program, that follows nature, will feel well and at ease—in a word, happy—because it is doing what nature intended.

When a plant performs photosynthesis, it is simply fulfilling one of its programmed functions. As we shall see, the duties of humans toward their offspring, their neighbors, and society as a whole are also natural functions. The reader should be warned that the words translated as "functions" (Greek *kathekon* and Latin *officium*) also mean "duty" or, as used to be said, "office." If the liver, in fulfilling its role in the metabolism of sugar, were conscious of what it was doing and were free to act or not to, it would be out of reason and a sense of duty that it would perform its function of storing glycogen. A being that exactly fulfills all its functions, neither going beyond nor shrinking from them, is a perfect being, excellent, or in the traditional translation, "virtuous." Virtue, for every being, is the perfect execution of its natural program. There is thus a virtue for plants: a tree that faithfully executes its "arboreal constitution" is, after all, called a beautiful plant, a well-developed one.

The tree, it is true, gets no credit for this. Neither does a cat who raises her kittens, because she has only obeyed her instincts. People, on the other hand, being of a higher rank than animals, do not act out of sheer instinct: reason dictates what natural functions must be fulfilled in order to become perfect, virtuous, and happy. Reason also instructs instinct on how to survive as a human worthy of the name: by taking shelter from the external world and its problems, whether alluring or appalling. For example, once the open eyes of reason take the place of blind instinct, the instinct for self-preservation yields to a lucid consideration of whether it is still worth the pain of living, or if it might be more worthwhile to commit suicide or, again, die nobly for one's country, a cause that reason approves as a natural function, or virtue. However, the objection goes, most mortals shrink from dying in this manner: is this a survival in them of animal instinct? No, it is an error of judgment, as we shall see later: they have reasoned incorrectly.

Reason, therefore, is the first facet of the human constitution (or program), and whoever carries it out fully will be happy. The outcome is that reason guides man toward a goal that is, in itself, reason. Reason is both the pilot and the port where security is found. It is easy to understand why man should live by reason and reason alone: in order not to be the victim of the external world, an animal has its coat or feathers or claws and its instincts; man—naked and weaponless—has reason. It taught him to sew scanty but sufficient clothing and to build huts made of branches. It also teaches him that if his attention is not dominated by external objects, he must submit his desires, his fears, the passions he feels, in short, all his emotions, to the critique of reason. Otherwise, he will become the hostage of things, of others, and of the hazards of Fate. Reason alone is exempted from these external forces because it judges them. For humans, reason guarantees their individual survival as, so to speak, independent nations. Reason is their fortress.

Only reason matters because it alone can judge what is good for the individual. What is good is not to be handed over to forces alien to the individual. Without going so far as to consider the Stoics as so many De Gaulles, in their view, it was essential to secure their own independence. For political independence, the sovereignty of the state and of the government is both means and end. For individuals, government is in the mind and soul of each; the Greeks called it "governor," or *hegemonikon*. To achieve total security the individual has only to take refuge in the fortress of the governor. Whenever danger arises, he will find shelter there, and with the help of reason, he may leave to fulfill his natural duties, perhaps to harvest some grain or to pluck a few wise pleasures. Here an evil spirit whispers, "Wouldn't you die of boredom in such a fortress?" Apparently the Stoics thought not.

The evil spirit, however, goes on: "But really, no one has ever seen or heard this nature. Do we have any proof, or at least a sign, that the strategy the Stoics attribute to nature is not the product of their imaginations and hopes?" Seneca replies that the requested sign exists: wisdom, once acquired, is never lost. There is no going backward, it works like a ratchet. Wisdom or virtue is like a building block that locks itself exactly in the right place and never moves again. How could Seneca have known this? Not from his own experience nor from those of the very rare sages who existed up to his time (the number of sages then could have been counted on the fingers of one hand). Hercules, Socrates, and Cato had not confided in him. Seneca affirms this on the faith of his sect.

Is it even possible to execute nature's strategy? Isn't it a chimerical project (and a mutilation, the evil spirit adds) to brave torture, mock death, conquer sexual passion? That would, in effect, be voluntarism, the Stoics respond, as if each of us were multiple and as if there were within us not only reason, but instinctual, animal, desiring, concupiscent components. Then might one exclaim:

My God, what savage war!
I find two men within me!

This is not, however, the case, they go on. The soul is unitary, not composed of different parts that could ignore or confront each other. The unity of the soul was veritable dogma for the Stoics, and for good reason. Without it, their doctrine would be an empty dream. There are not two enemy camps within us; our emotions are only the effect of an erroneous use of our reason. Passion is false reasoning, just like errors in arithmetic or spelling. The only difference is that by repeating the same error too often, one develops a bad habit, a vice. Human nature is decidedly well made, and as monolithic as can be.

Legend aside, the Stoics are not voluntarists, but quite the opposite. They believe that intellect is always decisive, and are thus "intellectualists." According to them, all you have to do to stop loving is to understand that love is nothing more than the friction between two epidermises. In their exhortations they never appeal to the will, which could never be self-sufficient; the intellect has as much will at its disposition as needed. The will is not a part of the soul that can desert the other part. Intellect by itself puts reason into play in full freedom. The intellect is neither the prisoner of ideology nor moved by a subconscious. It floats in broad daylight in a transparent world. Nor does perversion exist: the Stoics could not conceive the will to evil for evil's sake. The worst men are simply deranged; no one can be bad in a lucid state of mind—but let us consider these matters at a higher level.

The way to be secure, protected by reason from the surrounding world, is to be insensible to what the Stoics call passions and what we shall dub affects: fear, lust, and so on. The violence of the affects renders us hostages to things and to others; therefore, we must cut their chains—but is this possible? Aristotle thought that it was impossible, and that the best one could do was to moderate the passions and put them to use once they had been tamed. Anger, for instance, allows for more effective combat against one's country's enemies.

Stoicism, though, took another route. The capacity for affect is not a profitable part of the soul, but a parasitical phenomenon, destined to disappear spontaneously in the sage. Everything that is done with passion can be done as well and even better composedly. The Stoics, with no excessive subtlety, distinguished four passions: for a future good, desire; for a future evil, fear; a present good gives pleasure, while a present evil gives pain. What good, then, is there in getting so worked up? It is enough to wish composedly for those future goods approved by reason, and to forearm oneself calmly against evils to come. From a present good, the sage will not take pleasure, but a pure joy—that of having done his duty. (He knows no other good than the satisfaction of his conscience. If his country emerges triumphant from a just war, he will have only the joy of telling himself that he has chosen the side of the just. His joy will be no less if his country is conquered—for all that, he was on the right side.) Finally, the sage does not know the pain that present evils create in the mad (that is, normal), because nothing can touch him: evils are not part of "him."

Is it actually possible to decide that something that touches me profoundly is nonetheless nothing to me? Yes, because goods and evils are only the idea one forms of them; we are free to form any idea of them. A caution: one must not therefore conclude that these evils and goods are nothing, or compel oneself to act as though they were of no consequence. If the Stoics had thought like that, they would have been no more than vulgar preachers, not philosophers. When they say that we must persuade ourselves that death is nothing, their clear meaning is that in fact, death is, objectively and in reality, nothing for us.

This is their principle: every affect, however intense, is in reality an unconscious judgment, a dispassionate judgment, but an erroneous one. Fear of death is to have decided, wrongly, that it is to be feared. The judgment underlying every pain and every pleasure is implicit (although the doctrine supposes that it takes place), at times half-conscious, or on occasion even completely deliberate, but it is always there. When the cannon balls were flying too close to his person, Marshal Turenne would say to his trembling body, "Carcass, you tremble, but you would tremble much more if you knew where I am about to lead you." We should not imagine that he was afraid and that he got the upper hand over fear by force of will. A Stoic would make short work of explaining to us that Turenne trembled without experiencing the slightest dread in his soul. The trembling was a simple physiological phenomenon, like shaking with fever. The explanation of the phenomenon is that our body is a chemical combination of earth and water, heavy elements managed with difficulty by the soul. The soul, on the other hand, is a combination of fire and air, the latter cooling to a degree and slowing the former. The result is that although every person has as much intelligence as the next, some take more, some less time to achieve understanding. Turenne, we must believe, had a swift intelligence and had already long understood that death must not concern us.

Why death and desire amount to nothing must be explained. Suppose I have gone mad with grief because my son has died; I am submerged in despair and want to dynamite the planet. Epictetus would say,

> What is this really all about? The death of your son, a detail, nothing more. The scheme of the universe is unchanged, death is the most normal thing in the world. Try to take a loftier view. If your tribunal of judgment considers the matter objectively, you will see that this death is an everyday incident which has done your son no real harm. An objective view of things reduces them to what they are. When madly in love, all you need to do is say to yourself—as Marcus Aurelius did—'Coupling is an internal rubbing accompanied by spasm and the release of glair.'

What about torture and punishment? Here again, let us be objective. In an hour we are to be tormented, but because the suffering is not yet present, it does not exist. Let's not anticipate it for nothing, out of sheer dread. Nor should we be impressed by the supposedly intimidating display of the instruments of death. That is only a bad moment to be gotten through. Either the pain will be long and tolerable, or it will be excruciating but short with death arriving quickly. Let us experience the intimate joy of enduring courageously. "If suffering is violent, one will bear it; if it surpasses all measure, it will prevail. But during that time, the flame of virtue within us will shine like the light of a lantern in the violent eddies of wind and weather."[13]

What about death? Death has no effect on us because, if we fear it, it is because we are still alive and death is absent. If death has come, we are no longer there to know about it. Will the sage regret that his felicity will end? No, he lives in the moment, which satisfies him completely. The duration of a happiness does not increase it. Nothing helps us understand the Stoic idea of felicity better: there is no expansion of happiness, no *more*. It consists simply in being constantly at the level of the situation in which we find ourselves, in facing up to it, and in remaining in a state of security through virtue by transforming the material of the events with which the passage of time ceaselessly confronts us into that virtuous security. Therefore, if we die, we no longer receive material to transform; we are deprived of nothing and have nothing to regret. On the contrary: the task of living as a human is finished.

Finally, mourning: here the judgment becomes half-conscious. On the death of a loved one, we undergo the first shock of sorrow, a kind of physiological reaction. It may be an as yet uncontrollable movement or again an implicit judgment: "The death of a friend is a misfortune,"[14] but following this comes a second judgment, dramatizing the matter: "It is thought proper to afflict oneself grievously over this misfortune." Seneca tells us repeatedly that if we observe ourselves at a time of mourning, we will notice that we think it best to exaggerate our tears, either from a taste for tears or out of respect for public opinion. A Stoic is not someone who has become insensible to emotions, but someone who has succeeded in controlling them. He is also someone who defies conformism and received ideas.

Behind these detailed arguments about death or torture a more general consideration emerges. Our true self is our governor and nothing can reach us because reason is the judge of everything and nothing can harm it. As we see, a Stoic is not what we call "stoic," he is a king. He is not hiding in a whining crouch or behind a kind of resigned emotional extortion, ready to undergo every blow in victimized silence; he ignores the blows of destiny, for they are incapable of wounding his sovereignty as a king in exile. His is not a resigned silence, but a greatness of soul.

Although he remains proudly masterful in the midst of storms, that is only because he has passed judgment on their futility; he never forces himself. The fate of passions, the affects, depends on how they are judged in the court of reason. This court's sovereignty traces the boundary between "what is mine" and "what is independent of me."

Each of us must decide, following Nature's pattern. The sentence of our court is executed immediately: as soon as I have acknowledged that death is nothing, it is nothing for me any longer. Seneca never speaks of resignation: the words that come repeatedly from his pen are "disdain," "despise," or "defy."

Most people, however, are unaware of the existence of this court. They suppose that pain and pleasure are powers that cannot be brought to justice. The best one can do is to try to pacify them. They cry out, "The capacity for emotion is not nothing, it is the voice of nature. Fear of death, far from being an error, reveals our mortal condition. Desire, perhaps, is our touchstone of truth. As Proust says, desire is the greatest of life's pleasures for every creature. Emotions are visceral, and we are our viscera."

How is it that people see the capacity for affectivity as a mountain when it is only a molehill? From a prejudice rooted in childhood. The extraordinary importance of pleasure and pain is an inveterate error we have adopted as a bad habit known as a vice. Once error has become habit, it forces itself on us, seemingly evident and natural. We believe it neither could nor should be resisted. It is in this way that we contracted the vice of thinking death fearful and women desirable.

Such false judgments have consequences as spectacular as they are peculiarly their own: the burning, agitated, potentially tempestuous state of mind that we call affectivity, whose imperious heat is so diferent from cold judgment, a phenomenon so violent that it reveals that this world, according to the Stoics "not of us," nevertheless touches us deeply.

According to the Stoics, nothing of the sort; they have their own theory about affectivity. It is not the voice of nature, wont to reveal that our true connection to the world defies the judgments of the courts of reason. It is a purely local disturbance, devoid of significance, a parasitical phenomenon automatically accompanying judgments whenever they are incorrect. As soon as judgment improves its performance, the parasite shrinks away of its own accord.

To understand this, we must see what happens in the "court." Four actors sit there. Reason, handing down the sentence; representation (also called image), who has presented the accused; assent or approval, who may sometimes agree with the arguments of the accused; and, at last, movement (or impulse, inclination, tendency, etc.), who, based on the sentence, passes to action. For instance, an instrument of torture is presented to reason, who, on this occasion, not being at the peak of fitness or tone, judges wrongly and submits to the idea that the instrument is terrifying. Impulse therefore takes over and attempts to flee. In passing sentence, reason was in such a state of weakness that the error is self-explanatory. The same lack of fitness caused the whole procedure to unravel in a sort of frenzy—the frenzy, it would seem, of panic—directly caused by the spectacle of the gallows. Whenever the reader encounters words such as representation, inclination, and the like in Seneca, as well as those such as attention, or tension, it is a clue that Seneca, without being heavy-handed, is alluding to this theoretical construction, and that the words are pregnant with meaning. According to this theory of affectivity, the characteristic fact is the lessening of tone. Having lost one's head, it is impossible to judge the gallows objectively. However, when we judge with all possible dispassion, we do so reasonably and, no affective disturbance occurs. "Tone" is the soul's strength. To judge soundly, we must have a "muscular" mind; error is "assent through lack of strength."[15]

This is why Stoicism rejects with horror the Aristotelian position of moderating the passions in order to put them to use in acceptable doses. Seneca insists on this more than once: the point is not to moderate the passions but to root them out entirely. Let there be no mistake about the true meaning of this doctrine: we should not see in it some kind of vengeful fury, hoping to extinguish, once and for all, the beast within, or the sort of rhetorical exaggeration that asks for the impossible as a way of encouraging effort. Seneca is no rhetorician. It is necessary to demolish the affects because we can never be sure of having tamed them: in the end, they may unleash themselves and conquer reason. This counsel, though prudent, is only a down-to-earth way of portraying the matter. In reality, ordering reason to moderate the passions is not dangerous and difficult—it is impossible and contradictory because wherever passion exists, reason has perished.

Stoicism is as open to philosophical challenge as any other doctrine, but it does not simply enunciate platitudes. It does not suppose that one must extirpate the passions, it asserts that affectivity is only the symptom of a lack of tone in the organ of reason. Aristotle imag-

ined that one part of the soul, reason, would keep watch over the passions and keep them in their just bounds. However, say the Stoics, this
is absurd because the soul is indivisible, comprised of reason—vigorous
or enfeebled—alone. When reason is enfeebled and its muscles cramp
and tremble, engaged in an effort beyond their strength (this trembling
is an affective disturbance), it will naturally be unable to judge just
bounds soundly or arrest the transition to action. Passions do not
weaken reason: they are born of an enfeebled reason, and it would be
absurd to expect this invalid to keep them in check. It is not because we
have passions that we judge unwisely and tremble in our hearts with
desire or dread. It is because we have judged unwisely that we yield to
fear or desire. The parasitical trembling of enfeebled mental tone adds
to our imprudent actions that sentimental aura, that distress, fascinat-
ing or insurmountable to so many, which is called affective tonality.

We have been speaking of affective disturbance, of "cramping." The
Stoics also used another metaphor: the whirlpools of a river in flood.
This is more than a mere simile. Tone is indeed a kind of electric current running through the nervous system, composed of fire and air,
and called the soul—you either are or are not a materialist. Seneca
teaches us that in animals, beings less perfect than us, the motions of
the instincts are often disordered and agitated. This has important consequences because it allows a better understanding of the great promise Stoicism offers us, in Seneca's words: "a fully happy existence
passing in a regular flow," not as a torrent. Our author is simply paraphrasing the Greek word *eurhoia*, which must not be translated as
"prosperous flow"—Stoicism has no concern for prosperity, but rather
as "smoothly running current," or "regular flow." If our existence
passes without affective whirlpools, we will have real happiness, a true
existence reduced solely to the exercise of reason, at once excellence and
assured tranquillity.[16]

Henceforth, we will be only the serenely heroic part of oneself, the
only part worthy of the title of man. In truth, we are *only* that part,
except for our errors. We are fallible angels, true, but we have nothing
bestial about us. From time to time, Seneca, in the desire to kindle the
narcissistic enthusiasm of his readers or disciples, teaches that it is necessary to rise above animality and scale the ladder of mortal creatures
up to the supreme level reserved for us by nature, that of a reasonable
being. We must specialize in what nature has attributed to us alone,

reason. This would seem to be offered as a choice among angel, beast, and some mixture of the two. In reality, this choice between human and animal is only a manner of speaking. Seneca is not urging us to renounce an animal component no longer extant in us, but to forsake our all-too-human side and the vagaries of our blinded reason. We would choose this path for ourselves if our eyes saw clearly, because it is the path of self-interest, if properly understood. The beginning of wisdom, he says elsewhere, is "to become friend to oneself," that is, to pursue our own interest, which is to free ourselves from error and vices in order to become truly happy.

There is no beast in us, trying to save its skin; it is our human reason judging, because of insufficient tone, that dying is an evil. If reason only judged better, it would be free. Then it would desire only one thing: to remain what nature made it—an autonomous, reasonable being. Then we would be in an *absolute* state of security. We would never tell ourselves, for instance, that a passion could enrich our soul or even lead us to a discovery. We would never take the risk of attaching ourselves to an external good because it would result in its own inevitable downfall.

Those who are not Stoics run the risk of thinking that this assurance comes at a steep price. Things such as desire, fantasy, adventure, initiative, creativity, fashion, hope and even, as we shall see, cultural life and civilization—all these disappear from our horizon. Everything is rationalized, marked with signposts; nothing unexpected can happen. A Stoic will never experience the sensation of fainting before a miracle. Things are of no interest in themselves, because, as Seneca writes, "virtue has need of nothing, it makes its happiness out of what it has, coveting nothing it lacks." Reason gives no orders, but waits for cases to be submitted for its judgment. Reason is without content, and the fortress of government is indeed empty.

We read of this fortress in *Letter* 82, but Seneca specifies in advance that only an advanced education in philosophy can build it for us.

> Let philosophy erect around us the impregnable fortress which fortune with all its artillery will assault without breaching. If the soul has had the wisdom to extricate itself from external things and make itself independent thanks to this castle, it occupies an untakeable position. For this, we have only one means: knowledge of nature and of man.

Or, as we would say, of the philosophy of nature and of anthropology.

This is Stoicism's explanation of man's search for happiness and of how nature has prepared the path by bestowing the gift of reason as a guide. But what is this esoteric knowledge (called philosophy or wisdom), doing in the midst of nature?

BE YOUR OWN LIBERATOR

Every man leaves nature's hands as a sound seed, but the development of this seed is immediately warped by the sensations of pleasure and pain, and society makes this universal error reverberate in each individual. Could it be that nature is ill-formed? No, because nature made the elaboration of wisdom or philosophy possible, whose lessons it will be our personal merit to follow, thus rectifying our initial perversion. This wisdom, an immemorial knowledge common to all, has always been known deep down, and Stoic doctrine only recalls it—insistently—to our attention. Thanks to wisdom, we will lead happy lives and, if we do not become perfect sages, "our lives will at least become bearable and sheltered." On the other hand, without philosophy, it is impossible to live without trembling, impossible to be secure—*sine philosophia, nemo intrepide potest vivere, nemo secure.*

Irrational animals cannot go wrong, having neither passion nor vice, nor, for that matter, merit. What replaces instinct in man, reason, can make mistakes, but it is also bound to discover the central truths on its own. Everyone has an inborn desire for happiness, but recognition of the true method to attain it is not innate, nor is it a sensation in the way that colors or pleasure are. It is an idea that must be worked out, but happily, this occurs very early and universally because nature has given all of us a presentiment of virtue. "We are born without virtue, but for it." Nature created us "educable, by giving us an incomplete, but perfectible, intelligence." That was all nature had to do because reason is its own guide, it will know how to find the path.

I referred previously to the presentiment of virtue. It is a fact that we may cast about for a long time in our naïveté, wanting education, but in our very first lesson we understand what the good is, and blush. We recognize it without having ever seen it, and so we must have had the seeds of morality in us all along. "Nature has given all people the foundations and seed of virtue." The innate beginnings of the good are present in the newborn. Along with virtue, we have presentiments of a divinity. These "prenotions"—the technical term—of divinity and morality work as a kind of spark. When someone instructs us and reminds our senses of a duty otherwise unknown, the spark "becomes flame with the breath of speech." The image should doubtless be taken literally: words are made of air in motion, and only their meaning is incorporeal. In short, the shock of sensation is necessary for us to form the idea of virtue. This idea is quite different from individual opinions, which vary between one person and another, because they do not arise from a natural prenotion. Sufficient proof is found in the fact that all peoples have both a system of morals and a religion. We moderns are inclined rather to think that universal consensus is suspect—nothing is commoner than superstition, belief in spirits, or machismo—but for the Stoics, whatever is universal is natural (because chance would tend instead toward a diversity of opinion) and what is natural is true, because nature is too good to mislead us.

Sensation is a physical shock inciting us to form new ideas. A repetitive painful sensation causes us to form the idea of suffering. We see the connection between the sun and daylight, and the resemblance between fire and lightning. What, then, of excellence or virtue? We form our idea of it by analogy[17] alone because virtue is an extremely broad notion, the principle from which are derived the many varieties of virtuous acts, such as not eating or drinking too much or helping the victims of disaster. It is the natural seed that leads us to perceive the analogy between them. The very general idea of virtue allows us to rise above sense impressions, among them the welcome and the painful. It also allows us to respond according to a principle, not at the whim of circumstance. Thus, pleasure and pain are on one level, and virtue on another: our initial perversion is on the horizon dividing them.

This is also where we find wisdom. "You won't find anyone who doesn't think that wisdom is a good and that it is good to be wise," except for those who are not—the mass of men in their madness. Of course, what people say is a babel of confusion, so greatly do opinions vary. Rather than relying on mere talk, therefore, we should confine ourselves to discourses that matter: to poetry, the original language, to Homer and the classics like Euripides and Menander, or to the proverbs and adages taught to children. There the ancient storehouse of wisdom is to be found. Chrysippus cited Euripides for pages on end to prove by his words that men think with their hearts, not with their minds, and Seneca brings in schoolboy proverbs as witnesses with the utmost seriousness. Stoic philosophy is not a revelation—an event marking a turning point in the spiritual evolution of humanity—if it were, it would be suspicious. It only repeats what men have always known, although they have only rarely wished to know it. The acknowledged sages, Hercules and Socrates, came a millennium and a century, respectively, before the earliest Stoic writings. Civilization is nothing but a fashion or a perversion. Nature is ageless and knowledge of it is common to all.

Nature "causes each to be born free and unharmed; the vices that bind us are not natural." Unfortunately, although man is naturally good, reason often badly misjudges the true good. We must not exaggerate: the influence of the idea of virtue can be sensed in the ordinary course of life. People fulfill their duties, sometimes well, sometimes badly, they bring up their children, they give directions to a lost traveler, etc. Only their conduct is imperfect. They do evil as often as they do good, they are inconsistent because they are forgetful of the general principle from which all their acts should uniformly flow. Moreover, they possess what we call today "civilization," which is nothing more than an immense and unnatural excrescence of vices in the guise of collective habit. The general perversion of reason justifies the claim that, with the rarest of exceptions, all men are diseased, insane.

The founders of Stoicism, and Seneca following them, teach that this perversion has a double origin, in sensation and in popular opinion. It is produced from the moment of birth. The sensations of pleasure and pain mark the soul of the newborn; later, nurses and parents, by their own example (to say nothing of the poets' celebration of love and pleasure), habitually attach capital importance to pleasure and pain, rather than judging them by the light of reason. Their own initial perversion will be passed on to the child, as the child will do, in turn, in the next generation.[18] Scarcely has the infant left his mother's womb, leaving behind its warm prenatal humidity for this dry, cold world, than he is given a warm bath by the midwife! The first thing he learns is the difference between pain and pleasure.

No doubt, the physician Galen would object to the Stoics, how then does it come about that a baby attaches a certain importance to pleasure and pain, despite reason's disdain for them? Might it not be that reason is not everything for us? Might there be something irreducible in our sensations? It would have taken much less to enrage Seneca, who had no tolerance for the idea that pleasure might have any natural significance. What could he have replied? That sensation precedes the elaboration of prenotions by a step; that the ideological pressure of the environment is powerful; and above all, he would reply, I believe, that the soul of the newborn is still tender, and does not have sufficient tone to repel the lessons of sensation.[19]

After sensation comes the phenomenon of habituation. The importance of pleasure and pain is a prime error which, over the course of years, becomes a habit; like all habits, it resists us so well that we believe it is natural—an Epicurus could build an entire philosophy on the basis of this superstition of the pleasant. Habit reinforces itself a little more every time we yield to it. The Stoics did not believe, as their adversary Galen did, that there was an affective component of the soul, but they did believe in habituation. They imagined it, in their materialism, as a physical phenomenon, a hardening. Seneca repeatedly speaks of "hardened," "indurated," and the like, although the Stoics never dreamed of explaining how the soul hardens: daily experience (Chrysippus pointed to water turning to ice) made the process a matter requiring no explanation for them. By repetition we acquire the habit of errors of conduct (which are called "vices"), and in the same way, that of well-reasoned conduct, called wisdom. The soul remains single—not a team of two horses, one pulling to the right and the other, too easily led astray, to the left. The soul is drawn by reason alone, but reason can love pleasure, adopt comfortable habits, and harden, as though with a crust. Habit becomes second nature, an inveterate way of being (also called, in Latin, *habitus*), a chronic malady—an untreated cough becomes pneumonia, and Seneca, we may recall, was asthmatic. This is the necessary nuance to that which we were claiming at the beginning: passion is not only a simple error of judgment, but requires habituation. It is not enough to tell yourself once that the lover's embrace is nothing in order to stop loving—you must become imbued with this truth over a lengthy period.

Habit, combined with the initial perversion (which no one escapes), causes everyone to have vices, inveterate errors, which are literally diseases (Seneca loved using a medical vocabulary) of the soul. Considering all individuals, and on the collective level, all of society, whatever epoch we consider will seem to us like a colossal madhouse. The only proof of our original rectitude is the equally universal sense of shame, the homage disease pays to health. We should be wise enough not to feel irritated by this collective perversion: the guilty are, in the first place, victims, not degenerates who have abandoned wisdom. "A sage is made, not born." Seneca writes with irony of Rome's proverbial, supposed decadence: "There never was an age of innocence." Vices change from age to age, but their quantity is constant. In the period we are discussing, under the reign of the emperors, the main vice was luxury (an inadequate translation of the Latin *luxuria*, which consists of permitting oneself everything and denying oneself nothing). In the preceding age, that of the civil wars, it was cruelty. Every epoch has its dominant vice, its own form of civilization.

Seneca's vision of society is almost hallucinatory. He calls it a "gathering of wild beasts," worse than wolves because at least wolves do not devour each other. His rejection of social reality is as violent as the condemnations of bourgeois society, or of consumerism, or the *contemptus mundi* of the clergy would later be. This collective madness blankets the land and sea like a weed, covering civiliation, with its buildings, cities, and ships. (It is contrary to nature to go searching for exotic products, which divine providence surely made to grow on foreign shores.)

To find a state of society that might have been consonant with nature, one must leave history—and perhaps reality—behind. During the prehistoric golden age, men wished each other no harm, political power was exercised exclusively by good kings, and people were content with simple cabins or caves and clothing made from the skins of animals. Yet Seneca is strangely reticent in confronting such natural purity. These people, he writes, were not sages, but grown-up children. They knew nothing of error and their honesty was without merit because only a rectitude once lost and then, by means of philosophy, recovered, is meritorious. Perhaps Seneca had a subconscious desire to earn merit through pain; or maybe he was too fond of the mental bulwark of culture to admire a time when philosophy was useless. Above all, he thought that without the bulwark of philosophical reasoning, first innocence could not last, as it had nothing to put in the way of temptation.

The sicknesses of the soul have this peculiarity: the patients do not feel sick, and in their madness feel happy about their condition, so much so that "discovering that one is sick is the beginning of healing." A mental medicine called philosophy is useful: "How do I become a good person? By wanting to." In other words, I agree to consult a doctor and to follow his orders strictly.[20]

The first sentence of the *Letters to Lucilius* is this: "Yes, dear Lucilius, be your own liberator." Liberate yourself from the chains made of our indurate errors, our habitual emotions, of desire and of fear. Nothing is simpler than liberating ourselves because we are at liberty to go to the doctor. We only go there, it is true, if our intellect has allowed itself to be persuaded that we are sick and less happy than we thought. Self-love is not complacent acceptance of one's condition. You would not seek wisdom if you were not already slightly acquainted with it. The will, liberated by knowledge, allows us to regain the liberty of obeying our reason alone, and reason dictates that we do not enslave ourselves to any external object, precisely so that reason will be preserved as the condition of our independence and, thus, of our infallible security. The independence of what we may call "intellect or will" has itself as its goal and is the means of its own liberation.

How can we free ourselves from errors hardened by habit? By acquiring, through the same repetition, the truths opposed to them. With every repetition we progress in wisdom. Repeating a right pattern of conduct is not simply obedience training because we are also penetrated by the truth that makes the conduct right. This is not Pascal's method, to begin by making gestures, by "bending the machine," but its opposite. One would not perform a right act unless one had begun by understanding that before, one was doing wrong. Moreover, the rightness of an act is immediately recognizable, thanks to prenotions. Intellect comes first.

Once the error of desire or fear has been recognized, it becomes possible to interrupt the first, vicious movement. Seneca recommends this method at length in the treatise *On Anger*: refrain from acting and profit from this pause in order to pass sounder judgment on the object of irritation. In the words of the schoolroom verse:

Between your raging anger
And the tempest that it brings,
Put the interval of a night.[21]

He orders us to repeat this until it becomes automatic. This cure, accomplished through understanding of the universal truths of reason, is quite different from the psychoanalytical excavation of the lower layers of the sufferer's personal history. Everything is accomplished by the forceful intervention of reason and through habituation, and is completely without any pathetic or pathological overtones. The decision to tend to oneself does not have the brilliance of a conversion to wisdom, and the will to recover is not born of an unbearable illness. On the contrary, the afflicted person had been feeling full of health—the whole process is bathed in a tranquil intellectual light.

The same tranquillity is observable in the power of error, which is not a diabolical force; it is the same as the power of truth, but ill-employed. When an external object tempts us, stirring up our desires or inclinations, and we proceed to act, it seems to draw us to itself and to be the cause of our weakness. In fact, it is only the "proximate cause," just as opportunity creates the thief. Beholding Helen, Paris thus became the thief of love, but the true and efficient cause was none other than himself. He had not learned that there are no desirable objects, only fools who judge them to be so. Passion, according to this doctrine, is "pleonastic," it goes too far, surpassing its just limits. This is not from libidinous energy, but only from having judged the limits badly. Swept up in the occasion, we may go too far, but not out of some infinite desire with its own energy and expansive force, needing to discharge itself in one way or another. Man, as conceived by the Stoics, is far from Freud's vision.[22]

For anyone wanting to do good, the will to do so is never lacking. Seneca writes *"velle non discitur"*—willing is not taught. Whether we see truly or judge falsely, we pass automatically to the act, executing the sentence of our reason. Where we moderns speak of the will, ancient philosophy simply averred that living beings possess a natural capacity for action and are self-motivated, in technical language. Thinking that behind such spontaneity lurks a mysterious, anxious intention would be to multiply the thing itself with its verbal echo. If, in order to proceed to action it were necessary to will it, then to proceed to willing, it would be necessary to will to will. This is like Baron von Munchausen saving himself from drowning by lifting himself out of the water by his own hair. "To will" then meant "to decide" or very simply, "to do."

Of course, in order "to do," tone is necessary; analogously, it is needed for judging, too. In both cases, we will expend the amount of tone of which we can avail ourselves, neither more nor less: a great deal in order to judge well, and less to judge wrongly. However, it will never be possible to assert a lack of tone because tone owes its existence to the Stoics' need to explain that the soul was not only a passive receptor of information, but also manipulated it and acted in consequence. Energy is the dynamic counterpart of movement, the reverse of the coin, which is always the same size, neither larger nor smaller than the obverse.

In return, we can look at the coin from either side. At times Seneca says, "Be careful! Stretch your soul," and, he implies, "You will judge well." At others he says, "Judge better of it," with the understanding that in order to judge aright, the soul will stretch itself as much as necessary. Progress in this is not a question of will, but of practice. Chrysippus would say that the soul learns to stretch itself by practice, but also that with exercise, truth becomes habit and sets like ice.[23] Will and knowledge go hand in hand, as do understanding and action. Seneca did once turn away a disciple presented to him because his vices were too hardened to be curable, but neither Seneca nor any other Stoic would ordinarily accuse someone of a lack of will.

Action consonant with virtue was no longer conceived as the result of a conflict between different parts of the personality. The Stoic scheme rested on the state, healthy or diseased, of a unitary personality. The will carries out our decisions, and mental tone must assist, with intellect and will in lockstep, either inferior or equal to their task; the libido is without independent energy. Our impulses are only responses to the stimuli of the external world, and life is not a prodigal expense of spirit, as some later thought. Its motto is *"Je maintiendrai"*—I will stand firm. Creativity, initiative, attack, quest, the will to power—none of these exist. Every factor of our being is already in play; no potential energy is hiding in some corner, fraying its leash. Beyond will, intellect, and habituation by practice and exercise there is yet a third factor, always passed over silently: time—the time we take to understand, if we have sluggish minds; the time to unlearn our habits, if we have a vice.

Plenty of time will be needed. To be a philosopher, "the space between childhood and old age is very short. You must spend all the years of your life, learning to live." Even at sixty, Seneca was still going to hear a philosopher's lectures, adding that one would be truly lucky if, at the cost of incessant study, he arrived in old age at greatness and rectitude of soul. An entire lifetime "is barely enough as a mere apprenticeship in disdaining life." The dialogue *On the Brevity of Life* confesses frankly that many very great men realized on their death beds that they had still not completed the task of learning to live. Lucian mischievously ridiculed those Stoics who lived their whole lives trying to learn how to live.[24]

TIME AND ATTENTION

Becoming a sage, then, or less ambitiously, progressing toward wisdom, takes a long time. Oddly, though, the Stoic does not seem to be preoccupied with this. He does not wonder anxiously if he will be among the elect or if he will be taken away before reaching his goal. Apparently, sufficient unto the day is its evil. Seneca, like Saint Augustine after him, regrets only having discovered the truth so late. Concerning his future, though, he is neither impatient nor fearful.

This Stoic attitude toward time is at once curious and revelatory; we must stop a moment to examine it. As we shall see, it is not unrelated to an even more bizarre anomaly: the Stoics unabashedly admitted that the sage, who is the goal of their exertions and the raison d'être of their philosophy, may never have existed, or if at all, only in the rarest of circumstances.

To recapitulate: a Stoic puts himself on a trajectory that ought to lead him from the general, though abnormal, state of inmate in a madhouse, to mental health. This state of mental health, once grasped, will be final and definitive. It is consonant with nature, all of whose efforts tend toward it, and it is as rational as it is natural. It is as stable as a pyramid which, set abnormally on its pinnacle, falls at last onto its base, but not instantaneously: a little time is needed before the pyramid resumes its normal position. Likewise, time is needed to arrive at the rationally utopian state of the sage; it takes time for human reality to resume its theoretically normal aspect.

(Communism, as part of the current of history, also needed time to come into being, according to the laws of historical rationality.

Structurally, Stoicism and Marxism have this in common: time meas-ures—and annuls—the interval separating the real from the rational, reality from theory. History needs time to come to rest, but at the same time, the distance separating theory from reality loses all importance. This is not an argument against theory because it is only a simple mat-ter of time. No one would put everything in doubt for so little, espe-cially when there is no fixed deadline. The process could last indefinitely; perhaps no one as yet has attained the status of sage.)

Does all this leave the belief in the truth of Stoicism and the sage unshaken? On the contrary: the motions most obedient to rational mechanics are instantaneous only in dreams; in reality, they come about only at the price of extended interaction. Modern economics provides a framework that allows us to understand the Stoic's belief in the sage. This theory describes a state of the market in which supply and demand have at last come into equilibrium, which (as is mathe-matically demonstrable) has the happy result of maximizing the shared interests of the community. This final, optimal state is reached only at the end of a certain amount of time because of the interactions within the system. But even if true equilibrium has never been reached, the the-ory allows us to comprehend the movement of prices (they tend toward equilibrium) and to prescribe the most rational policies (lower trade barriers, free competition, etc.). So, if you asked an economist, "In all of recorded history, has this equilibrium ever been reached?" he would reply without the slightest embarrassment that, no, it probably never has, but that all in all, that is unimportant. By aiming at equilibrium and applying rational policies, we progress toward the optimum state and escape from the economic doldrums. The Stoics brandished the ideal of the sage in the same way, thinking of individuals "in progress" toward wisdom—Seneca called them *procedentes* and he himself was one of them, obviously not a sage.

Stoicism, Marxism, and economic theory are rationalist systems subject to interactions over time, so to speak. The first two doctrines are both intellectualizing. The "oppressed masses" and we, the "men-tally ill" have no inherent quality preventing us, in principle, from fol-lowing our interests and liberating ourselves. Our soul is undivided and we only need time to become aware of our unhappy situation, to con-vince ourselves of the remedy, to educate ourselves in their daily strug-gles, and to relieve ourselves of the ideologies that initially blind us.

Time is needed to explain all of this, but there is no need for delay. If we seem to be dawdling, it is only because no one has sufficiently explained (a sacred term in Communist cell meetings) the truth to us, or because the doctrine has not penetrated the masses deeply enough, or impregnated the soul of the person progressing toward wisdom. In the end, everyone will understand because all are equal in reason, but it will take more or less time (because time, for doctrines dependent on interaction, is always indeterminate). It is customary to praise Stoicism for acknowledging that slaves were reasonable beings, but it went further yet. Seneca admits that women, "those thoughtless beings, restive, incapable of resisting their desires," were nonetheless educable, at the cost of the most strenuous instruction.[25]

As for the perfect sage, Seneca writes with magnanimous humor that he is as rare as the phoenix, glimpsed once or twice a millennium at most. This was official dogma: in all time there were one or two— Hercules surely and Socrates, probably. Some added the Cynic Diogenes, and Seneca patriotically included the Elder Cato among their number. The sect did not grant the status of sage to its own founders.[26] This was understood: "To this day, there has never been a perfect sage, nor a consummate orator," wrote a cultured expert on farming,[27] evoking the two rival human archetypes, the philosopher and the rhetorician.

But even if the sage could never exist, his model (in the sense that we speak of mathematical models in economics) justified the efforts made to approach this state and the rational path to follow. In beautiful, almost lyrical pages, Seneca draws the sage's portrait again and again to arouse our enthusiasm and illustrate the point at which all our parallel efforts converge. Therefore it is not altogether true that Stoicism was an elitist doctrine imposing sainthood as the norm. It did no more than Catholicism with its teaching that everyone should endeavor to imitate Jesus Christ, not in the hope of equaling such a god, but to follow in his path, because it is good. Seneca confines himself many times to a more accessible ideal, that of the "good man," which everyone ought to be able to attain. However, he still flaunts the loftier image of the sage as a point of revolutionary honor, distinguishing his sect from the popular reformism of prudential systems of morals (Rome offered a proverbial morality of wisdom and of uprightness, which was taught in the schools). Similarly, authentic Stoicism was easily distinguishable from the eclectic exploitation Cicero made of it in his efforts to educate the Roman people. The ideal of the sage is almost completely absent from his adaptations.

Seneca truly believed in the reality of the sage as a real possibility which, even if rarely achieved, was provably coherent and of daily usefulness. It is demonstrably true, for instance, that it is possible eventually to suppress emotion because theory shows that emotions are always the consequences of an act of judgment. The time it might take to reach that point does not enter into consideration, being deemed both beside the point and a given, as well as external to the rational model. Pure economic theory similarly loses sight of time: in it, the economist waits absent-mindedly for the equation of supply and demand to reach a stable balance; in the long run equilibrium will be reached. This caused Keynes, a confirmed empiricist faced with the need to reduce unemployment in England in the 1930s, to remark, "In the long run, we will all be dead." And a Stoic dies before becoming a sage.

The paradox of the extreme rarity of sages—or even of their nonexistence[28]—has attracted almost no commentary, being mentioned simply as a curiosity, an example of Stoic extremism. This is not in the least extremist, however, but rather revelatory of the deep structure of Stoicism. Taken literally, the paradox seems huge: it comes down to saying that Stoicism exists, but there have never been any Stoics. Everything dealt with by this doctrine went right over the heads of its followers, except for a few pages treating those in progress (the *procedentes*) and the degrees by which their progress was measured. They were often reminded that the last gap between the most advanced practitioner and the true sage remained so large that it was practically impossible to cross it: the sage was a being of a different order entirely. Seneca has recourse to an all-or-nothing comparison: you can drown just as easily a few yards offshore as in the middle of the sea. You are either in the water or on land; there is nothing in between.[29]

Let it be clearly understood that the real difference between the sage and the rest of humanity is on a metaphysical level: it is the distinction between pure rationality and empiricism. Stoic rationality, however, does not hover in the heavenly realm of ideas: it resembles instead a thread of pure gold entwined in the depths of reality like a vein of ore. Empiricism is an approximative rationality, closely approaching pure reason because it is from reason that it receives its orientation and value. Remember that the Stoics had no thought of conveying the revelation of unknown secrets to mankind; they thought they were only untangling the implicit and incomplete meaning of human conduct.

Consequently, the sage's exaltation did not entail the devaluation of the rest of humanity, quite the contrary. Stoicism was not an elitism, still less a hyperbolic provocation. The model of the sage was made inaccessible only in order to preserve its pure rationality, because it was only that pure gold that gave meaning and value to the all-too-human conduct surrounding it. They elevated the sage to unreachable heights only to elevate ordinary people. Empiricism would have no meaning if it were thought that sagedom could be reached by approximation.

The Stoics had a taste for the paradoxical that their contemporaries, not understanding its import, found amusing. The paradox of the sage's nonexistence was a way of expressing their concept for a rationality embedded in empiricism in a period when neither mechanical rationality nor economic theory existed, and every distinction between the real and the rational ran the risk of being interpreted as a radical separation in the tradition of Plato. This was an awkward situation, as a passage from Musonius reveals. How can we believe in the possibility of virtue if it seems to be beyond the capacities of human nature? The only proof that virtue is possible is the existence of sages; Musonius, rather than naming the sages, declares that it is not impossible that sages may exist—one day.[30]

Far from being ruinous, the admission of the sage's nonexistence was comforting, and another widely decried paradox became understandable. All faults are equal: it is no worse to kill your father than to steal an egg. Seneca defends a corollary paradox: whoever is not a sage simultaneously commits every conceivable fault and vice. Certainly, in courts of law, not every fault merits the same punishment, but for philosophers, whose only concern is to distinguish the rational from the real, a course of conduct is either in conformity with reason or it is not—a single point makes all the difference. For those interested in the diversity of human character, a miser suffers from a different vice than a glutton, and a person who had all vices at once would be a prodigy. In the eyes of a Stoic, however, all vices are equal with respect to their nonconformity to the rational conduct of the sage, which Seneca expresses in his own way: whoever is not a sage has all vices, but only virtually; in practice, every real individual has only his own.[31]

We find the same all-or-nothing paradox in Kant, intended to illustrate the gap between a rational model and its empirical embodiments. Not a single act, he writes, has ever been accomplished out of a pure moral sense. In this, Péguy saw a sterile rigor. "Kantianism," he thought, "has clean hands, only it doesn't have any hands." This is to mistake a philosopher for a preacher. Kant does not decide in our stead that one must keep one's hands clean even if all the world should perish. Rather, he analyzes the phenomenon of morality as a chemist analyzes sugar or an economist, the market. He is not seeking to advance his own morality at the expense of another, but rather wishes to know what morality *is*, as it is found in the real world. To do this he proceeds in two steps. First, he declares that a rule is a moral one whenever it is obeyed because it is the rule: duty is categorical. Then he extracts from this a rational model, that is, one that is apt to bring such categorical obedience into reality:

> *If* what people want is that morality function categorically, *then* it would be necessary for them to obey rules out of sheer docility, not out of charity, a taste for perfection, altruism, the pleasure of acting rightly or, at best, out of a sentiment of respect. This is because, should these self-interested motives disappear, there would be no impetus to obey the rule.

At this point, Kant is claiming two things: that this coherent model is the one that, in reality, people aim for, thinking that only the will is good, ready to sacrifice its own interests to the sense of duty. He also is claiming that this model, in its theoretical purity, is applied only by means of emotional motives. It is in this sense that no act in conformity with pure theory has ever been produced, but it remains the case that, by means of moral conduct such as the philosopher observes around him, he is able to uncover an approximation of the theoretical model.[32] For instance, the Stoics themselves fulfilled their duties not because of duty alone, but, as we shall see, out of a desire to bring their individual selves into conformity with the great Self, the universe, or as we have already seen, because they wished to be happy. They nonetheless expected that everyone would do his duty, even if it resulted in suffering.

These all-or-nothing paradoxes, it should be remembered, ultimately lead to a valorization of the efforts of those in progress, advancing little by little toward a goal beyond the realm of experience, that will never be reached. But their actions have meaning, and they are not wasting time when aiming at a pure rationality. The ideal model must not be confused with salvation: not becoming a perfect sage and being damned are two different things. Salvation is a judgment that declares that everything one has done up to one's last day is gained or lost. Prior to this final test, all hangs in the balance. On the other hand, every step closer to the model is an immediate and irrevocable gain, even if the theoretical model is never attained. The steps of progress are immediately recognizable, and never placed back in doubt.

This is the source of the absence of anxiety or impatience we spoke of. The life of the progresser, that of every Stoic, is transformed by it, and is positive in every direction. Even though the "revolution" of the sage remains visible like a lodestar over the horizon, guiding the disciple's efforts, the tasks of the moment and the habit-forming exercises, are his sole concern, and they are enough. The recovery of mental health is the grand aim of the Stoic's life, with every other design joyfully renounced because only true happiness matters. The Stoic dedicates himself solely to this, and Seneca does not let up until he has persuaded his disciple Lucilius to resign his high financial offices in order to devote himself exclusively to wisdom. Recovery consists in following the outlines of a highly systematic plan, much more extensive than a five-year one. Lucilius will therefore need to organize his efforts as a function of a highly organized model. At every moment, existence suggests duties to us and assails us with solicitations and temptations. Will I divert myself at the theater this afternoon? Should I go into town to fulfill a social obligation? I can't leave this to chance because I have a supreme task: I must submit my duties, whether real or imagined, to the sole judgment of reason; the slightest temptation endangers my internal security; the slightest action accustoms me somewhat either to good or to evil. Living each day just as it comes, one becomes habituated to an irrational mode of life, that of the "madmen" that we all are. The Stoic's existence is one of incessant control. As Seneca says, "Every hour, an infinity of incidents arises, demanding our consideration; it is philosophy from which we must ask advice." Happiness is dependent on the "internal fortress" decreeing a permanent state of siege.

This is a revealing text. In the life of a Stoic, every minute counts. Time is precious not because it is short or because we fear we will not have enough of it—every minute has its sufficient profit, which is to have been spent rationally—but because it must not be spent without reflection. Let us imagine how an ordinary, reasonably decent person (but not a convert to Stoicism) spends time. This person has a certain number of social obligations to fulfill, along with his duties to the state, as head of a family, as a member of society, etc. Between these fixed duties imposed on him by the routine of existence, he will have free spaces where he has no need to give an account of his time. The course of his life is punctuated by isolated duties, between which there is neutral ground. For a Stoic, however, no stretch of time is neutral. If, for a moment, he has nothing to do, how will he employ this space rationally? He has every right to rest, but reason must still determine if rest is really necessary. The Stoic is like a driver who must never take his eyes off the road for a single instant because at any moment a signal may appear or an accident may occur endangering his safety. The driver must never let his attention lapse for a single instant; he must continuously focus his attention. This is a key word—attention—meaning to put under tension or tone as we used it earlier.[33] The goal of the first letter to Lucilius is to put the disciple immediately into a state of attention, which will not permit even a minute to pass distractedly. The letter's message seems to be that time is not an indifferent, fluid medium: letting it pass without reflection, drop by drop, undermines the principle of its use according to plan. We need to maintain "a soul always ready and tensed like that of athletes in boxing matches."[34] The principle of planning having been stated, the second letter begins to address the proper employment of time. Every day it is necessary to accustom oneself to the idea that poverty and death are nothing by steeping oneself in readings supporting these notions. A minute lost is more than the loss of time, it marks the onset of the loss of the habit of attention. If I decide to take a walk, I will, doing so, act fully virtuously, so long as the decision is made prudently, that is, with discretion.[35] Not losing time means using it so as not to be the pawn of circumstances, and thus to maintain oneself above time. It is not too mischievous to imagine that a Stoic would always be doing three things at once, for instance: eating, controlling his eating, and making a mini-epic out of his eating.

Thus we wage "an incessant war against pleasure and against fortune." If we granted ourselves a moment of respite, "we would be retreating and exposing ourselves to even greater danger." Completely unlike Vigny's attitude of resigned expectation, Stoicism is combative because its positive project is to bring mankind into conformity with what nature prepared it to be. Philosophy is a course of conduct, not gratuitous knowledge; it is an enterprise, a new mode of living, indeed the greatest of enterprises, "the great work" for which "gods gave us the capacity, without giving us consciousness of it." In *Letter* 53, which would scandalize even the seventeenth century's Christian Stoics, Seneca goes so far as to say that the sage's merit "surpasses that of God," who only had to go to the trouble of being what he is.

Total devotion to this great work is required because philosophy is "a queen who does not suffer her courtiers to dedicate only a portion of their attention to her"; a continual tension must be exerted on the soul, "otherwise its spring will relax" and we will give up the ground gained the day before. We must also fend off all kinds of pursuits that might distract us from an assiduous course of study, including daily meditation. What does "study" mean? Evidently, not acquiring information, but self-formation.

The program of this formative study could be expounded in many different ways. Seneca's *Dialogues* approach it from their own particular angle, and the *Letters* follow a progressive plan that is more pedagogical than systematic. All in all, the study of wisdom consists of giving the soul a schematic form, that of the four virtues, which are in reality one.[36] For his part, Seneca enumerates them only a few times, but all his writings presuppose them, as the virtues imply a practically complete inventory of our moral world. Broadly speaking, Temperance concerns what one hesitates to call the "desirable," because it seeks only what is truly good and flees the objects of lust of all kinds. Courage is opposed to weakness in the face of death, or before philosophical effort and the like. Justice concerns, obviously, relations with others. Prudence or discernment is first among the virtues because it recognizes the truth of what is good or bad (that is, what is desirable), what is to be feared, and what is unjust. Mankind exists in a world where all is temptation or menace, and nothing is completely indifferent. Because virtue is all-enveloping, nothing is haphazard except whether "the number of hairs on my head is even or odd." No object or event escapes the jurisdiction of the virtues, all jointly dictating everything we ought to do, all our duties, including whether to take a simple walk. Our lives are entirely organized, the numbers of our hairs aside, by this committee of the four virtues.

The sage is a person who has accustomed the "neurons" of his soul to function according to a plan obedient to this scheme, what Seneca calls "having an ordered soul." He also writes that when "this order holds sway," our souls are "harmonious" after the old image of a just man's soul being comparable to a well-tuned lyre. This is doubtless more than metaphor: the Stoics' representation of the nervous system constituting the soul was comprised of "currents" under tension radiating from a center, the governor—Seneca alludes to this in *Letter* 113. The currents dispatch information derived from the senses to the center and transmit the order to act to the limbs. If these currents are "tensioned" appropriately, the soul will be in harmony.

How do we arrive at such harmony? By creating a habit through repeated exercises. "Exercise" is our translation of Greek *melete* and Latin *meditatio*, in English "meditation." A meditating Stoic is not trying to solve a philosophical difficulty or considering an idea from all possible angles. Rather, he carries an idea within himself for a time in order to imbue himself with it. Such meditation is a daily affair. The spiritual exercises of the Stoic are purely intellectual, and the emotions, obviously, have no place in them nor, for that matter, do our imaginings of truth. There was no Stoic Ignatius of Loyola to teach us to render inwardly and vividly the travails of the sage named Hercules. These exercises, were far from codified, known from tradition, or reinvented as evidence because they did not form a body of instruction. Partly, they were left to individual initiative and arose by occasion. When Seneca had a thought-provoking object before him, he profited from it by considering the truths it suggested to him. To form yourself according to truth, you must incessantly inform yourself: read the works of the sect's writers, attend philosophical lectures, keep a journal of meditations (like Marcus Aurelius) or, like Seneca, write in order to spread the good word and to be penetrated more deeply by it.

To all this we may add what is roughly termed the examination of conscience, although it was far from a general practice. Seneca describes it as peculiar to a thinker named Sextius, whose sect had died out. Every evening, Sextius inquired of his soul, "Which of your maladies have you treated today? Which vice have you resisted? In what respect have you bettered yourself?" He was not examining himself about his sins, but rather summing up his progress, doubtless so as not to lose the habit of performing the daily gymnastic exercises to straighten the soul.

The examination of conscience seems to have been a Pythagorean institution, while Stoic rationalism was little inclined to rites and institutions, with their whiff of superstition. At most, Stoicism endorsed a special theme for meditation consisting of putting oneself imaginatively in an unhappy situation like illness or exile, in order to accustom oneself to such a contingency.[38] The practical exercises Seneca recommends, like sleeping on a pallet or dining on coarse bread, are also a way of actively premeditating ruin and poverty. His recommendation comes, however, with a caution: he fears that an element of ostentation and snobbism may mix in. Generally speaking, Stoicism never developed its therapeutic side: the founding fathers mainly developed a general theory of the diseases of the soul, and Seneca himself is more of a clinical observer than a healer.[39] We might better say that he encourages his disciples to practice a universal therapy never reducible to specific remedies: impregnating oneself with truth.

These brave efforts will ultimately result in an attitude (a word combining thought and action) that will necessarily be immutable, spontaneous, and systematic. Stoicism cannot be lived except by commanding the doctrine as a whole, connecting each precept with the rest. These changes will find their reality in a physical transformation of the soul in its entirety. Each person's conduct will become constant and internally coherent, no longer changing with mood, lack of reflection, or hesitation. It won't be a case of one day saying, "I'm going to get married," and, the next, "I'll make do with a concubine." The sign of error is that it varies and is multiple, while "the good is never incoherent or irregular." The phenomena of fashions enraged Seneca and were enough to damn so-called culture and civilization in his eyes. Fashions amount to imitation, and in them we reencounter the social pressure underlying the initial perversion of the individual. The great principle of "living uniformly with nature" in practice comes down to simply "living uniformly."

Rightly judging everything that arises and acting correctly in response will therefore become as spontaneous as a reflex. There will be no further need for reflection or for a pause halting a first, but false, step. Truth will present itself to the mind "of its own and without delay." The proper precepts will be "at hand, ready to be applied," even in the most trying circumstances. Truth, as we know, over the long run, has a physical effect on what must be called the body of the soul, and philosophy is analogous to a potter or a smith, "giving shape to the soul, fashioning it."

The transformation will either be complete or not at all. It is not enough to acquire precepts one by one: in addition, one needs to acquire the view of the whole where their justification is to be found. The whole cannot be understood without an understanding of the precepts, but a precept cannot be understood apart from the whole. This seemingly vicious circle troubled some Stoics greatly, but we moderns call it the hermeneutic circle and realize that there is nothing vicious about it. If there were, no one could ever learn a language or understand the shortest sentence, in which each word takes its meaning from the whole. In fact, it is enough to begin at one end, and the whole eventually comes along. It is possible, therefore, to learn both foreign languages and Stoic philosophy. Nonetheless, we will never have stably and definitively assimilated it until the whole has been understood and, as a corollary, our soul has been totally transformed. The physical solidity of a soul become Stoic goes hand in hand with the logical coherence of its thinking. An individual precept, poorly linked to general principles, will soon be forgotten and its habit unlearned. The Latin word *solidus* also means "all of a piece," "coherent," "faultless." Stoicism has a taste for the monolithic.

A perfectly conceived program, without faults or gaps, can neither be added to nor modified. This realm of obsession was likely to attract people troubled by their impulses or their internal multiplicity, who needed to simplify their characters and restrain themselves. The world of Stoicism, with its clear-cut boundaries was reassuring to them, albeit at the price of so narrow and monotonous a rationalism that some have found in it a juvenile ignorance of life's painful or wonderful realities and an impoverished idea of the human. Nature, taught the Stoics, is as simple as a well-wrought machine, and man is simple in nature's image. Every act has an end—by definition, man's happiness. Man is mad enough to complicate this straightforward scheme, and thus is unhappy; but he has only to eliminate these complications, and he will be authentically happy.

There is no variety of aspect in this world, no inequalities, and no vacuum. Perfect things are equivalent to one another: there is no way for one sage to be more perfect than another. Virtue fills the soul, leaving no empty space that it might covet. The universe is not expanding because "matter cannot spread further once it has reached its natural size; the vault of the heavens maintains the same dimensions forever." Regardless of perspective, things remain what they are and do not conceal unsuspected aspects. From every possible angle, "virtue is the same as if one could see it from all sides at once." It is so regular a solid that, perceiving one of its faces, we might believe we were seeing its ground plan. Time causes things to last, but cannot make something more perfect or reveal in it any novelty—and so much the better.

This world, with no exterior or gaps, is uniform. None of its parts has its own color, or sounds its own little tune that might make our ears prick up. Excellence covers the whole like a coat of paint. Pleasure is only an aggressive futility, and desire must be eliminated as a crime of indefiniteness or infinitude: "It loses its way in formless and boundless immensity." Moral progress is not an adventure—we know where we are going, laboriously it is true, but with the soul of an accountant, simply figuring the balance. "I have acquired this, but yesterday I lost that." An hour of music would add nothing to the credit side of the ledger. One day Seneca was in Naples, where he was attending the lectures of a philosopher. A musical contest had been organized in the theater—Naples, still an entirely Greek city, was a cultural center of international repute, and many foreign virtuosos had come to take part in the contest. Seneca recounts the event in these terms:

> I am ashamed for the human race every time I leave my doors. To get to
> the lecture hall, you have to pass the length of the theater. It was packed,
> and vigorous discussions were going on to decide who would win the
> prize for best flutist. One trumpeter, a Greek, and another, Latin, also
> had their fans. But on the benches in the school of wisdom, practically
> no one.

To be sure, vain pastimes of this kind are worthy of condemnation, but the Stoic openly grants that we do need relaxation. Rest is a natural function, and so a duty, but our initial perversion is such that we often do not attain complete relaxation. "Sometimes our mind is occupied with gladiatorial combats, but in the midst of a spectacle created to amuse us, it so chances that a slight shadow of melancholy steals into us."

But such shadows cannot insinuate themselves into the sage, with his self-sufficient security. He puts into serious practice an ironic aphorism of Pascal: "All of mankind's unhappiness comes from a single thing—not knowing enough to rest quietly in a room." The thought that living like this would lead to death from boredom never even crossed the Stoics' minds. The Stoic behaved like a heat regulator, reacting to every leap in the ambient temperature to maintain the central heating at a constant level. Stoicism was one kind of homeostat, and Epicureanism was another.

The ideal of the Stoic sect, and of all other ancient sects, was quietude. For the Stoics this was a well-regulated state of the soul (with its tensions harmoniously tuned like a lyre) and "there is no peaceable quietude unless it is regulated by reason,"[40] that is, by judgment, the controller of emotion.

No philosophy could be farther from our own. We no longer believe that the objects of our fears or desires are simply placed before us, being nothing other than what they are. Instead, we believe that with no objective reality of their own, they are what fear or desire causes them to appear to be. Their reality is our doing, not blunt, neutral fact, and it is not our judgment, true or false, that makes them seem frightful or desirable. According to whether we are frightened of death or view it with cold objectivity, we are not imagining the same death, and an objective vision of our beloved does not destroy the loving vision we also have. We are, so to speak, no longer dealing with the same person, so much so that no objective judgment will ever subdue our amorous intent. We do not think with our conscious mind, but with our body. It desires, it fears, and if it stops fearing, judgment has nothing to do with it: it is the body that has become courageous.[41]

Human nature reduced to the choice between right or diseased reason, with emotions that are no more than false judgments about objects external to the true self—so simplistic a conception of man is incapable of perceiving the most obvious evidence. Stoic moral accountability, with its cut-and-dried balance sheets, cannot accept the slightest deviation by imagining, for example, that a fault one has not committed can entail a far greater deficit, ravaging a whole life through frustration.

Accountability is the issue, and this explains what can only be called the insipidity of Stoic ideas on death. Yes, considered from the point of view of the Beyond, death is nothing because once dead, we are no longer around to realize it. If, on the other hand, we look at death from the side of life, with eyes of flesh, the idea of nonexistence is as unbearable as looking straight into the sun. This anguish is not an illusion that mental exercises can dissipate; it is inscribed in the depths of our existence. Our existence does not, so to speak, draw a line under each instant's reckoning, but unrolls in a false, instantaneous present which is, at the same time, a perpetual future. The terrifying idea that one day there will be no more future for us is inscribed in the heart of the present. Whenever we begin to speak the shortest sentence, whenever we are in the process of speaking it, we have in mind the sentence as it will be when completed, or if not, the embarrassment of not having the words to complete it on our tongue. Time is not lived as a succession of minutes (except for washing machines and other automata), with no advance thought of its progress, living events as they occur. Men are different, always pulling toward the future the fleshly burden that death will mutilate at whatever moment it arrives.

The Stoics pretend not to know this, which is in itself very revealing. They want to believe that they are only responding, minute by minute, to what time brings them: a duty to fulfill, a temptation to resist. Deep down, a Stoic is not interested in anything—he only reacts.

"Stoicism," to paraphrase Hegel, "found itself embarrassed when asked what was true and good. The response was thought itself, with no content at all. Rationality comprised by itself truth, the good, wisdom, and virtue. Though edifying, this language quickly begets boredom, since no positive content could arise from the good or from virtue."[42]

This is a severe judgment, but it expresses the overall impression well. In detail, though, it is unjust. In fact, the Stoics attacked the problem of content on two fronts, each time able to develop a response, for whatever it is worth. We may amuse ourselves by giving the two questions in the drolly paradoxical form the Stoics favored:

1. Because death is nothing, why will a Stoic crossing the road and seeing a reckless driver bearing down on him, not let himself be run over?

2. Because death is nothing, why does a Stoic rush to the aid of a neighbor, the victim of an earthquake, instead of leaving to the neighbor's governing faculty the burden of deciding whether the misfortune is external to him and no danger to his security?

Given its appetite for being a totalizing doctrine, Stoicism attempts in this way to reconcile its dogmas with the fact that external reality does count and that we do feel concerned for other people. This is at the cost of some inconsistencies and of a reorientation of the fundamental project of the doctrine, as well as of a broadening of the Stoic attitude with respect to the cosmos.

IS THERE NO GOOD OTHER THAN THE IDEAL?

In truth, even according to the Stoics themselves, people have a strong interest in certain things. The instinct for self-preservation is natural, for instance, and not all of our inclinations are as wrong as empty fears or carnal longings. Some are in conformity with nature, and therefore our rational judgment cannot help but approve of them. It is natural to prefer life to death and health to disease, to seek health as a desirable state and to be averse to sickness or suffering—at least as much as excellence, or virtue, allows (as expected, Stoicism takes back with one hand what it grants with the other). Health or survival were thus called, if not good (since only the trio of virtue, reason, and morality are inherently good), at least preferable and advantageous. Disease is the opposite, Seneca qualifying it as an inconvenience contrary to nature.

The same Seneca who exalts the bravery of the sage under torture will thus not hesitate to say that it is preferable—and equally virtuous— not to be tortured. His language is as clear as possible.

> The Good is the same whether you are lying on a bed of roses or being burned alive. There remains an abyss between joy and suffering and, if you asked me to choose between them, I would seek the former, which runs in the same direction as nature, and would avoid the latter, which is contrary to nature. Nevertheless, from the point of view of virtue, suffering and joy are equivalent.

Just as clearly—and with the same final restriction—he writes a few pages later

> How is this? In the case where health, tranquillity or the absence of suffering are not obstacles in the way of virtue, won't you seek them? But of course I will! Only I won't regard them as goods in themselves. I will seek them only because they are in conformity with Nature, and I won't adopt them until I have passed right judgment on them.

Life and health are not the only things to be preferred. Everything that makes a person a perfected, but still natural, being is to be sought after. It is better to be victorious than to be vanquished, better to have virtuous children, better that our country be saved rather than lost. In case of misfortune, it is preferable to bear sickness or exile with serenity, but it is still more preferable not be sick or exiled. Bearing illness serenely is good, but the occasion of this absolute good, its "matter," is nonetheless a state contrary to nature, disease, and its suffering. When Seneca was exiled to Corsica, he said to himself that exile is only an apparent evil because we are citizens of the whole world; at the same time, he solicited pardon from a minister because he could ask for it without dishonor. This is not irony: from the point of view of doctrine, such a double attitude was correct.

Another advantage is living in what we might call a natural state of civilization. Water is found everywhere, along with minimal nutrition and shelter. (All antiquity fantasized about cave dwellers, although modern archaeologists no longer believe in them.) These easily obtained advantages are called in Latin *parata*, resources already prepared, to which we have only to extend our hands. This was a technical term the Stoics had in common with the Epicureans, expressing the ideal of a simple, natural life, and implying that nature herself had prepared the resources destined for man's use. We must take pains to distinguish the vicious excrescencies of our so called civilization with its futile and perverse refinements, from what we may call natural civilization, of which agriculture is a part. Nature traced (in outline, as ever) the path toward the discovery of cultivating wheat. She acted so that we might be able to discover the means of making the earth our field to cultivate. It is readily apparent how opposed this naturalism is to the modern idea of human progress. Far from being advantages, the technologies added to nature serve our vices. From time to time, the Stoics have been presented as humanists, bards of the mastery of man over nature. This is a complete misconception. On the other hand, some personal refinements are authentically advantageous to man's preeminent dignity on the scale of beings. The sage is courteous, full of urbanity. He never speaks ill of his neighbor and meticulously observes the prescriptions of honorable civility.[43] According to Seneca, he even dresses suitably "since man is by nature a neat and elegant animal." Finally, because man is also a social animal, he prefers that his offspring, his fellow citizens, and all other people have the same advantages he hopes to have for himself.

All natural advantages and preferable conditions have another name—a misleading one. The Stoics also called them "indifferent." This did not mean that advantages were without importance or should leave us coldly unmoved. It only meant that by themselves, they were neither good nor bad, but neutral, without any moral tint of their own, even though preferable. They became good or bad according to the circumstances, or rather according to the use our virtue made of them. Life, preferable as it is, is neutral, and it would be an evil if we were to save our skin at the price of dishonor. In brief, preferable conditions are neutral because they are only the substance of excellence or error. To give another example: nature in its immensity, in which earthquakes and microbes are also completely natural products, may send us an illness, and this will obviously be opposed to our individual nature (the two must be kept distinct), but our reason will transform such an "anti-preferable" or inconvenience (disease) by deciding that our virtue has only to triumph over it, rather than whine about it.

As we see, the judicial organization of the human being has been slightly complicated. It functions on two levels: the lower issues propositions that the higher endorses or rejects. Down below, our nature has utterly natural preferences and aversions. On the higher level, our reason has loftier requirements. It finds the preferences of the lower level neither good nor bad in themselves, waiting to pass judgment on the use that virtue makes of them. Thus we understand why virtue, reason, and morality form the sole good: because they judge and measure the value of all the other goods which, compared to these three, are simply advantageous. In the end, as we might have expected, the ideal remains the only true good.

Still, it is true that for an instant a truth has been revealed, glimpsed like the view of a naked breast as someone changes shirts. The sage is not made of wood: he is concerned with himself, and Stoicism, despite its harshness, addresses the individual above all. (It in no way intends, for instance, to create a well-made city out of love of public order and at the expense of the citizens, as Plato does with an unbelievably good conscience.) Despite the very numerous points of view from which Stoicism may be regarded, it was truly and essentially a recipe for happiness, which only exists at the level of the individual—what would happiness be if it were never experienced in the world by an individual? Stoicism claims that some states are preferable, even though they should not always be preferred, and that these are advantageous, but not in themselves good. Preferable for whom? Not for angels or for some anonymous truth, but for an individual seeking well-being.

Let us ponder the novelty that the theory of the preferable brings. It is the affirmation that we matter and that we do not exist in order to immolate ourselves for an ideal or to resign ourselves to a grinding reality. If, on another level, the preferable is not always preferred, it will be in our better interest at a higher level. Preferable things are natural, they are *us*, not judgments falsified, like emotions, by the ambient ideology. Nor are they sensations, data external to us, in the way that physical pleasure and suffering are. Things that are preferable (health, homeland, friends, family, bodily well-being, lack of suffering and poverty) are our nature, as representatives of the human species; they are our most profound hopes. We are fundamentally individuals in search of natural well-being.

This is Stoicism at its purest. It is diametrically opposed to its vulgar image. A Stoic, supposedly, is a person who remains "stoic" in misfortune: Epictetus looks on dispassionately as his master had his leg broken; Emile Bréhier, the historian of Stoicism, digs down into his convictions and finds the strength to bear the loss of his arm during World War I and to continue to write. The fact that ancient Stoicism was something quite different from this is proved by its doctrine of suicide.

We know that happiness is as possible under torture as on a bed of roses, but the bed of roses is much to be preferred. Let us imagine, then, that I contract a painful illness, or even just a disagreeable one; or that I lose all I possess and am reduced to begging. What ought I to do, as a Stoic? Generally, the answer is to bear poverty and illness virtuously and, thanks to virtue, happily, even if it is preferable not to suffer misfortune. To put it another way, virtuous happiness will carry the day over our taste for the preferable. The ancient Stoics' response would have been quite different, however. They would have said, kill yourself, put an end to your days. Seneca, in *On the Happy Life*, replied to his critics, who made ironic fun of his immense fortune, saying that if he found himself reduced to begging in the streets, he would not make a fuss about it. He would, simply, kill himself. In the amazing *Letter 77*, a man afflicted by an "illness that, though not incurable, was painful and drawn-out," receives advice from a Stoic friend to put an end to it. This he did, by starvation, "not without experiencing," he says, "the sort of pleasure that some swoons afford."

Could this be a heretical deviation on the part of Seneca, obsessed as he was by the idea of suicide? No—it was the sect's official doctrine.[44] We should leave life, it taught, with the same happy indifference that we leave a banquet. One leaves a banquet for one of five reasons: (1) if a loved one needs you; (2) if a boorish guest shows up, giving the party an ugly tone; (3) if the food and drink are spoiled and make the guests sick; (4) if there is no more to eat or drink; or (5) if drunkenness has toppled reason. Similarly, there are five cases in which it is reasonably permitted, and even required, to leave life: (1) if it is necessary to sacrifice one's life for friend or fatherland; (2) if a tyrant forces you to say or do dishonorable things; (3) if, afflicted by an incurable or painful disease or mutilation, the soul can no longer rely on the body; (4) if you are prey to destitution or poverty; or (5) if you become mad. Therefore, it is better to kill yourself than, for instance, beg; survival is not counted among the preferable conditions. Prosperous life is preferable, while death is of no account. To live for the sake of living, just to live, has no independent value. There is no reason for displaying futile heroism to endure poverty or suffering.

How the doctrine reconciled this with the affirmation that bearing them, one would be as happy as it is possible to be, I do not know.[45] In any event, as we have seen, if the sage sacrifices his life, it is not to virtue but to those whom he loves or to his own physical and economic well-being. Thus he preserves his irreducible portion of animality and individualism. Nor is the sensation of pleasure alien to him. Of this, there is a curious proof, one of those formal asymmetries so striking to mathematicians and philosophers: corresponding to the four evil passions

there are only three good attitudes or "constancies." Faced with present
or future goods and evils, the madman experiences, respectively, pleasure or desire, pain or fear. The sage, on the other hand, with his more
constant governing faculty, will feel pure joy, a reasoned preference,
fearless defiance, and nothing corresponding to pain. Before present
evils, he is not sorrowful. As long as they were yet to come, he defied
them, but from the moment they are present, he feels nothing. Is this
because he is insensible? No, for present goods fill him with joy. Thus
we see the extent of the sage's security: painful states are foreign to him,
and the joys he knows go beyond the satisfaction of a duty accomplished. Joy, of which Seneca speaks often, is the superior form of the
satisfaction (the result of an inversion of the will to live) experienced by
an animal when, sheltered in its lair and belly full, it feels the current of
life beating regularly in its veins. The sage experiences at every moment
the well-being of realizing his soul is well ordered, fortified in its proper
disposition and functioning in accord with its natural constitution.
Such joy may come at the cost of the most frightful tests, but it remains
no less the joy of an individual.

Herein is a contradiction we cannot ignore any longer. Stoicism
affirms simultaneously that natural goods, such as health, are desirable
if we are to be happy, but that reason shows us we can do without them.
Either man is an animal and cannot forego health and remain happy,
or he is pure reason and his share of animality does not matter. Animal
or superior reasoning machine—the choice must be made.

In his *Letter* 92, Seneca was so aware of this contradiction that, in
an excess of zeal, he tried to choose by proposing a desperate solution
for the human animal: we must become angels of rationality in order to
become aware of our position at the peak of the scale of living beings.
He had already written Lucilius several letters repeating to him that it
is more natural to be healthy, but that health, contrary to Epicurus, still
does not constitute happiness. If he repeats himself in this way, it is less
in order to convince Lucilius or to wear him down—Lucilius is only a
straw man here—than because he was unable to extricate himself from
the difficulty. Here is his argument: nature has so ordained matters
that it is better for us to be healthy, to be elegantly and neatly attired,
than not to be, as reason reveals to us, but it also reveals to us that we
can be deprived of these advantages and still be happy. What gives value
to decent attire is not so much the natural pleasantness of well-being as

it is the rational character of the choice in favor of well-being. The true pleasantness is the mental superiority ratifying this choice, the pleasure of correct reasoning. Should one be in tatters and worn with disease, there remains the satisfaction of bearing oneself as a rational animal, the only naturally occuring rational living being, outside of the gods. Being rational consists in saying inwardly that disease is not an evil.

This argument strikes us as hollow and insipid. For us, it is hard to wax enthusiastic at the idea that we are superior to dogs and horses. Our snobbism is not satisfied with acting like the most distinguished members of the flora and fauna. Doubtless, the ancients felt the same way. Seneca's argument, we suspect, stemmed from a hidden impulse: egoism, self-censure, sublimation—call it what you will—ancient thought speculated so much about nature that the argument, false as it was, was not regarded as insipid. Nature entered human imagination with sufficient consistency that such zoological snobbism could seem seductive. This is referred to as "snobbism" because nature created the scale of being: plants at the bottom, and man, the rational animal, at the top, distinguished from the lesser animals by reason alone.[46] He should therefore attach value only to this distinguishing characteristic. Every living being, as Aristotle had written in the opening of the *Ethics*, has a certain way of functioning that is also a "function" or duty that must be fulfilled. Plants simply vegetate; animals live more actively and follow their instincts, while man has reason, which (if he takes it as his sole guide) can make him more than just another animal. The proper function of each being is the one peculiar to it. Reason—this means of choosing well—becomes the chosen thing. Or so, at least, *Letter* 92 concludes.

Seneca has often been called an exaggerator, a rhetor, a bombastic mind, or a typically Roman voluntarist, shriveling the will to a more or less empty heroism. It might be better to say that he understood the contradictions of Stoicism only too well, and that he tried to force his way through them at the risk of bringing down the whole edifice. Stoicism promises the sage felicity, but adds that only one or two people will attain sagacity in each millennium. It promises a naturally prosperous existence, but teaches how to forego what it promises. Seneca's only recourse, living amidst these contradictions, was to take refuge in the extremism of a zoological snobbism and, as we shall see, to stake his all on suicide and the art of dying well.

As such a naturalism, intellectualizing even in its joy, which is to be rationally self-governing, Stoicism remains an individualistic doctrine, albeit a highly idealized one. The individual finds ultimate security only in a kind of excellence or virtue that attaches value to morality or honor alone, but what is the content of this morality? We must not be lulled by grand terms like reason, virtue, and honor, which recur like a litany on Seneca's every page. What exactly do they mean? Seneca pounds out the refrain that there is no good except what is honorable.[47] What does he mean by this? Is he taking the word in its ordinary sense? What does "reason" mean? Were the Stoics rationalists in the modern sense of the term, believing that the human mind possesses an internal light and a fixed set of principles permitting the discovery of scientific truth and triumph over error? Yes and no. The Stoics believed in truth and were profoundly interested in the sciences. Among Seneca's own works are the *Natural Investigations*, but when he uses the word "reason," this is not what he is thinking about.

1. In the modern sense, reason is a kind of code of laws: universal determinism, the principle of sufficient reason, the regularity of phenomena, and so forth. This is not reason in the Stoic sense of the word, where it uniquely denotes the exercise of free judgment. Reason is only the "court" applying a code of which it is not the author. This is a simple matter of semantics: the code exists, but it is called nature or honor (because the court of reason judges, above all, cases of good and evil).

2. If reason is the court applying nature's code, excellence or virtue is what we call the act of respecting the sentences the court passes on matters of good and evil. This presupposes a certain bravery (and indeed, Latin *virtus* can also mean bravery) as well as an effort brought to bear on oneself. (Common sense recognizes acts as virtuous in part by what they cost their author.)

In any event, Stoic virtue, though it encompasses the common understanding of virtue (thou shalt not kill; thou shalt not steal; thou shalt honor thy father and mother), is much more comprehensive. It resists vices like greed, egotism, ambition, and lust, but it also stands fast before suffering and disease. It allows us to be happy and to submit to nothing, "dominating from far above chance and accident."

3. Honor and morality go far beyond what non-Stoics understand them to be. Honor is the very content of reason, the natural code

applied by its court. It is, moreover, a code in which justice is not forgotten because following nature means espousing the order of the cosmos, itself organized for the benefit of all men. In the end, though, honor fights against fate and death as much as against sin. When Seneca wants to speak of a virtue, the example that flows most readily from his pen is that of steadfastness in the face of torture. It is evident, however, that Stoic moral philosophy could encompass common sense morals. The honorable Stoic, though superior to vulgar ideas of the good, will scarcely fail to respect a contract. It was commonly acknowledged that philosophy, like religion, tended toward disinterestedness.[48] Also, any failure of duty to others is at the same time an egotistic weakness; to be unjust or cruel is to cede to external temptations; to be an egotist (in Latin, *avarus*) is also to be avaricious, and risks happiness for ever-uncertain wealth.

We can see that there could be no other good than honor because nature prescribes—for our own benefit—that we behave disinterestedly and in a manner superior to any and all events. Honor is the sine qua non of happiness, but Stoicism did not rest there—it laid down two other requirements. Honor is not only a necessary condition of felicity, it is also a sufficient one. Every happiness must be honorable, but conversely, honor is enough to make us happy. It would not be possible to be virtuous and unhappy. We shall see why, and we shall also see the underlying supposition of the ultimate requirement: doing good is not enough in itself; we must do good knowing it to be good—what is commonly, though loosely, called a morality of good intention.

The first maxim (no happiness outside of morality) guarantees us *certain* security because happiness not based on virtue will always be threatened by reversals of fortune, which are always possible. "We wish not to suffer, but to suffer courageously; misfortune is not to be wished for, but the virtue allowing us to bear it is." A tragic hero will at least have conscience on his side, even if he would prefer to have luck, too.

We may know this perfectly well, but why is it the case? The reason is economic.[49] "Virtue is the value and origin of all the other goods." Economists say that money gives value to other goods, and that paper currency is backed by bullion. Gold has a sure value, removed from the chance variations of the market. I may become rich, but this advantage is neutral and will become a good only if I put my money to good use;

no one can ever take that from me. A piece of paper—say the commission making me governor of a province—will be valueless unless those under my administration feel that they have returned to the age of gold under my rule. "Good flows from honor, which flows only from itself." The value of morality is absolute because it is its own measure; other goods are measured relative to it. "Winning a victory or not losing one's children do not make us more virtuous, and therefore do not make us happier."

Conversely, being defeated does not increase unhappiness because being virtuous is sufficient for being happy. This second maxim insures that our security will be *absolute.* "Well, would it come down to same thing if the Republic and her champion Cato, faced with Caesar, were conquerors or conquered?" Or if Seneca should convince Nero to follow the right path or not? The answer is "Yes." There is no such thing as an unhappy hero. This, too, we know—but again, why? Why does the conquered sage receive the palm of triumph, as though he were a holy Christian martyr?

It is because absolute security demands that we picture happiness as the supreme state of being of which Kant speaks, not merely a more nearly complete state. Kant may have been remembering Carneades, who said that felicity consisted of enjoying either *every* good or the supreme good.[50] With less delicacy, one authority distinguishes "effective happiness, human, coarse if you like" and "beatitude, a product of the imagination and condemned to remain unreachable."

Let us grant, indeed, that the Stoics' discussion of happiness is in large part purely verbal. Virtue alone causes felicity, but natural advantages like health and long life also matter. This only leads Seneca to repeat more insistently that these advantages can add nothing to happiness. Many of his letters, which can be found a bit longwinded, hammer away at this decree more than they clarify it. "Better not to be tortured, but if not tortured, one will be none the happier . . . "

All can be explained, I believe, if we admit that this is less a fundamental issue than a quarrel over the meaning of the word *happiness,* a quarrel in which a verbal caution is necessary. Every Stoic admitted that felicity had virtue as its necessary condition, its sine qua non. But every Stoic also admitted, without stating it explicitly, that happiness had other conditions, what we would call facultative ones. They were the "preferable neutral conditions," whether biologically natural (good

health, not being mutilated) or the advantages of fortune (not needing
to beg). Every Stoic granted that even if these advantages were preferable, one could also do without them. "*Facultative*," then, is a fit term for
them. Within the sect, all agreed to this point, but beyond, a schism
opened. Some heretical Stoics claimed that the virtuous man is happy,
but that a man both virtuous and prosperous is happier yet. To this,
Seneca reacted with revulsion, and at length. We can see the basis of the
quarrel: must we restrict the use of the noble word *happiness* to its sole
necessary condition, virtue, in order to say that virtue alone causes happiness, and that a virtuous man will be happy even if he is a cripple, or
should we stoop to include within happiness its facultative conditions?

That, as Kant says, comes down to knowing what meaning we will
decide to give the word *happiness*. In common use, the word had a sublime meaning—"Happy are those who have fallen in a just cause"—and
a more modest sense, "Being at once virtuous and prosperous, he is the
happiest of men." This is where Seneca's verbal caution comes in. He
fears that if facultative conditions are taken into account, the sine qua
non condition will be ruined. If we begin to say "He was a hero, but he
suffered the misfortune of being tortured," people will think that it is
just as important for happiness not to be tortured as it is to be a hero.

Toward the end of *Letter* 76 we encounter a page whose exaltation
and minor inconsistencies are revelatory. Images of ascension are dominant, and under the name of happiness, Seneca ends up speaking of
greatness. "Wouldn't you gladly die for the safety of your country?"
asks Seneca, who supplies his own answers. Because Lucilius had
already been asked to raise up his soul, the response is in no doubt.
"Not simply with resignation, but with joy!" Seneca seizes on the
answer.

> So you see very well that you believe that no good is equivalent to honor
> by itself! Thanks to it, during the moment preceding your imminent
> death, you will live in absolute joy, and you will think that others, rich
> and powerful are not truly happy, even if their good fortune lasts. Why
> aren't they, unbeknownst to themselves, happy? Because in reality they
> are dwarves, even though they draw themselves up to their full height.

Stoic happiness arises from the sublime alone.

The last maxim is the oddest. Doing good is not enough, you must
do good being fully conscious of the reason for it. We may immediately

remark that such exigency proves that Stoicism, at base, not only aims to make men happy or make them conduct themselves well, it aims to transform them, out of a love of transformation itself. It wants to create a new man—but at this point, we must proceed step by step.

We recall that every living being, from plants to men and even god, has natural functions to fulfill, called offices or duties. Among them are to grow, to prosper, to perform photosynthesis, to be a good spouse and citizen. Whatever the functions, each being has nothing more to do, and should do no more. Intoxication, conquest, and in general doing anything not corresponding to one of these functions is a fault. All normal conduct corresponds to a natural function, and so the complete list of functions would be endless. To be a sage is a duty, but so is to preserve one's health. In certain, very unusual circumstances, self-mutilation could become a duty. Asking questions (if they are pertinent) and answering them (if it is proper to do so) are also functions[51]; indeed, every action is or can be a duty. When we carry out a function correctly, we perform a "right action," inspired by the "rectitude of the soul," to use Seneca's language.[52] Every right action is the perfect execution of a function and can not exist without the function.[53] Nature has definitively foreseen all of them. When we fail to fulfill a duty or carry one out badly, we commit a faulty action. The sage fulfills all his duties, not omitting even a single one of them, including being a person of refinement.[54] Thanks to his wise soul, he is also almost the only one to execute them with rectitude. The right action is his distinguishing mark and his privilege, while the majority of people only approximate it. To sum up Stoicism in a few words: "The happy life is made of right actions."

If we accept this, what are the conditions under which an action is right? To read Seneca and his masters, one might think that right actions are as rare as miracles, but the conditions they impose are in reality obvious enough. To fulfill a function, we must take into account the circumstances, the environment, and the best way to act on them. Showing one's beneficence is a duty, but the treatise *On Benefits* takes pains to discern what should be given, to whom, when, and how. "In principle, you must return a deposit that has been entrusted to you, but I shall not always, nor everywhere, nor in every circumstance return

one," because it may happen that its return will rebound to the detri-
ment of the depositor.[55] "In the same way, on the subject of benefits,
I shall take account of the why, the when, the how and the to whom."
I will not, for instance, return poison deposited with me by a friend if
he is depressed when he demands the return of his deposit. Even the
most compelling duties are subject to the force of circumstance. A
father, for example, wants to become tyrant. His son must denounce
him because the well-being of the nation surpasses that of his father.[56]
To sum up, "If we fulfill our functions at the wrong time, we will not
be happy."[57]

All of this seems rather simplistic, but the Stoics nonetheless maintained that a right action is an astounding feat; doubtless they had
their reasons for this. Duty, they say, is only the matter[58] or the occasion
to act well, and only the sage is able to employ this material perfectly.
This was another of their paradoxes: only the sage is capable of being
king, cobbler, orator, navigator, and all the other occupations you like.
He is the best in every domain because he alone knows how, when, and
why one must don the robe of royalty or cook a meal. (Unlike cooks
who are not sages, I suppose he will repudiate gastronomy and serve
only natural, freely available foods, the so-called *parata*.) Better still,
only he knows how to be a connoisseur of fine wines and a lover of
pretty boys. (On these two points, however, Seneca, grave Roman senator and prude—who surely would have had plenty to say on the psy-
choanalyst's couch—refused to follow the older Stoics, with their
provocative audacity and Hellenic notion of passion being restricted to
love affairs with adolescent boys.) The rejection of our decadent civilization arises from the same principle. The arts and technologies not
prefigured by nature prove that their inventors had judgment—reason—but Seneca stipulates, not "right reason." They invented the
milling of grain and navigation without asking if they were not harm-
ful or if they were truly useful. The sage might be the best navigator but
he would not, I imagine, navigate unless the well-being of his country
demanded it. Navigation, kingship, and all the other functions, including beneficence, are "middling" advantages (*mesa* in Greek), because
they are only matter to be perfected.[59] The mass of men perform them
imperfectly, while the sage is a perfect benefactor—or, we might say, a
benefactor, period.

We can begin to understand the reasons for this sectarian attitude when we go on to the other conditions of a perfect action. It must be executed, Seneca tells us, "willingly, without hesitation, fear or delay, under penalty of the loss of joy." This is asking quite a lot of alacrity from someone who may be about to sacrifice his life for his country; it is to suppose a superhuman soul, the soul of a sage. Right action implies the possession of the four virtues or, to put it another way, being a perfectly virtuous man.[60] Finally, rectitude is not a matter of acting rightly a single time, in passing, so to speak. Rectitude is a general idea, a principle, and it would be contradictory for a principle not to be applied in every instance. An isolated right action is not, in reality, right. It is only a stroke of luck, as though an inept archer hit the target by chance. Seneca puts it well:

> Without knowing *why* it is necessary to act as one must, to have done so is pointless; you will not do so every time nor according to a uniform rule. From time to time, by chance or by effort, you will offer a proof of rectitude, but without having the rule that allows you to draw a straight line of conduct, or to be sure that what you do is right. When you have shown yourself to be a good man by chance, there is no guarantee of staying one definitively.

Only the sage can accomplish a right action because every one of his actions implies, on principle, that all of existence, woven as it is of duties at every turn, is righteous. Moreover, even a right action taken in isolation presupposes a righteous soul, unless it is a chance effect, which does not count. Right conduct is one faithful to its own principles, coherent with itself. At the first sign of error, it becomes evident that the agent was not imbued by principle and, until then, had struck the target only by chance. Because all men are ill, an isolated spike in fever might well seem unimportant to the lay person, but the physician would see in it a symptom revealing that the patient was not really cured. "An action will not be right if the corresponding decision was not; and it was not since the soul was not in a good condition." Conduct in conformity with its rules in every action indicates a well-formed soul, one that is changed and indeed cured. "Right action is both the practice and the proof of virtue."

Clearly, the state of the soul is more important than the actions themselves. The Stoics were not moralists exacting that duties should be fulfilled or the social compact be respected. They were physicians whose every action was aimed at the patient's recovery of health. To them, what mattered was the state of mind in which a person acted. That an insane person (and we are all insane) steals an ox or an egg is a serious matter to be sure, but that is not what interests the psychiatrist—the healer of souls—who must consider the state of mind of the patient. *Animus* is the Latin term for state of mind and, unfortunately, was a close equivalent in Roman law for "intention." In that context, the jurists said that when phrases in a will were ambiguous, it was necessary to take the departed's intention into account. However, the Latin term *animus* is more vague than "intention." It meant only that in order to understand what the testator meant to say, it was necessary to know with what intent he had written the disputed sentence. Did he intend to free the slave Smith or his homonymous slave Smyth? From this we have inherited the habit of translating *animus* as intention, and to imbue Stoicism with a morality of intention, when its morality was really that of mental health.

Why, then, was good conduct not enough for Stoicism? Why did it ask in addition that good conduct be engaged in for good reason? Was this merely a kind of ideological fanaticism, or the snobbism of intellectuals for whom clear thinking was a point of honor? No. The reason—the very important—reason was what we have been writing of all along. It was because Stoicism did not teach common morality, but instead a method of achieving personal happiness. "Virtue" forms a complete science called Stoicism, one that creates happiness for its possessor. The phrase quoted above needs to be taken at face value: "If you do not act perfectly, you will not be happy." In fact, those who do not have this science will act well or badly, but without it, he will not be happy even in acting well. He will suffer fear, undergo passions that are by definition painful, he will fear death, he will be neither tranquil nor serene. The knowledge that leads one to correct conduct is the very same knowledge that procures happiness. To be sure, if an ignorant person does good, it is a benefit for society, for his beneficiary, and for moralists whose only concern is morality itself. For them, doing one's duty is the important thing. However, the Stoics were not moralists. Doing one's duty haphazardly, without knowledge, will never lead to the final good of Stoic wisdom: happiness. Imagine an upright fellow who neither steals nor kills out of fear of the police or of the lessons he learned early in life—not for scientific, Stoic reasons.[61] He will behave properly, but he will be, for want of knowledge, "unhappy" and fearful of death. So, doing good is not enough to make one happy.

It is time to pause and try to take stock. Did the Stoics believe in the exaggerated morality of intention and conviction (*Absicht* and *Gesinnungsethik*, as the Germans say) that has been attributed to them?[62] No, they did not set themselves up to make people *act* in a certain way. They wanted to make them *be* secure and in a state of calm by making them superior to the chances and concerns of a fallen world. There are, of course, many things that must be accomplished, the functions or duties, but the goal of Stoic doctrine is to permit, through these actions, a permanent happiness, whether in success or failure. If like Cato you lose a war of liberation or like the captain in *Letter* 85, you see your ship tossed on the rocks, it is, as Seneca writes, the captain that has failed, not the sage—they are two different people. As a sage, the unlucky captain meant only to remain happy, thanks to his virtue, even in the event of shipwreck. This was what was in his mind, what his *animus* intended.

This has only the name in common with a morality based on intention, able to distinguish between murder and involuntary manslaughter, wondering if good intentions excuse an inept pilot, proclaiming "Let the empire perish, not a principle!" Stoicism, for its part, is concerned not with merit or responsibility, but with felicity—one void of content. One's personal happiness could never be staked on the success of an endeavor large or small, professional, political, charitable, scholarly, or artistic. As we saw above, Stoic felicity can be reduced to keeping oneself at the same level as life's accidents, and to respond to them without investing oneself in any particular project or vocation. If Seneca had invested himself in the enterprise of guiding Nero, what would have been left for him in 63, when the cult of the imperial personality came to dominate political life in Rome?

Given all this, why has it been possible to attribute a morality of intention to the Stoics? They owe it to their own constant repetition that an action cannot be good if the state of the *animus* is not well formed, and to our habit of translating *animus* as "intention." Why do they repeat this phrase? Because as practitioners of corrective therapy, they thought—out of their own intellectualism—that their disciples ought to mold the form of their souls after wisdom. If you think well, you will wish well and act well. Only chance allows a fool to hit the target from time to time.

Stoic materialism led to a completely mechanistic notion of psychology. Good plans of action (in Greek, *katorthomata*) can only be formed by molding oneself on a correctly formed state of the soul; in turn, that state will be correct if the soul itself is molded on the truths taught by wisdom. Just as with computers, we might say: a correct response follows from a correct program, according to theory. For the Stoics, the soul was a bodily organ located in a part of the heart so minuscule that doctors had never yet been able to discover it. A soul is composed of what we would call neurons and, as we also know, neurons work well if the wiring plan among them is correct. A right action (*katorthoma*) and a rightly formed soul correspond like a mold and the cast formed by it. An insistence on moral rectitude is the same thing as insistence on the rectitude of that "state of mind" (*animus*) misleadingly translated as "intention." The progress of the one is parallel to the progress of the other. Stoicism never declared, "An act is not truly moral if the intention behind it was not pure." Rather, it insisted that "You can never act in a fashion at once moral and well calculated if you haven't brought your soul into conformity with moral theory."

The very idea of intention, probably arisen from the biblical world of the Psalms, was foreign to the Greco-Roman tradition. Classical antiquity did not care for a humble, whining purity of soul, did not delve into bowels and hearts, did not sniff at the soul's aromas. If you did good, it was because you had reason to, and this reason was simply love of the good. There was no distinction between heaven-sent commandments ("Thou shalt be beneficent") and the chore of applying them, which was left to our own perspicacity. If you practiced beneficence unwittingly, you did not deserve the title of benefactor, even if your intentions were the best in the world. Seneca develops a whole dialectic of good deeds: you must understand when, how, and to whom to give.

Stoicism, in its every fiber, ruled out a morality of intention. What has mislead commentators is the resigned attitude of the Stoic. It is, though, one thing to resign oneself to misfortune and failure out of love of cosmic destiny, and another to seek an excuse or comfort for failure in the purity of one's intentions. The Stoics were intellectualists, professing the unity of the soul and the virtues, and this made the doctrine foisted on them triply impossible. For an intellectualist, will, good or bad, goes without saying and is indistinguishable from reason. If people want this or that, they do it, and, if they want it, it is because they have reasons for desiring it, be they good or bad. Should they later complain, "This isn't what we wanted, our intentions were far purer," that is because they acted witlessly.

Fulfilling one's duties isn't enough: they must be fulfilled perfectly. Perfection, in this regard, is measured less by the objective way in which one acts than by the perfect disposition of the soul of the agent. In truth, the two amount to the same thing. Only the finished sage will neither stumble nor commit those minor errors of understanding that reveal imperfect discernment or courage. Nonetheless, it remains the case that Stoicism measured perfection of action less by the objective result than by the internal state of the individual. Insofar as the individual had not undergone a complete internal transformation, Stoic doctrine had yet to attain its final goal. Stoicism remained a doctrine firmly centered on the individual.

This, however, was the source of its fundamental inconsistency. How can it be possible to be simultaneously an individual and to believe in a universal, impartial reason that makes no allowance for persons? Is it possible to remain oneself and yet be just and impartial? Stoicism, in its firm conviction that the world was well wrought, believed this was possible. It even believed that the individual would draw his convictions from the enormous powers of universal reason and equitable justice.

On this point, though, we may have our doubts. We may imagine, on the contrary, that an individual is essentially an abyss of egocentrism, and that reason cannot be divided among a number of persons without ending in tragic conflicts in which it will be necessary to sacrifice either justice and reason itself, or the preference of each individual for his own interest. The least conformist philosopher of antiquity—he was called Carneades—recognized this divorce between truth and life, requiring but a single case of conscience to demonstrate it. Let us imagine that after a shipwreck, two sages have come to hang on one life buoy, able to support the weight of only one of them. Who ought to sacrifice himself for the other? Life is nothing, and both would accept self sacrifice, but what does justice say? Our two sages are, by definition, equal in virtue, and so justice is unable to draw the line. If each one were charitable, they would both drown themselves. If they were evil, the result would have been no less unjust. Before a plurality of mutually exclusive individuals, justice fails. This case of conscience is no mere speculation. Imagine, for instance, an international conflict revolving around the golden word—oil. Christian charity runs up against an equally insoluble aporia, the one that begins with itself and refuses to grant that one should sacrifice one's own eternal salvation for that of one's neighbor.

We moderns, on the other hand, believe that the thing dearest to the human animal is desire, even if it leads to unhappiness more often than to happiness. (We have renounced any philosophy of happiness.) We picture a humanity whose clans and masses argue over rare goods (rarity being the fundamental concept of economics, since the notion of marginal good was discovered). It is a world in which every consciousness wills the subjugation of every other one, whether by jealousy or by means of conversion and conformism. Stoicism, in its belief that the world is well ordered, saw things differently. This is what permitted it to proceed to a first synthesis of its concept of virtue (which could also be called a recipe for happiness) and of a morality of duty to others. Stoic morality would also encompass commonsense morality.

1. In the first place, this was because our nature demands little. Only the wicked wrangle over goods that will obviously always be in short supply, out of their perverse desires, which eventually become infinite. By our nature we require only spring water, the grain the seasons deliver to us, and a cave or a hut of branches. To put it another way, for the Stoics neither the law of the jungle nor the struggle for life exists.

2. Secondly, this peaceful state among men (nature's wish for the human species, as we shall see), is also a state of serenity for each individual. Serenity, the absence of passion, is the basis of happiness. A thief or murderer is unhappy; one kills out of cruelty, the other steals from greed, and cruelty and greed render the soul unhappy for the simple reason that, rather than resting in peace, it inflames and torments itself. Even a satisfied sadist is not happy because he is prey to a passion—sadism. Briefly, happiness is the absence of desire, and we were right to say that the fortress of the soul was empty.

THE SAGE VERSUS THE GOOD

It is a solemn moment: we are about to reveal Stoicism's great promise. The human soul is at birth a completely rational, coherent mechanism. In it, there is no opposition between desiring and rational parts, and it has, at every instant, exactly the amount of energy that it needs. The soul never gets carried away. Alas, this native state lasts but an instant and the mechanism loses this lovely theoretical purity. The friction arising from its upbringing makes the machine seize up. Eventually, the machine realizes that it is jammed, because rational judgment and liberty recognize that they are defective, and free themselves from a want of liberty. The machine attempts to free up its sticky parts, but it takes time to get the rust out of the mechanism. When the gears are as pure as their theoretical blueprint, the machine merits the title of sage. When it is still being cleaned up, it is said to be "in progress" toward sagacity, and for Seneca is called "good." A decisive stage in this progress is the moment when the machine, although not completely unstuck, is nonetheless unable to slip backwards and seize up again. As long as the machine labors to free itself, it monitors its least motions, but when its motions have attained the purity of theory, and there is no more friction, this attention is replaced by comfort and serenity, even a sort of unconsciousness. The machine no longer perceives its functioning because everything is running smoothly. Better still, according to Seneca,[63] the machine is unaware that it has become a sage. The moment the last speck of rust is gone, this state of comfort and unconsciousness settles in like an enormous silence. Not that all sentiment has disappeared: as every living being takes an interest in itself and finds its happiness in performing its natural functions, the sage is permanently in a state of joy, whatever happens. Fully in conformity with truth and nature, as perfect as theory itself, the sage has become *true*: he is no longer perverse. Now, it is impossible to see what nature intends unless one has oneself become in conformity with it. Objective knowledge and self-transformation presuppose each other: the true scientist is also a sage, and the sage is the only scientist. What would an entirely external science amount to? A truth that we do not interiorize is not a philosophical truth. At best, Seneca explains, it amounts only to education, vulgar curiosity, erudition (which the ancients called "grammar" or "philology"—words, nothing but words). We are very far from modern rationalism, the cult of scientific truth for love of objective truth.

The perfected sage is not the tense, willful, obsessive being we might imagine—in fact, he is exactly the opposite. He has ceased to struggle, he lives in a state of joy and semiconsciousness, one the ancients thought superior to the gropings of an anxiously seeking mind. His sagacity is always at his fingertips. Whether he is judging and condemning desire and fear, ruling that preferable neutrals are good or bad, or enduring physical suffering, groaning but not weakening, he does so without having to think about it, with utter spontaneity, like "someone reading without being aware that he is reading."[64] Like god, he "cannot not act rightly." He lives in a perpetual present, with never a thought for the future. He is serenely impartial with regard to his condition as a human being and the order of the cosmos. He no longer knows pain. His joy, "that privilege of the gods and their emulators," is not intermittent like that of demi-sages. It is never interrupted because no external event, no stroke of fortune good or bad, can touch the sage. His joy does not stem from external matters, but from "the awareness he has of his virtues."

This great promise was widely known, well beyond the boundaries of the sect. Educated people, the curious, and the philologists were aware of it. The common people considered the sages (by which they meant flesh-and-blood philosophers) to be heroes of conviction, afraid of nothing, boldly addressing kings and emperors. To stalwarts of the prevailing order, they were trouble makers, with no respect for legitimate authority. The Stoics themselves delighted in parading through the streets in their professional trappings, flaunting virile airs—the malicious said this was to compensate for a poorly repressed femininity. (Seneca was said to love, not tender lads, but grown up males.) Finally, everyone wanted to know the truth of the matter. If a sage was not supposed to groan on the pyre, his reactions were scrutinized all the more maliciously. Once, on a boat making the fearsome crossing of the channel of Otranto, between Albania and Brindisi, there were two passengers: a Stoic, strict master of his young disciples, and a rich Greek from Turkey, of effeminate, luxurious appearance. During a storm, the sissy remained all smiles, while the philosopher was pale, trembling in silence. On board, everyone observed their faces to see what to make of it.[65] Once they arrived at Brindisi, the sissy mocked the philosopher, who replied coldly and then justified his conduct to a less malicious and more cultured passenger. Seneca recorded his justification as follows:

He began by forcefully affirming that the ideal of the sage is in no way utopian, and does not demand the impossible. "The sage conquers evils, but not without feeling them." It would be scant merit simply not to feel pain! That is not where human dignity lies; to those knowing how to will it, a happy life is both greater and more accessible. Stoicism and sagehood would be unattainable only if the soul and the body were not two separate things. The division passes between them, not between two distinct parts of the soul. The body feels and the soul decides. We must not oversimplify: the sage certainly senses physical pain perfectly well; in return, though, if there is any effect, it is on the body, which pales and trembles. The soul does not even experience fear.[66]

Suffering (being burnt or wounded, say) is a sensation just like color or taste. By nature, it is common to all mankind, a physical given furnished by reality. Judgment is neither applied to it nor capable of lessening it—you cannot decide that you are not suffering. The body faithfully registers this given and transmits it to the soul, whose highest duty is not to succumb to it. Pleasure, too, is a sensation. Out of excessive zeal, some Stoics went so far as to maintain that the sage was immune to the effects of wine. Seneca discounted this, saying that if it were true, the sage would also be able to resist the fatal effects of poisons.

Emotions, on the other hand, along with desires and fears, are not sensations. They are, rather, judgments or opinions, and for this reason vary from one individual to another. One man might hold fast against his desires but tremble before a scarecrow. Death is only an evil if it is so judged. In this, the emotions and passions are only judgments.

However, they are not so at first, and the doctrine was not such a caricature for all Stoics. Seneca, Epictetus, and before them, Chrysippus, believed that the first moment of passion was unaccompanied by any judgment, presenting itself to the imagination first as stark temptation or terror. Passion is not immediately false judgment; this judgment occurs in a second moment.

The sage judges correctly and once the first moment has passed, experiences neither desire nor fear. He does not even have to resist them as sensations because his judgment has nullified them. However—and Seneca insists on this repeatedly—the sage is not the impassive being people might imagine. True, he does not treat death as an evil and does not give in to his torturers, but in his flesh he trembles and goes pale. Therefore, what the Stoics called *incommoda extrinsecus*—inconveniences coming from the outside world—do affect him.[67] Before the abyss he feels dizzy; if someone delivers bad news, his face falls, he trembles and becomes pale, hair standing on end. But these surprises of the senses must not be confused with a passion such as anger. Having a fit of anger is not a surprise of this sort, but a voluntary event, dependent on our will, one which we can control or even abrogate. This control becomes easier once we understand that indeed we can control and judge it. In the same way, the sage may tremble, but does not fear.

The sage never flies into a rage, but he may tremble and shake, experiencing, as Seneca reiterates, assaults from without, as though to remind him of his condition as a simple mortal. "This assault, though, is minor, and only scratches the surface of his being," because the sage does not add to such scratches the approval of mistaken judgment. Passing through the half-mile-long tunnel that connected Pozzuoli and Naples (even until around 1900), Seneca shuddered in the flesh, but without any violent emotion and without fear, having judged that there is never anything to fear.

Would it be enough, then, simply to decide that a danger basically amounts to nothing for it to deflate like a pricked balloon? Yes, because the decision is not gratuitous. In spite of appearances, what we call danger is not the enormous thing we think we see, but a sort of double entity, touching us personally only at a tangent, with the smallest part of its volume. The rest of its enormous body is not a concern for us. *Letters* 28 and 29 give some examples. What difference does it make if we are pursued by not one, but thirty persecutors? It adds up to a single persecution. What difference does it make if you are assaulted by a whole battalion of assassins and have twenty daggers planted in you? A single blow is mortal, and death lasts only a fraction of a second. Again, what does a tyrant matter to us, surrounded in his magnificent palace by a thousand henchmen and hangmen? Before such grandeur we must ask ourselves: how does this affect us personally? Not at all—it all comes down to a single sentence: "Off with his head!" Beings are circles that touch each other at purely incorporeal tangents. For instance, the moment my head is struck off, the tyrant affects me only at that one point of contact. What does it matter what the tyrant's private thoughts about me are, or what he intends his gaudy trappings to make me think?

All this is so because, where ordinary people and the rest of the philosophers see one thing—a tyrannical regime, an assassination plot—Stoics see two: a substance, grossly material, flesh and blood, the tyrant or assassin; and the purely incorporeal effect produced by that substance, the sentence of exile, the mortal blow. Incorporeal, I say, because they are events, something that happens invisibly and passes like the wind. That a tyrant exists in flesh and blood is of no possible interest to me. What does interest me is what he can *do*. We must acquire the habit of separating what exists (the substances with their properties, like steel with its edge or the tyrant with his cruelty) and what is done or happens, a slightly disagreeable, and incorporeal, moment to endure. We must distinguish the actors on the world's stage and the play they enact. Only at this price will we accustom ourselves to neither admiring nor fearing anything, to letting ourselves be amazed at nothing—*nil mirari*. The Stoic's *sang-froid* rests on this distinction between the corporeal and incorporeal; it is not (or does not think it is) a gratuitous or willed decision.

But how long will it take us to get used to making this distinction between corporeal and incorporeal, to look on the torturer with indifference as he prepares his tools? It is time to recapitulate, and to reflect. Physical suffering exists—we can do nothing about that. But what of fear, anger, desire? They are at once false judgments (a decision that fear is justified is wrong) and emotions, with all the violence and color we associate with them. The heart of the problem is to learn to dissolve emotion through judgment. Chrysippus was no naïf: he fully realized that the sight of a hangman or a beautiful woman evokes a "pre-emotion" in us, of fear or desire, and that the "matter" of the proceedings submitted to our judgment "provokes" us, to use Seneca's own terms, setting in motion an impulse that will carry us away if our governing faculty is in less than perfect form. False judgment will follow the provocative sight. In fact, it is necessary to admit this idea of a pre-emotion because otherwise, all emotions would be the same, and fear and desire would not be distinguishable. They would be reduced to an internal weakness, a kind of asthenia, and to a single colorless unease.

However, this is not the way things are. Fear rests on the pre-emotion of a tightening or constriction of the soul, while desire on a different one, that of thrusting forward. The principle remains the same: only in the case of asthenia do the pre-emotions determine our decisions. If we are fit, taut, our judgment of them will be more just and will determine that this unease of the soul is only an error. In the final instance, passion, despite the real existence of the pre-emotions, is only false judgment. In *On Anger*, Seneca applies—and misapplies—Chrysippus's subtle analysis. He slows the film down, taking the analysis of the constituents of a single act as a succession of distinct episodes. When a furious pre-emotion boils up in us, we must take the time to bring ourselves back under control.

In reality, though, the pre-emotion in question did not boil up except in virtue of an already formulated false judgment, and was a single act, both premeditated and voluntary. So much so that, when we are beside ourselves, the problem is not to think of regaining our *sang-froid*. We are beside ourselves only in virtue of a false, if formal, judgment of our internal tribunal. Chrysippus was not a preacher of voluntarist sermons, and made no speculations on regaining *sang-froid* while there was still time. Rather, he postulated a long, progressive habituation of the judging faculty toward judging rightly at first, from the pre-emotion. Inasmuch as we fail to attain this perfect, instantaneous sagacity, the pre-emotions sweep us away and make us suffer. With respect to them, we are in a permanent state of asthenia, and the result is that at every blow we judge erroneously. If this asthenia is continuous, habitual, it is a disease, and the diseases of the soul are called "vices." We yield to our passions because of a weakness of judgment that has become habitual. The vast majority of men are ill.

Let us grant this: in the final analysis, we are all ill. Such as we are, our emotions matter. The fact is evident, and a reasonable person could deny this only as a kind of Don Quixote. The Stoics reply that we must imagine the larger picture. We have a choice between two strategies. One, to continue to be as we are, is lowly and will not earn us happiness. The other is difficult, but will certainly pay off. If we shed our asthenic habits, our vices, we will attain absolute security—but when? Will we live long enough for the necessary, lengthy effort to be recompensed?

This is an inescapable question, and neither Chrysippus nor Seneca dodged it. Fragments of Chrysippus (separated from a context we can

no longer recover) say, in fact, that "it wouldn't be worth stretching out
a finger to get wisdom lasting an instant" and that it would be wasted
effort "to extend a finger to possess prudence for only a moment, or at
the end of life."[68] Seneca, for his part, takes care not to invoke this calculus of returns. He repeats that it takes a whole life to learn how to live
and that sometimes we do so only on the eve of our death, but he is
painting a different picture. He is placing his bets on the final scene, on
the mode of dying or of killing oneself. We will never be sages, only
transformed into honorable men, or good men (which is a lot). The
final instant, however, will prove that wisdom is possible. We will be
sages in the process of ceasing to be at all. Seneca renounced the possibility of becoming a perfected sage in his lifetime. He affirmed, indeed,
that it is possible to rid oneself of one's vices and to become a good
man, but that only the sage succeeds in ridding himself of the troubling
pre-emotions.

The "minor assaults," such as shaking or pallor, vary from one person to the next, because they arise from temperament, that is, the manner in which each individual's nature has tempered the four elements
within him. People made of more earth than of air will shiver less than
others, but will also be slower witted. There are even individual differences among the sages. One may be more affable, another more impassioned and eloquent. No one can combat these material differences,
these innate necessities.

Far from being impassive, then, the sage lives in a state of joy, feels the
effects of physical suffering, and experiences emotional reactions based
in his body and his individual temperament. Seneca's sense of psychological reality only extended these ideas. He meditated too long on the
ideal of wisdom and had explored the approaches to it too thoroughly
not to have formed a more concrete image of it than that of a theoretical blueprint. He makes allowance for emotional reactions when they
are pure; the examples he gives go beyond the rule. The sage will weep
for his friends, and not only the tears that are the bodily counterpart of
grief, not subject to the control of the will; he will also grant himself
consented tears, bearing the sweetness of memory, only forbidding himself the ostentatious laments spilled to be witnessed. Surely Epictetus
would not have admitted such a breach of principle.[69] At other times,

Seneca, without openly attacking dogma, enlarges on a point of detail in a way that upsets the balance of the doctrine. He dedicated an entire book, his longest treatise, to the exercise of beneficence. He makes special allowance for this virtue, the only one capable of uniting individuals, whom the virtue of justice leaves in isolation. Orthodox Stoicism made no such exception for beneficence, which was only one virtue among others practiced by the sage because he practices them all. Seneca, somewhat forgetful of man's initial perversion, makes beneficence a simply human attitude, a value apparent to any open mind. *Letter* 109 on the subject of friendship between sages goes beyond the letter of the doctrine as well. How can the sage have friends because being perfect, he is self-sufficient? Because being perfect and encompassing the whole realm of the possible are not the same thing. One sage does not know everything, and two sages do not know the same things. Their perfection is inscribed in a finite space, and each completes the other. Even if friendship were of no use, it is a natural joy. The sages proved to each other by their own example that excellence exists, and thus multiplied their joy. Perfection cannot rest idle. Virtue needs to be practiced and preserves itself only by exercise and with the stimulus of others. That last claim, contrary to the dogma according to which virtue cannot be lost once it has been solidly acquired, agrees with experience, which clearly shows that wisdom "does not maintain itself at the point we leave it, but slips backwards like an over-wound spring as soon as we let it go." This claim conforms to orthodoxy, but the emphasis is new. Under cover of metaphor, *Letter* 39 imagines a dynamic peculiar to the soul, which is like a flame with an internal impulse to rise: the greatness of the soul becomes a principle of action. Seneca tempers—or enlarges—the letter of doctrine and escapes the economy of a Stoicism closed in on itself and the project of self-preservation.

Ilsetraut Hadot has written of the visionary power in those pages where Seneca exalts the ideal of the sage, at once inaccessible and, it seems, at our fingertips.[70] In their torrential lyricism, these pages, intuitive as they are, are no less firmly supported by a framework of highly articulated ideas, probably Seneca's debt to Posidonius. What is a sage? A man who, thanks to his internalization of the four virtues, lives in a perpetual state of joy because he possesses the three excellences: greatness of soul, confidence in himself, and security with regard to the outside world.

1. The sage no longer sees things except from the vantage of absolute truth. Reality, as people imagine it, no longer matters for him because he identifies entirely with his ideal. Because the soul can mentally enlarge itself up to the scale of the cosmos, the sage judges everything from its point of view, from the point of view of god. His own person no longer matters to him. He sees on a grand scale, and acts grandly, not in accordance with the tiny corner of the universe he happens to live in.

2. If the sage is tortured, his physical suffering is just as terrifying as that of any man, but he will not yield to it. Better still, he is certain ahead of time that he will not yield; he knows that he can have confidence in himself.[71] Because his greatness of soul attaches importance only to the good, he will be happier to have virtuously triumphed over his ordeal than to have escaped it in terror.

3. Finally, the sage is not only without vices; he fulfills each of his duties and has reduced the external world to an incorporeal membrane. Above all, he has taken the step Seneca regards as all but impossible, not to say chimerical: even the emotions, fear, shame, anger, desire, and so on have lost all density for him. We have seen how these seductive emotions solidify, in ordinary people, into vicious habits. The good man, who has been transfigured, has grown unaccustomed to these vices, but is not entirely secure from the effects of the emotions. He continues to feel them because they are part and parcel of human nature; if these pre-emotions did not exist, we would not be able to distinguish between desire and fear, only experiencing a vague sense of unease. The sage does not escape human nature, and he still receives the emotions of desire and fear, but they are reduced to a minimum. There is just enough left of them for him to be able to distinguish among them. Certainly, the sage experiences a slight twinge seeing the outline of the hangman or indeed of a temptress—his emotions have just sufficient presence so that he will not confuse one with the other—but once having distinguished the two silhouettes, the sage turns away with indifference.

These passages of Seneca, in their nostalgic unreality, aware of their self-delusion, are among his most beautiful because they are immersed in his internal experience and in a fictional world simultaneously. His imagination extrapolated them, starting at the roots of lived experiences attempting to rise above themselves. Seneca is so in love with this exalted image of himself that he decks it out with the least egocentric virtues, beneficence and the spirit of friendship. Forty years of work on himself and uncomplacent observation of himself were crowned by this fresh enthusiasm, as youthful as it was experienced. In it, his adolescent fervors come back to life: the crisis of his twentieth year, his enthusiastic conversion as a young man, and the spiritual vocation revealed at the dawn of adulthood.

In 63, as black clouds gathered on the political horizon and Seneca began his two greatest works, the *Letters* and *Moral Philosophy* (unread nowadays, and perhaps never finished), Seneca felt that his efforts had been worthwhile. He also felt as close to his ideal as one could be, and rejoiced in his creations—and in his self-creation. Then, at the opening of the sixth *Letter*, a solemn declaration resounds, one of the two or three most momentous occasions of his lifetime. "Lucilius, I feel it clearly: I am not merely improving myself; I am transforming myself. . . . I wish I could make you feel the effects of so sudden a transformation. . . . You can't imagine how much visible gain every day brings me."[72] In *Letter* 94 Seneca unambiguously describes such a transfiguration, citing his sources.[73]

> Philosophy, says Ariston, is divided into consciousness of the truth, on one hand, and a certain state of the soul on the other. If you only seek instruction and understanding about what to do and what not to do, you are still no sage. For that, you must have transfigured your soul according to the truths you have learned.

Seneca is not a perfected sage because he has not been transfigured. He is in the process of transfiguration—the change is in progress, but the goal was, or seemed, less distant. This was his state as he was writing his greatest works, with two years left to live.

We still have not seen, concretely, what the state of a transfigured person is. The *Letters*, while abounding in confessions and self-observation aimed at instructing and edifying the reader, also provide us with a few theoretical landmarks. *Letters* 71, 72, and 75 distinguish three degrees of progress. The first involves having stripped away the grossest faults. In the second, the subject has no faults, and has put an end to the most violent emotions, though without so complete a transformation of the soul that the possibility of relapse is excluded. The third stage, that closest to wisdom, includes an inability to relapse, even though passing emotions of regret, false shame, and the like are still felt. This stage is that of the transfigured person, the one at which Seneca had arrived.

His confessions prove it. Seneca, who obviously denies being a sage, but had nonetheless passed through the tunnel at Pozzuoli without fear, had many occasions to put himself to the test. One night he arrived at one of his villas, starving. There was no white bread, and he had to content himself with the brown bread of his farmers. He took this in perfect stride, an assured token of his progress toward virtue, because unexpected trials are better judges of a man than those against which one has had time to prepare the soul. Another time, in Naples, he rented an apartment right next door to a public bath house. Try as he might to ignore the clamor and cries, he was only partially successful. He could work despite the noise, willfully ignoring it, but he could not completely overcome the annoying sensation and resolved to move out. The worst trial milord had to confront was shame before his peers. One day he set out on a trip, not in the rich carriage suiting his rank, but on a peasant's cart, with only two or three slaves escorting him. "What I had to endure, in order to accept that people would think this was my own conveyance! The perverse shame for doing good still is with me. Every time a more splendid cortège crossed our path, I blushed—I couldn't help it!"

As we see, a transfigured person still experiences passing emotions; the treatise *On Tranquillity of Soul* calls this the state of rolling or slippage.[74] What exactly is the abyss separating the perfected sage from the person who is merely transfigured, whom Seneca usually calls the "good man?" Lack of security would be Chrysippus's reply; more subtly, Seneca calls it "slipping."

In conclusion, like the sage, the good man continues to experience sensations such as physical pain, but he faces them with courage. Like the sage, he distinguishes between the bodies of executioner or courtesan, terrifying or seductive, respectively, and the brief, bodiless moments to which these appearances may be reduced—the moment when the axe falls or the swoon of pleasure. The good man, then, enjoys the same three constancies as the sage. Knowing how to choose among pleasures, he admits of only reasonable joy. He is prudent and knows how to protect himself without succumbing to fear. He knows how to exercise the will in full awareness, and resists the blandishments of unnatural desires. All this is because he has succeeded in getting rid of his bad habits or vices. The good man, like the sage, has reformed himself on the bases of doctrine and virtue. Finally, he deploys all of the four virtues at once, and correctly accomplishes all his duties.

May we say, then, that he enjoys the three excellencies, composing the happiness of the sage? Certainly, those who have been transfigured possess the first of them, magnanimity, and everyday miseries no longer affect them becasue they have reformed themselves according to doctrine and thus see the big picture and take the point of view of the whole, even when it might be against their limited self-interest. At the point about which we are writing, Seneca had recently learned that he personally had tranquillity with regard to external threats or seductions at his command. He had undergone an asthmatic crisis so violent that he had persuaded himself he was about to die, yet the spectacle of death did not frighten him. "Take what I am about to say to you like a prescription written expressly for you," he wrote to Lucilius. "I shall not tremble at the last moment; from now on, I am ready." Under Nero, acquiring such assurance was not an idle matter, and events would prove that Seneca's presumption of secure tranquillity was not mistaken.

The third excellence remains to be discussed: the internal security or assurance of not backsliding or falling again into one's earlier errors. Chrysippus believed that the person in progress, even if he were the most honorable man in the world, would still not have solidified his good habits in the mold of doctrine.[75] If not, what would distinguish him from the sage? The Stoic in progress was still, so to speak, in a semifluid stage and could therefore fall back into sin. Seneca cites this opinion in *Letter* 71, while tacitly opposing it with his own. There comes a point, he writes, at which the good man comes very close to the sage, but without the possibility of becoming aware of it. What screen, you may ask, disguises this proximity? We may conjecture that it is the state of slippage, the little humiliating incidents that seem to prove that basically, the human essence has not been transformed, and that cause fear of relapse. What does this "slippage" consist of? I imagine it consists of not having yet succeeded in reducing the emotions to what we have called the minimum level of identifiability. Does one ever succeed

in this? If a true sage, perched on a rubbish cart, encountered the handsome carriage and haughty glances of people of his own circle, he would
identify it as an incident apt to humiliate any other man, but he would
not experience the slightest twinge of shame. The most honorable man
in the world could not say as much. Slippage is, in itself, a small thing,
but it is enough to ruin happiness and to make us apprehensive about
the security of the progress we have made. It is a thin screen, but one
that is practically impassable. Once a millennium, a sage succeeds in
revolutionizing his innermost humanity to the extent that this seasick-
ness ends, and he can traverse the open seas in complete serenity.

In 63, as Nero was veering toward tyranny, Seneca no longer
dreaded the greatest trials; he knew he was an honorable man, but
knew, too, that the all-too-human in him was far from dead. When he
writes that no one will see him weaken at the final moments, he was
pledging much. Perhaps his pledge was made public to insure that he
would have to keep it. In him, we sense an anguished haste to be put to
the test. It is one of his favorite theories, and one that has resulted in
his treatment as an exaggerated rhetor. A calm life is actually disquiet-
ing because we are unaware of whether we would remain strong in the
case of a tempest. If we have not confronted bad fortune, we have not
really lived. Is this mere boastfulness or the Roman taste for glory?
Might it not be, rather, a secret anguish, a "retreat forwards?"

A retreat forwards, a giddy madness, perhaps haste to be done with
it, and certainly pride—these were all sources for the strange declara-
tions of Letters 66 and 67. Is it enough to live honorably, but in peace?
Is it certain that an existence without heavy trials is neutral and preferable to one more sorely tested? No, Seneca answers. A too-calm existence is like a dead sea. In such exaggerations some have seen mere
rhetoric or a sort of moral estheticism.[76] It would be better to speak of
a hasty desire to receive baptism by fire, and of a military taste for
glory.[77] "Let us serve as examples for others," is a favorite saying of
Seneca's, but so is "Let us take stock of our force of character."

Seneca states: "the day of death will pass judgement on our whole
life" and, "I will trust my death to tell me how far I have progressed."
On that day, we shall see if our virtue was on our lips or in our heart. Of
course, this has nothing to do with the Catholic idea that a good death
redeems a whole lifetime. Rather, it is a truism: whoever has spent his
whole life rising toward wisdom will have reached his highest point at

the moment of death, but it is above all the conviction that how we die is the supreme test, and the only truly probative one.

As J. M. Rist has well said, for Seneca, suicide is the act par excellence.[78] It is almost the simplest way to achieve wisdom, at once final and instantaneous. No doubt it also a symptom of an anxious haste and of secret doubt concerning the possibility of achieving wisdom. Die as a sage, because living as one may only be a utopian dream.

Such an extreme attitude is typical of our author. Stoic orthodoxy did not go this far. Like all pagan antiquity (at least until the revival of Platonism around the year 100), Stoicism approved "well-reasoned" suicide, that of the conquered hoping to preserve his moral integrity or of the invalid wishing to spare himself useless suffering and the spectacle of his own degradation. The frequency of suicide among the Roman aristocracy is well known. Still, we should not speak of a kind of *mal du siècle*, Romantic melancholy before the fact.[79] What Roman law called *taedium vitae*, weariness of life, was more simply what present-day psychiatrists would call a depressed or suicidal state. The number of suicides in Seneca's day was also a function of circumstances. Faced with the threat of a conviction for lèse-majesté, senators preferred killing themselves to waiting for the executioner with his torments and to seeing their estates confiscated. Other times the emperor suggested that they put an end to their lives. In Tokugawa Japan, hara-kiri (or seppuku) was the noble substitute for the death penalty.

Still, this is not enough to explain the veritable delight with which *Letter* 71 describes a suicide for which euthanasia could only have been a pretext, nor does it explain the frequency and complacency of the praises Seneca addresses to death, which he calls the "door always open" and the "key of true liberty." Reading these veritable hymns, the imagination dizzies and we almost believe ourselves inclined to die, so persuasive is Seneca's prose. Seneca's extremism is not gratuitous. In the final analysis it only reveals Stoicism's profoundest truth, which is to see life from death's point of view and to make its followers live as though dead. Nothing is of significance but a disembodied self, just barely personal, whose existence can be snuffed out without any disadvantage because this self is not waiting for anything. Let us observe that wherever we open Seneca, where he speaks not of death but of happiness, magnanimity, or of those things to be preferred, we withhold our faith from this blatantly false conception of man and of life in vain, remaining nonetheless under his spell. We continue our reading, at last divining the source of his charm: as long as the literary illusion lasts, we can imagine living in a world at once weighty yet light, because our thoughts are no longer burdened by the subconscious omnipresence of death. More than a century ago, Jean-Marie Guyau, a gentle, all-but-forgotten Nietzschean put it well: "Death, release from the tension, the endless, aimless toil that is life, this is Stoicism's final word."[80] We must admit that Epicureanism was equally empty, equally jejune, but it did at least allow the interval between birth and death to be passed in a more relaxed way.

It is time to glance back now over the territory we have traversed over the course of the last several sections. We shall see the details of the landscape come together in three large ensembles which, in their turn, are joined together in a single whole. Stoicism will thus take on that systematic unity and coherence that professional philosophers hail as an achievement and have tended to consider as, in itself, another proof of the truth of a doctrine.

We have seen that everything in the world exists in a state of tension. We have also seen that over the course of time the most important thing is to maintain attention constantly; by means of this tension, the soul attains self-transfiguration or transformation. Finally, we have seen that whoever is so transfigured accomplishes only right actions, the *katorthomata*. Nothing can be more right than what is right; rectitude is, or is not; it is a question of all or nothing, allowing no degrees; this is why all errors, serious or not, are equal. A line is straight or crooked. If it is straight, it is perfectly straight, and can be no straighter. It is, in this sense, perfect. These, then, are the three poles of the Stoic system: tension, form, and rectitude.

Now hear what a difficult ancient specialist in philosophy, a commentator on Aristotle, had to say: "Form, according to the Stoics, is due to tension. For instance, this is the case of the interval separating two geometric points. Thus they define a straight line as a line under maximum tension."[81] The three poles are really one.

This is the coherence of which I spoke, verbal coherence if nothing else. The rectitude of a course of action (which we call "right" metaphorically, and as a manner of speech) is the same as that of straight line in geometry, which only exists on the blackboard or, strictly speaking, as a mathematical ideal. This rectitude is also the same as that of a piece of string stretched from both ends. Stoic materialism is a system of analogies.

LITERARY ILLUSION AND FERVOR

This section's title is unfair, to a degree. It would be better to speak of a demi-illusion. No Stoic ever achieved supreme happiness, but no Buddhist ever achieved nirvana either, nor has any Taoist become an immortal or ridden the tiger. Still, Stoicism and Buddhism both help us to live. We dream of the sage and forget about death, or we give our days over to ritual, or we mange our interior conflicts better. It is common to do one thing while thinking another, so that we deceive ourselves only halfway.

Those enormous excrescences of the self, constituting all doctrines, may serve to reestablish an equilibrium of character, but they also, and above all, represent elaboration for its own sake. Man is too formless and unpredictable for everything to be reducible to the rather curt logic of compensation and equilibria, with ideology replacing religion, the circus, politics, and soccer—the divine, as though everything was reducible to everything else. This "everything" does not exist, and such explanations are so much wheel spinning. We are, in fact, not so machinelike. Instead, we resemble clouds, extending tendrils inexplicably toward unforeseeable objects: the passion for tulips, the triumph of a philosophy, or nationalist movements. We have the capacity to be enchanted by such half-fictions, none of which allow us to foresee its successor. Against all expectation, some of these fictions, especially religions and occasionally philosophical doctrines, can maintain their success for half a millennium or more.

Whether they are durable or not, these excrescences are still *us*, they are our very flesh, they swell our being, and we rebel if someone wants to suppress them; we regard those without them with disdain. In fact, is it really we who have them, or it is they who have us? Beliefs, doctrines, and historical passions are *objective dispositions*. We think through them or, rather, it is they who do the thinking for us, summoning the actions we perform while we think them our own. In so doing, however, we are not thinking at all, just as the significance of a rite lies in the ritual act itself. When food is placed on a tomb, we do not imagine that the dead will come and eat it, nor do we imagine the contrary. The ritual act "thinks" for us. Where, then, are our external boundaries? This is impossible to say: every individual is a chaos, and chaos has no more boundaries than structure.

For this reason, it is not surprising that no one has ever explained the slightest cultural or religious mutation and that, after a century of the sociology of culture, the net gain has been zero. We shall not investigate the historical or social causes of Stoicism, still less its psychological roots, because any number of such roots would be discovered.[82] Psyches are only separable with difficulty from what the objective dispositions make of them. The verbal formulas of doctrine become our own selves, and we draw from them our fervors, which in turn are our sources of energy. Even so, we fail to reach the goal of unifying our internal chaos, whence the perpetual malaise of which *On the Tranquillity of the Soul* speaks.

At least it is possible to imitate internally the heat of such localized ferment. Rousseau, in the eighth book of his *Confessions*, permits us to relive the intellectual ferment Stoicism had been seventeen centuries before:

> The news that my *Discourse on the Arts and Sciences* had won the prize of the Dijon Academy reawakened all the ideas that had dictated it to me, animated them with new force, and finally set fermenting in my heart that first yeast of heroism and virtue that my father, my fatherland, and Plutarch had planted there in my childhood. I judged nothing greater or more beautiful than to be free and virtuous, lofted above fortune and men's opinion, and to be sufficient unto oneself.

Plutarch is named only out of loyalty to his childhood memories; what is characterized here is the Stoicism of Seneca, and these are among his fervors. Here we witness the capture of an individual (as one speaks of the capture of the waters of a river) by an objective disposition. What comes next is easily foreseen: Stoicism incites a passion for Stoicism just as psychoanalysis, even if it fails to cure the patient, at least procures a new passion, that for psychoanalysis. No, a Stoic will never become a sage; he possesses wisdom only virtually, and can do no more than to sketch his feats and prolong them in thought. This is enough, however, for in the case of man, potential beings have a present impact, and virtualities are of equal value with realities; we expend considerable effort on virtualities that will never be realized.[83]

Because virtualities excite just as much fervor as realities, the Nietzschean critique of Stoicism remains true but inoperative. As a reader of La Rochefoucauld, Malebranche was familiar with the wiles of amour propre.

> When someone struck Cato in the face (an allusion to *Letter* 14), he did not in the least take offence, did not in the least take revenge and he also did not pardon. He proudly denied that he had been dealt an insult. . . . Not being able, or not daring, to take real revenge, he attempted to take an imaginary one, flattering to his vanity and pride, which gives him a greatness of soul making him comparable to the gods.[84]

Malebranche was too clear a thinker to accept the Christianized Stoicism that had seduced so many of his contemporaries. Indeed, it would be misleading to forget that Stoic religiosity (whatever religiosity may mean here) was addressed less to the gods than to the sage, with the result that it was the object of its own veneration. Thanks to wisdom, man becomes the equal of the gods. "The gods are in no way jealous," and allow mankind to equal them in their happiness and security. The only difference between the sage and Jupiter is that the supreme divinity will endure indefinitely, but we have seen that the duration of happiness does not increase it. Whoever learns to be content with cool water and gruel will never be hungry or thirsty—"Jupiter possesses no more than this." Moreover, the sage lives without cares, while Jupiter labors to maintain the cosmos and rests in his thoughts only during the intervals of chaos between successive cycles of eternal return.

What rouses Seneca's wonder is the contemplation of so well ordered a cosmos and of wisdom itself. The sage, with his four virtues and all his other qualities, "that humanity so rare among men," his greatness of soul, his delicacy and kindness, strikes us with holy respect and religious enthusiasm. If we were to see such a person face to face, we "would fall down in ecstasy, as though at the appearance of a god." Those great uncoverers of truth, Socrates, Plato, Zeno, and Cato, arouse an almost equally lively fervor. "Let us devote a cult like that of the gods to them; why should we not celebrate their anniversary days" as we do those of temples or of the genius associated with every human being?

The gods do not care whether "we sacrifice fat calves to them, or slip coins of gold into the chests of their sanctuaries." Likewise, wisdom demands no other form of piety than that we conduct ourselves as justly as it does: this rectitude is the only true religion. What good are temples, then? "The entire cosmos is everywhere a temple" because it is everywhere the product of perfect reason. The Stoic religion has neither a cult, nor a notion of the supernatural, nor any inequality between the human and the divine. Its god is a "great artisan," the perfect cosmic architect.

A god to whom one is equal is neither father nor master. "*Non pareo deo, sed adsentior.*" I do not obey god; I partake of his advice. Such a god would not be able to give in to prayers because he has already done all for the best, and because he respects his own laws. No more could he cause us harm. The relations between Seneca and his god are those of two free citizens of the world, with equal rights, mutually independent, and obedient only to reason. The rights and transports of religion would be, in this view, servile as well as absurd. Lighting lamps on the eve of the sabbath or going to salute the gods in their sanctuaries every day at dawn are the acts of slaves, and "god has nothing to do with slaves." We justly wonder at the good handiwork of this artisan-god, in which our reason sees its own image, but for god himself we experience no feelings.[85] A strange religiosity indeed, one that has no idea of the love of god or any personal relation between creature and creator.

Equally absent is the idea of the supernatural. If we are unwilling to make religion a catch-all for everything that goes beyond the bounds of common sense—the communist faith for instance, or the passion of a soccer fan—all religious attitudes have one very precise characteristic. They have no empirical basis, no connection with the real.[86] For a true believer, providence is neither the author of good fortune nor a defender against real misfortunes. If bad luck strikes, the believer will not leap to the conclusion that providence wished to spare him from a worse fate or that he is being put to the test. Before coming up with this kind of rational explanation, his first feeling will be that somehow, inexplicably, in some other world, this all-too-real misfortune is not absurd or senseless. If such a believer feels "safe in the hands of god," he has spiritual security that is proof against the accidents of the real world, and not translatable into any practical effect. This is the polar opposite of the Stoic view of a providential god who is literally and physically the central nervous system and brain of a cosmos that is itself an enormous, perfectly spherical organism.

The Stoics are deists, but their deity was simply the incarnation of reason, a way of explaining the order of the universe. According to them, commonsense ideas are approximations of a higher knowledge, and religion, with its myths, rites, and fervors, is the naïve expression of a far purer truth. Like them, Voltaire eventually said that the priest explains god to the people, while Newton demonstrates god to the sage. In *Letter* 41, Seneca expresses the awe felt in sacred woods or at the sources of mighty rivers in admirable phrases, but from it he draws only an argument a fortiori: how much more majestic must the spectacle of the sage's unshakeable soul be! It is precisely the sage who excites a form of religiosity, in the narrow sense of the word, in Seneca, because in the end, the sage does not *exist*. The sage is only the object of an expectation (like the longing for a messiah) that in the end does not want to be fulfilled, for fear that if it were, the ideal image would become trivialized and too real.[87]

The only true Stoic religiosity, then, is this adoration of man by man, enlarged to the dimensions of the cosmos, of which man is the microcosm. The Platonic ecstasies attributed to Seneca are reducible to this, along with his avowed desire to attain a belief in the immortality of the soul. It is also the source of what we might term Seneca's cosmic masochism.

People have spoken too hastily of a tendency in Seneca toward a Platonic spirituality, and of Plato's influence on him. The question is not whether he cites Plato, but why and in what sense. The *Letters* are not a theoretical treatise. Seneca aims to convert and educate his reader, and his strategy sometimes leads him to state the universally revered name of Plato. He also has occasion to cite Epicurus in support of Stoicism: the least suspect testimony is that of a sworn enemy. This does not mean that Seneca was influenced by Epicureanism, any more than he was by Platonism.

At first glance, Seneca is close to a Platonic sensibility when he repeats that the body is a prison for the soul and that our existence is a forced exile or a stint of military service (as Socrates spoke of it in the

Phaedo), so that we will take our leave of the body without regret, or even, perhaps, will force the issue by committing suicide.[88] "What is our body? A weight on the soul to torture it." We long to climb back to heaven, whence we came.

How will we climb back? After death? No, we will climb back while alive, through the study of nature and in contemplation of the whole, by assimilating wisdom. If our body oppresses us to the point of wishing for death, it is because it limits our field of vision. Our eyes of flesh allow us to perceive only the smallest part of the universe and our fleshly desires and fears cloud our reason. To climb back to god is the same as becoming a sage through the development of the seeds of truth within us, with the soul-enlarging study of nature as an aid. The body is not some concupiscent contaminant disturbing the soul's purity, but a limiting factor on our capacity to see the whole and to follow truth. It is certainly true that our soul is a part of god, a divine spark, as we read in the treatise *On Leisure*, but in what sense? We know the answer already: these sparks, these seeds of truth, or pre-notions, kindle into flame when they contact the facts of sensation and induction, leading us to recognize wisdom. This is rationalism, not spiritualism, without the slightest care for a world beyond this one. Aware of the divine origin of the seeds of our soul, we will "equal the gods" during this mortal life, during which we are "promised to heaven."

Still, if the soul should chance to be immortal, that would be even better. It could not be immortal in the fullest sense of the world because it will disappear, like everything else (including the lesser gods) in the cosmic catastrophe separating the cycles of the eternal return. Nonetheless, we would have lived over the course of several millennia as disembodied souls, fire with no admixture of earth, air, or water. We would have contemplated serenely and at length the splendor of the cosmos in all its vastness. Can we hope for this quasi-immortality? Before giving Seneca's answer, it is necessary to describe the terms in which Stoics before him imagined the destiny of the soul after death.

We might think the question of the immortality of the soul mysterious, disturbing, and sublime, but the Stoics were so little disturbed by it that they scarcely spoke of it at all, never arrived at a firm conclusion about it, and posed it as a problem in the most prosaic terms imaginable. Our soul is composed of air and fire, the latter of which tends to rise. At our death, the heavier elements, air, earth, and water, will remain on the earth, while the fiery part of our soul will go to rejoin the fire burning in heaven. It will rise in the form of a small sphere (bubbles rising from the bottom of a pond take on a spherical form). In any event, this fire will rise only if it finds an aperture. Imagine a man dying crushed under a landslide—there is no guarantee that his soul's fire will find a clear way out.

That's real materialism. The question, then, is not to find out whether one believes in the immortality of the soul or not, but how one believes in it: as a physical phenomenon too prosaic to raise much passion, or as a sublime metaphysical fiction. The Stoics could view it only as a physical phenomenon, on whose reality their opinions differed. The soul is but one of the parts of the body, and is itself a body among the rest. As such, it is subject to the same necessities as other bodies. For the Platonic tradition, on the other hand, the soul is of a sublimer nature, a divine being or, as Plato termed it, a *daimon*, lodged temporarily in an earthly body. Its supernatural destiny is different from the imperatives of bodies. Man has important duties toward this supernatural being residing in him like a traveler staying at an inn or, rather, like a prisoner held captive in the jail of the human body, whose happy destiny is one day to escape. Seneca remains comfortably distant from this Platonism, feeling duties only toward himself and other people in this life. However, not very consistently, he is unable to accept that the soul is subject to physical laws, even while believing that the soul is corporeal. In *On the Tranquillity of the Soul*, he writes admiringly of a Stoic who, condemned to death and awaiting execution, caught sight of the soul escaping from one of his fellows in misfortune at the moment he was decapitated. (In the same way, Queen Margaret of Navarre, a good, even an enlightened Christian, watched for the instant when the soul would emerge like a gasp from one of her companions in her death throes.) But Seneca refused to believe in the strictly positivist view that the soul, rising like a breath or bubble of air, could be impeded.

Such positivism went beyond what Seneca could support. Not enough of a Platonist to be convinced of the immortality of the soul, he was Platonist enough not to put up with so banal a statement of the problem. The future destiny of the soul was something too sublime to be blocked by corporal contingencies; body and soul were of different orders. Supposing that a soul could be trapped under a rock was as ridiculous as supposing that a queen could be deprived of her coronation for catching her feet in the train of her dress. Seneca, tempted to abandon himself to his dream's desire, makes the immortality of the soul a fiction liberated from all physical realism.

Though tempted, ultimately, he does not yield. He speaks in many passages about the fate of the soul after death, but without reaching any conclusion, confessing his ignorance, without concealing his desire to believe in it. "I have just spent some magical hours, submitting complacently to the opinion that the soul is immortal, surrendering to so beautiful a dream." A true dream, or "a fable for fearful minds," as he asks in his tragedy *The Trojan Women*? Seneca is too intelligent and honorable to have allowed himself to make a conviction out of his wishes.

He goes further: *Letter* 102, starting with this beautiful, magical dream, goes on to enlarge the question so far that it loses all real consequences. Why do we want to believe in immortality? Because our soul is greater than the body and this lowly world. "The human soul is great and generous, and does not accept boundaries narrower than those confining the gods." Despite the body, the soul lays claim to all of space and time. Dying is a rebirth into eternity. Seneca does not, of course, imagine for an instant that there is a judgment of souls, with immortality reserved for the meritorious and infernal punishments for sinners: even children no longer believe in such old wives' tales. Has he really resolved to believe in an afterlife? No. His purpose was to elevate his reader's spirit, and the close of the letter draws a moral from this beautiful dream for life here on earth. The hope of Rabelais's *"grand peut-être"* should incite us from this point forward to conduct ourselves in a way acceptable to the gods. Our conduct should be worthy of their potential future companions. What does this conduct amount to? Not killing and not stealing, to be sure, but that is more or less assumed. The true conduct of the earthly gods that we (potentially) are is actually to become such gods, raising ourselves above the narrow limits of the body thanks to wisdom and the study of nature. We must become spiritually as cosmic as the gods. Avoiding the insoluble problem of the fate of the soul after death, Seneca subtly suggests to us the dissolution of the idea of the individual by means of a pantheistic fervor. Man shall be a god if he sees on the scale of the cosmos of which god is, after all, the soul—and man's soul is as immense as god's.[89]

In his reflections on man and nature, Seneca senses that our soul is, in effect, as immense as the cosmos, while at the same time suffering from the all-too-real limits of our finitude or, as he says, of the body. In his imagination, then, he attempts a "retreat forward" in order to loose his terrestrial bondage. In short, he entertains what contemporary usage would call a masochistic fantasy. Nature was bound to make man a being subject to death because matter itself does not allow the immortality of bodies. It was consolation of a sort to imagine that the great whole, the universe, is periodically destroyed before being reconstructed by god (something he has done, literally, an infinite number of times already, since both cosmos and god are eternal.) For Seneca, it would be a profound pleasure to be alive at the instant of such a periodic destruction and to be engulfed in universal ruin. "The day that god decides to demolish a worn-out universe to build it anew, we will be just a detail in the great catastrophe."

"It would be an excessive love of life to refuse to perish along with the entire cosmos," he writes in the tragedy *Thyestes*. In accepting such a death, we can imagine that the intoxication of self-sacrifice would give us the right to become the great whole that perishes; we would have paid the toll, and the price would be less than a lifelong effort most probably doomed never to succeed. It is like Samson, entombing himself along with his enemies under the ruins of their temple, or like Hercules who, in the tragedy *Hercules on Mount Oeta*, becomes a god by committing suicide on his funeral pyre.

We have been forced to use the word "masochism," with its contemporary aura of fascination: once said, all is said. Its allure, however, is not constant; many wares are proffered under its tent. There is the masochism of abjection alongside that of grandiosity, and it is far from evident that the word, always paired with sadism on paper, is so in reality, or that every good masochist is a sadist on the flip side. In fact, it is downright false—or always true because sadistic also means everything and nothing. All in all, the old term "active-passive" was no more imprecise, and less specious. Seneca's masochism was that of grandiosity, the sacrifice of the self that tops off the sentiment of the sublime, to use another archaic, but still useful, term.

1. The sublime, in fact, makes itself felt more forcefully when we dissolve ourselves in it. Telluric powers fascinate Seneca; his *Natural*

Questions exalt seismic activity, and to die in an earthquake he says, litot-
ically, is nothing, "since we must die one day in any event, we ought to
be happy to perish victims of so enormous a cause." (*Natural Questions*
VI, 2). All his dreams are of volcanoes. While Lucilius is in Sicily, to
Seneca nothing seems preferable than to scale Mount Etna. The tempest-tossed sea fascinates him to such a degree that one day he winds
up throwing himself into it. Between Naples and Pozzuoli the sea was
swollen and the captain of his ship could not land because the coast
was steep and rocky, so Seneca dove into the water, struggling to reach
the shore (*Letter* 53).

2. Seneca had been tested, and wanted to test himself. The need to
test our capacity to immolate ourselves as sacrifices to a superior
power, in the doubtful belief that too smooth a life is a lifeless sea, is the
same as when we feel unsure of ourselves until misfortune has tested
us; or the idea that god likes pitting a strong man against misfortune
in order to enjoy the grand spectacle of these two gladiators. Here, narcissism amounts to identification with the spectator-god. Spectacle
meant much to Seneca, who wrote (*On Leisure* IV) that the study of
nature is necessary so that so great a work will not go unwitnessed, and
that god needs us as testimony of his existence. Seneca's powerful personality oscillates between narcissism and self-immolation in the sublime. The dense world of Stoicism must have caused him a continuous
sense of suffocation, accompanied by the convulsive shiver of orgasm.
We feel this shiver in phrase after phrase, oscillating between an egocentric care of the self and devotion to the cosmos.

3. Seneca was suicidal, but in a quite personal way; we should not
yield to the facile connection between suicide and masochism. There
are certified sadomasochists for whom suicide has proved an impossi-
bility, and we ought not seek to unify a personality's chaos. Certainly,
Seneca was courageous, most likely under the guise of *sang-froid*: among
other things, his death proves that. Moreover, he always coveted suicide
more than he was obsessed by it. He calmly sensed, under no compul-
sion, that suicide was his choice. Psychiatrists tend to deny the existence of such calm at the availability of death. Unconsciously
naturalists, they claim that life cannot will the destruction of life except
in the presence of depression, pathology, or disease, but what if this
naturalism is a mere myth? What if there were people apt to kill themselves, who see death as the supreme escape, without this delectable

idea taking on the character of obsession? They sense that, if the need should arise, suicide would be a solace, even a sublime pleasure, and that is enough for them.

4. Another character trait in Seneca—which we would do well not to try to connect with the above—is a well-hidden taste for authoritarianism, a delight in governing the consciences of others. This betrays itself only rarely because the ancient direction of conscience had nothing of the paternal authoritarianism so dear to Catholicism. A director of conscience was not a priest: among well-born pagans you were among equals, free men who understood how to maintain the courtly tone of the interlocutors in Cicero's philosophical dialogues. There is one passage, though, and only one, that sets one on edge: the preface of the *Natural Questions*. This preface also serves as the book's dedication to Seneca's dear Lucilius. However, to the reader coming to it after reading the *Letters*, where Seneca is always consummately polite and amiable with his disciple, the dedication's tone is surprising. Seneca had seen Lucilius giving way to a session of flattery directed at Gallio, the beloved brother of his master. Such flattery was perfectly innocent, no more than the worldly civilities every senator had a right to expect from a lesser lord such as a simple knight. Nonetheless, Lucilius had given Seneca a reason for a sudden attack of rigor; having a weapon against him firmly in hand, Seneca makes him feel the sting of it, and feel it before the public of readers. He narrates the anecdote in detail, then condescends to pick him up again, increasing his domination even more. He does not let him go until playing cat and mouse with him for several pages redolent less of anger than of a somewhat cruel delight. The façade of liberal convention has cracked, and Seneca is unrestrainedly "acting out." This suggests that the senator and friend of the prince, in his nonwritten relations with his disciples and friends, must have appeared at times imperious and even slightly perverse in the name of the virtue he professed.

5. Finally, Seneca had an immense and enthusiastic capacity for elevated ideas, neither acrimonious nor proselytizing. To this he owes his finest pages, and we might call it religiosity if this fervor burned for god or for the supernatural and not, as it does, for the spectacles of nature (providential, no doubt, but even more, powerful and ingenious); for the human heroism of the lay saints of Stoicism, Socrates and Cato; and above all, for the ideal image of the sage and the splendor of his

wisdom. In the *Natural Questions* and in the last letters to Lucilius, this naturalistic, anthropocentric fervor leads Seneca to such a level of exaltation that, with a little luck, he may well have swayed in an authentically mystical experience, an ecstatic state in amorous apprehension of the sage, identified with God-Nature.

This fervor for such sublime objects is the hidden sense of his masochism, which we must call by its ancient name, magnanimity. We recall that the sage takes pleasure in the three excellences, one of which is greatness of spirit or magnanimity, characteristic of what today we would call an intellectual, sensitive to the whole universe and to great ideas, and which bore in those days not on world politics, but on the destiny of the cosmos. This breadth of vision completes the synthesis between Stoicism's individualism, aiming at security, and the importance, equally great, that the doctrine attached to morality and the duties owed to others, in short, to the love of mankind. Not being egocentric, the Stoic could not be egotistical. The quality of magnanimity also explains so-called Stoic resignation. The militant intellectual, a patriot of the cosmos, accepted whatever misfortune comes his way because the good of the cosmos demanded it. He cheerfully sacrificed his humble person to the progress of the great cosmic army. Stoicism is a recipe for securing individual happiness, but it also passes, as both a fatalism and a demanding moral code; it is magnanimity, whether we understand by this greatness of soul, sense of the sublime, or masochism, that makes these three poles ultimately coincide.

THE SOLDIER OF THE COSMOS

To this point we have been able to assume the wager of presenting Stoicism as the response to a defining question: how can we guarantee the happiness, or rather, security, of an individual? The remainder of our explication of the doctrine will respond to the same question, but by unbounding it on all sides, or rather by submerging it in a cosmic vision. The individual will enthusiastically embrace his role as part and, indeed, a microcosm, of the great All. In its breast he will forget his misfortunes and reencounter the rest of humanity, so that honor will not be limited to a heroic egotism. Rather, the social virtues, justice, benevolence, and humanity will contribute to it. Morality, in the Stoic sense of the word, will contain within it morality in its common sense. Stoicism will be at once an individualistic search for happiness and an altruism that, among the popular preachers of the doctrine, at times approaches conformism. In the words of Emile Bréhier, Stoics were conciliators at the expense, it must be said, of the coherence of their system. The other major philosophy of the fourth century B.C.E., Epicureanism (a sister doctrine, but one of sororal enmity), was less conciliatory and remained more strictly true to the quest for happiness in security.

From this the reader should not conclude that Stoicism was just another philosophy, or that reducing it to a single, central, question was only a jeu d'esprit on our part. It is only that, like some architectural composites, Stoicism flowed over the boundaries of its project from the very beginnings. Above all, there is no such thing as "just another philosophy." The tent of philosophy covers a range of merchandise with little or nothing in common, just as there is no "general" novel, not even if we confine ourselves to the realistic bourgeois novel: Balzac bears no resemblance to Proust. Around 300 B.C.E., the problem of happiness in security *was* what philosophy was understood to be, an historic fact in its own right, and as such, destined never to be repeated. If it emerges again, it will not be owing to any inherent, eternal signification, but only to the random churning of all things in the course of time. The profound relatedness of Epicureanism and Stoicism allowed Seneca to lay claim to the "quadruple remedy" in which Epicurus distilled his teaching: the gods are not to be feared; we will not survive to know our own death; suffering is either long but bearable, or hideous but brief; all we need is readily at hand.[90]

Seneca's Stoicism is comprehensible only from the starting point of the very particular question to which it is a reply—this is his project, his generative gesture. If you view philosophy as the sum of typical responses to eternal problems, you will misunderstand the nature of Stoicism. Instead of embracing its initial gesture, you will divide it into three areas—those consecrated by corporate custom: (meta)physics, theory of consciousness, and morality. Because Stoicism employs the words "virtue" and "honor," it must have had a conception of the one true morality, like Kant and so many others. Stoic morality is one among many, but it is astounding that this morality should be what it

is. A century ago, Victor Brochard merited the distinction of remind-
ing us that ancient morality, contrary to the Kantianism then reigning, had as its foundation the search for happiness, not the categorical
imperative. He might have added that Stoicism—to speak only of the
one school—had no aim to found morality *per se*; it was not the tran-
scriber of heaven-sent commandments to which we must sacrifice
everything. Rather, it had *its* morality, which was simply an art of living, and it exhorted us to adopt a method concerned with well-
being. This is why Stoicism was constructed as a practical discipline,
contrary to many modern philosophies, which remain confined
between the covers. It was not a description of the world, but a prescription. Foucault was right to speak of the "care of the self," and not
to have concerned himself overly with the care of honor in ancient
thought.[91]

Taking the Stoics' method of security as the basis of morality, some
are saddened that they gave the moral imperative so self-interested and
unreliable a basis. At times, as in the case of the great historian of
thought Victor Goldschmidt, this detail was simply altered. Ancient
morality amounted to nothing more than eudaemonism, and from this
Goldschmidt goes on to a reconciliation between Stoicism and Kant.
Others have recognized that this morality had something distinctive
about it, but got things backward: Stoic morality had a "much larger
domain"[92] than ours because it embraced functions conforming to
nature such as eating and drinking. Others, finally, confine themselves
to the raw historic datum: for ancient thought, honor and happiness
were inseparable. No doubt, but we must digest this datum. How could
the ancients have thought this? What were they thinking of? A thought,
after all, is not impenetrable like a stone. Didn't this way of looking at
things involve specific difficulties?

If the Stoics were able to refuse to separate honor and happiness, it
was, at first, because of a play on words. They understood by honor the
attitude that situated the individual in the state of happy security, but
at another moment they wished to enlarge their doctrine to include
honor in its current sense. They did this at the cost of a detour through
the cosmos and of several difficulties because *their* morality and morality *per se* retained two opposing statuses.

What is the source of morality in the common sense of the word? Nature herself: she watches over the well-being of the human species as a whole no less than that of each of its representatives. She reveals our duties toward others to us in two ways: instinct (*aphorme* in Greek) and the seeds of reason. The same instinct that makes every living being self-interested makes us interested in our offspring and relatives, as well as humanity in general. Man is the friend of man. Nature has also given us prenotions or, as Seneca writes, "seeds" of justice, to be developed by our reason. Thus, she has sown in us an aversion to crime—remorse is the proof of that. Men are social animals, made to live together, and nature created us to help each other in the same way she created dogs to help men.[93]

This is an idyllic painting, one in which morality would be as natural as the instinct for feeding or the development of language in children. Nature ensures public order within the human species and regulates rivalries according to the virtue of justice. In the stadium, Chrysippus said, the runners do not trip each other (or at any rate, they should not, we are tempted to add). Epictetus elegantly says not to steal your neighbor's wife because "our portions have been divided and distributed." At meals, you do not eat the pork off your neighbor's plate.[94]

Are these "men who do not trip up their fellow" men as they exist in reality or are they men as they ought to be, and indeed would be, if their instinct for altruism and their seed of justice had not been falsified by their upbringing? Here, the Stoics seem to have forgotten their theory of initial perversion, the *diastrophe*; forgotten, that is, that all men have gone mad and that they, the Stoics, are on hand to propose a method of reeducation to any who have come to understand their own dementia, and hope for a cure.

Seneca's portrait is of a corrupt society in which man is a wolf to man. Here, the incompatibility between Stoic morality and common morality is evident. Aren't the Stoics, after all, a handful of heroes of self-transformation? As for the rest of humanity—is its conduct more or less honorable, minus the inevitable fringe of adultery and petty crimes, or is it really mad? If so, what ought the Stoics' attitude be toward the society in which they are immersed? Did they become Stoics to assure their individual recovery or to practice altruistic virtue for the benefit of an insane world? This uncertainty becomes acute when applied to matters of politics. Should a Stoic take part in public affairs, as altruism and the sense of duty prescribe? Or should he flee politics entirely because the city is obviously corrupt and the only practicable politics must be reprehensible to his conscience? Would it not be better to devote oneself entirely to the study and spread of Stoicism? We shall see that Seneca, under Nero, asked himself these questions at the risk of his life. Despite the Stoic taste for reconciliation, this was an insoluble dilemma. Chrysippus wanted to have it both ways: the sage will not involve himself in politics unless his city has a better constitution than others,[95] but he and others also repeat that the sage is patriotic and loves his city—but which city? His real city, or an ideal city mentally uniting the few existing sages scattered over the globe? It seems that the sect never backed its members into this internationalist case of conscience. The Stoic texts relating to law imply that if the true law, that inspired by wisdom, reigned, words such as city, law, and contract would dissolve spontaneously, and the problem would disappear without having to be decisively encountered. In fact, though, the Stoics never could bring themselves to decide the question. On one hand, they regarded the positive laws of different societies as the material for an immense history of folly, while at the same time recommending the observation of justice in everyday life.[96] We may ask with Rist[97] how the Stoics, who accorded value to human beings strictly in proportion to the moral excellence of each individual, could simultaneously think that there was both affinity and amity between themselves and the rest of mankind?

This ambiguity dated from the foundation of Stoicism, and shows itself in the cynical component that was aggressively part of the doctrine from its very beginnings. Zeno and Chrysippus published political utopias in which they exaggerated the extremes. Alongside a devastating rationalism, abolishing private property, money, and the courts, and which justified manual labor for free men, along with unisex clothing, bare legs, and communal marriage; further authorizing the sage to become a pimp to earn a living and allowing him to eat the corpse of his father in case of famine, their utopia, with exaggerated refinement, forbade its youth a furrowed brow or languid glances, and ordered them to avoid long conversations with men in the barber shop. *This* was a city in which it would be acceptable to take part in public affairs! Seneca makes no allusion to the cynical substratum that earned his sect lasting ridicule; he must have hated it as much as the paradoxes of the sage as connoisseur of drinks and boys.

This, however, did not lessen the difficulty. Should the sage's course of conduct be traced according to a society in his own image, a city of sages, or was it necessary to situate it in his role as a resident of actual cities? The closing pages of *On Leisure* make this hesitation clear. The question is to know whether an aspirant to wisdom should take part in public affairs. Some answer that he will do so in cities that are not excessively depraved, where his participation will be neither futile nor compromising, but Seneca asks which cities fulfill this condition. It does not take long to learn that no real city is virtuous enough for that.

The lengthy dialogue *On Benefits* is founded on the same hesitation. For Seneca, the term "benefits" has a much broader significance than we mean by beneficence or services rendered. (The custom of gift giving played a major role in ancient society.) Basically, however, the sense of the words have not changed substantially: a good deed is a service that is neither obligatory nor recompensed—the baker who sells me bread for money is not my benefactor. Seneca claims that beneficence is fundamental to society, creating the social bond. His claim, we may justly remark, appears to be greatly exaggerated: the cohesion and relatively good order of the human flock are guaranteed above all by the pressure of institutions, the division of labor, and economic exchanges.

The exaggerated importance Seneca attributes to beneficence can be explained. He situated himself, as though in a dream, in an ideal society, a city of sages where the social bond is love—the love that, according to Zeno,[98] contributes to maintain civic life. Where love is active, institutions, courts of law, and money become useless. The love of man for man is sufficient to ensure social cohesion. Once we go on to actual cities, imperfect images of this ideal world, we still find loving, that is, free and disinterested behavior that we call good deeds. Seneca then proceeds unduly to attribute to beneficence, a marginal behavior, the importance Zeno had assigned to friendship or love as the cornerstone of human society. In doing so, he reduced sociology to a psychology of virtues and vices, and emptied it of its substance.

We should, therefore, be wary of assimilating Stoicism into a political ideology or even to one having political consequences, as we might with more justification do with a Christian sect. Christianity invented both proselytism and a church that feels invested with a legitimate authority over all mankind. The church is not confined to offering itself to each person, but rather feels founded on a mission to intervene and control, not just wait for potential converts. To us it seems evident—wrongly—that a doctrine valid for every person should have claimed, by the same token, to modify humanity as a whole, both in thought and reality. This, however, is not the case: it is a Christian innovation. The universal content of a doctrine is one thing, but a doctrine is not only its content. Its tacit ambitions are something else, and we err by repeating that every religious or doctrinal conviction is totalitarian by nature, by the force of its convictions. It is only the example of Christianity that makes us believe this, and the air we breathe is so permeated by this conviction that socialism itself has imitated Christianity's proselytism and authoritarian ambitions without wanting to do so or knowing it has. In the pagan world, matters were different. There was no church of Bacchus or of Isis, and one city's temple of Isis had no more connection with that of the next city than the bakeries in adjoining villages did. Stoicism had no more of a pope or hierarchy than did the religion of Isis. The Epicurean Diogenes of Oenoanda had a summary of his doctrine inscribed on his tomb in southern Turkey so that everyone could read it. Because all men were in error, "love of humanity" prompted him to propose Epicureanism to them as a remedy. As we see, he was opening a pharmacy for the soul and waiting for customers—no more. Neither the Epicureans nor the Stoics thought for a moment that the whole world would one day become Stoic or Epicurean. If someone had predicted this to them, they may (although perhaps not on reflection) have seen it as a possibility because, after all, their doctrine was good for every individual. The thought would never have occurred to them spontaneously in the absence of a church or of any proselytizing ambitions.

The Stoic attitude toward society confined itself to taking it as it was, and to await individual converts one by one. The only problem that could arise was this: was the sage originally external to the world as it was, and did he enter it only after reflection, if he entered it at all? Or was that which was at stake not scribbling a dreamed Stoicism down on paper, but rather teaching the doctrine to disciples who had been born in a real city and already belonged to it? For the sage, Seneca concluded that the matter would be settled in the future; in the present, it was between you and me. Was this individual revolution or conformist complicity?

The Stoics did not really want to have to decide. They were "more ambitious than anyone to govern both individual and social life."[99] They quailed before collective obligations because they were ready to be admired as the best, but little inclined to be pointed to as rebels, contrary to the Epicureans, who fled public office and did not consider man his own best friend. Epicureanism escaped the contradictions of Stoicism because it derived morality from a clearly recognized egotism and from fear of the police. No one likes to be harmed, therefore men have agreed among themselves not to do to another what they would not like done to themselves.[100] This is a cold doctrine, while the Stoic was a man who needed a certain ethical heat while congratulating himself on his disinterested zeal. Thus, Stoicism was more successful than Epicureanism because ethical zeal is a widespread passion.

Unfortunately, ancient thought had a certain difficulty imagining disinterestedness, and often got tangled in a verbal debate over egotism and altruism. Why would we do another good if we did not take personal pleasure in it? It was understood that everyone inevitably sought his own happiness (while good deeds, Seneca says, are willed actions). How can it be that individuals care about posterity, are concerned about what will be said of them when they are no longer there, and attach importance to what another thinks of them in his head, when they are not in his skin? For some Stoics, every good stops at the boundaries of the individual and cannot cross the frontiers separating one body from another. Seneca's thought is visibly more evolved, but he limits himself to saying that both sides of the debate over this difficulty have their supporters, and the question remains open.[101] Nonetheless, it was hard to reconcile altruism and the care of the self, which remained fundamental—hence the Stoic detour through the cosmos. Paganism did not have our idea of love: the encounter with "You" in the midst of "Them." We may cite Rist again: our relations with our neighbor are indirect, in obedience to the great All. They derive from the only thing that directly matters to us, in Rist's words, "our own isolated moral excellence."[102] The individual will enlarge his *I* by identifying with the cosmos; however, he will forget his *I* and his personal misfortunes by identifying with cosmic fatality, sacrificing his nature to Nature.

This will be the new way to preserve our autonomy and our security, and this security will be total because we accept the Great All in advance. We accept it because we cannot withdraw ourselves from it; in the Stoic universe, everything is fated. We are all in the same boat. In the calculus of individual security and respect for the public order of the cosmos, self-interest and obligation have the same standing, so much so that I do not *obey* the divine government of the world; in thought, I *am* it.

Our claim, in fact, is that within the cosmos, nature is ordered. Reason, which imposed this beautiful order (the Greek *kosmos* means both "world" and "order") pleases our own reason, or faculty of judging and organizing. It is out of respect for cosmic order that we will not play dirty tricks on others. Nature, writes Seneca, created us as brothers, and this ought to encourage us to be just and benevolent. Here, Seneca is summarizing, somewhat rhetorically, a less direct line of argument. Nature, or a providential god (which are the same thing under different names according to what function is being fulfilled) watches over the preservation of the cosmos, and our reason verifies this. Reason has a liking for whatever is, like itself, ordered, harmonious, and in accord with itself. When our reason sees the cosmos so well governed, it refrains from raising recriminations and categorical claims, if I may say so. Reason sees everything from the governing point of view, that of the public good. Being reasonable, it respects an order as reasonable as itself. The Stoics refused to believe for an instant that reason could ally itself with an individualist egocentrism, and teach it to play tricks, no matter how well planned and Machiavellian, on our rivals. They seem to believe that reason has a liking for reason; we imitate and love what resembles us.

Man, as a reasonable individual, resembles the cosmos. Man is a microcosm, a small empire contained within the great empire. In being governed by a rational capacity for organization, man is equal to the universe and therefore adopts a universal point of view and behaves accordingly. "In man, the soul is the same thing as god is in the cosmos." When we behave as good fathers or good neighbors, all we are doing is following an instinct. When we respect the cosmic order, we follow the bent of reason, which understands and approves that order.

Even though the Stoics exhort us to follow nature, they tell us at the same time that we *are* microcosms and love the public order of the world—and that we *ought* to be and love in this way.

To this point, Stoicism has taught us to rescue our *I* by banishing fear and desire. Now it exhorts us to respect others by looking at things from a lofty perspective. There is a virtue—greatness of soul—which disdains the petty reasons for fear and desire, and which sees the large picture.[103] This virtue does not get attached to details and remains proudly impassive before both good and bad fortune. For Seneca, it occupies a strategic position among the virtues.

Strategic is the key word. Again and again, Seneca, wanting to make the Stoic attitude before fate and the cosmos palpable, develops or indicates a military allegory with a single word. A man is a soldier of the cosmos. Mankind is a perfectly organized army under the command of an undefeatable general, the providential god who, for the safety of the All, assigns each one his post. From the private's point of view, chance or fortune seems to preside over the distribution of life's unequal roles, but what difference does that make? In the army, in any aggregation of individuals, we know in advance, without a word spoken, that there will inevitably be the ill favored and the sacrificed. Some will find themselves assigned to more dangerous or painful missions than others, but if the soldier is animated by patriotism for the cosmic city, he will joyfully accept his mission and even his own sacrifice. Chrysippus said he would accept disease if he knew that destiny (which is one of the functions of god) had decreed it for him. What is health or life compared with the safety of the great city? He would sacrifice himself with joy. The focus is to see things from on high, through the eyes of the governing god.

> Everything that happens to us by means of the cosmic order, let us
> accept it with greatness of soul. We are bound, by our enlistment as sol-
> diers, to bear our condition and not to trouble ourselves over what is not
> in our power to avoid. We were born in a monarchy: obedience to god,
> who is its king, that is liberty.

These are the terms in which Seneca exhorts us to freely obey cosmic fate.

And fate there certainly is: god's providence is also destiny, and everything that happens in our private lives and in universal history was fated—precisely because the universe is well made. It would be badly made if events occurred according to chance, without cause. That would mean that the world is not completely organized, that the march of the cosmic army was halting, and that god does not control everything, but this is nonsense: his providence does control everything, and so everything is for the best. God's providential government is, nonetheless, in no way totalitarian. He leaves us free to make our own decisions, although they are not, for that reason, any less fated. Even Jupiter, Epictetus says, could not succeed in making us do something we did not want to do. How can man be at once free and determined? Isn't this a contradictory doctrine? These questions are still being debated, but we will leave this vexing question—one Seneca never mentions—aside.[104] He confines himself to saying that "Destiny guides those who follow it and drags those who resist." Stoic fatalism is, or thinks it is, more reflective than resigned. Once the providential god organized the world, he did not abandon to its own devices. He controls its evolution strictly, leaving nothing to chance. Everything that happens is providential. The Stoics do not value submission to destiny because it is inevitable; they subscribe to it because it is rational and calculated for the good of the human species. Seneca convinced himself that accepting destiny is above all a source of calm.

> What is the price for having our lives flow regularly, without emotional turbulence? You shall know it: a perfectly virtuous man never cries out, 'Damned misfortune!' Whatever happens to him, he does not take it as an evil. He tells himself that he is a citizen of the cosmos, of the whole world, and that he is a soldier. He bends to chores and hard work as though ordered to his duty.

We have just remarked that the Stoics considered themselves citizens of the world, in Greek *kosmopolitai*, but we have also seen in what sense they meant this. Patriots of the cosmos and its destiny, they love this native land of all men, and show their love by respecting the public order of the cosmos—justice—and by courageously accepting their own destinies, whatever they may be. The problems confronting ancient philosophy are not our problems, and we must not try to find traces of politics in our sense of internationalism here. Should the sage take part in the public functions of his small city? That was how the question was phrased, but there was another question: if the sage

decided to participate in them, would he be exercising his public functions justly, as demanded of him in his capacity as citizen of a just cosmos? If his native land were to be conquered and annexed by a rival city,
he would endure this fate with greatness of soul, whether that meant
suffering in silence or committing suicide. It is hard not to project our
own ideas and preoccupations on the ideas of another age, falling victim to anachronism. Stoicism granted that the human race was one,
and that all men were equal by virtue of their having reason, the only
thing that counts. What, then, was their position on the scandal (to us)
of slavery? The Stoics believed in providential destiny—did they imagine that the triumph of Roman imperialism and the victory of
Caesarism over liberty were consistent with the flow of history? No,
they imagined nothing of the sort. Their cosmopolitanism and fatalism
were unconcerned with those domains.

CITY OF THE WORLD, DESTINY, SOCIETY, AND POLITICS

In those distant times, the panorama of reflection was not regulated, as
it is for us, by the two horizons we call society and history. The ancients
fought as many wars as we do and were equally active politically. They
forced themselves to kill for Caesar or for liberty, but when they
reflected or spoke, Nature, and Fortune or Destiny were the horizons of
their mental world. No one ever dreamed of abolishing slavery; the idea
would not have occurred to the Christians or the Stoics. Whatever century they live in, it is impossible for men to look beyond the changing
scenery that forms the horizon of their existence and see the bare walls
of the theater's wings. The reason: there are no walls.

Everything seemed to be getting off to a good start. Stoicism is uni-
versalist: every man, whatever his condition, ought to be, and is fundamentally a soldier in the cosmic army, under the command of a
providence wishing only for the good of the human species. Reason
tells us this because that army is the army of reason. To belong, it suf-
fices to be a reasonable animal; no other title than "man" is required—
not wealth, nobility, or free birth. Even women—how could one dare to
refuse—were accepted! Stripping the matter bare (in a highly philosophical manner), membership in the human race has reason as the
only admitting criterion. Why are men just and beneficent toward each

other? Why should we "show the way to a lost traveler and share our bread with the starving?" Because "this world you see, where gods and men live together, is one; we are the parts of this great body; we are all of the same family, since Nature formed all of us on identical foundations, and for the same destination," that is, on reason and for blessedness. Consequently, "What could these words mean: a Roman knight; a freedman; a slave? They are only words, springing from pretension or injustice." Seneca's sincerity is not in doubt, but it does not prevent him from breaking into laughter at the decrepitude of an old slave who had watched over him lovingly in youth—in the slave's presence, no less, as though before an old dog. Seneca himself tells the story quite unwittingly, then begins a meditation on time.

The unity of the human race was not a discovery of the Stoics. It had been known for two million years, since the times of the first hominids, because all superior animals understand that they are representatives of a single species. A cat recognizes another cat and distinguishes dogs from cats very easily. Every featherless biped, endowed with language, is a human being, a beautiful discovery that yet remains to be put to use. The Nazis must have considered Jews as human beings because they treated them as an inferior human race, the dregs of humanity. It is not enough to have principles, we must be faithful to them (for example, we have the rights of man and the hydrogen bomb). It is perhaps even more difficult to discern all their consequences. Seneca professes that all men are brothers and assigns a high value to the virtue of humanity, yet writes sentences about gladiators that make our jaws drop. He also wrote a humane and generous letter (*Letter* 47) on the duty to treat slaves as humble friends. It is worth pausing a while to consider it.

First of all, we must realize that the prescription of humane treatment for slaves was in no way revolutionary, and was not unique to the Stoics. For four centuries, the fashionable morality of the rich and powerful required that one manifest one's concern to appear simple toward inferiors, open to all, and clement to the vanquished—at least if it were possible without wronging oneself. This virtue was called humanity. It required that, when there was a choice, one should take the most humane attitude possible. This meant giving to charity without diminishing one's heirs' patrimony; or leaving the vanquished with their lives, if national security did not require sending them to the sword. For where there is necessity, one is no longer free, and there is no margin in which virtue might make itself known. Humanity was practiced in what we might call the "charitable margin." A slave remains a slave, but we will treat him humanely, without going so far as to cast doubt on the legitimacy of slavery itself. The pagans had two attitudes here, as did the Christians. A master who demanded impeccable service from his slaves and punished them ferociously (there are examples in *Letter* 47) could also set the deserving ones free in his will and leave them a small income. It was more humane to have your slaves love you than fear you. Among friends, it was proper to say that slaves were men like us, and children learned this at school when they were made to study the maxims and proverbs of popular wisdom. Slaves had a dual attitude, just like their masters. A good slave loves and admires his master, to the point of sacrificing his life for him.[105] Stoicism took up the virtue of humanity, along with its marginality; not contesting the legitimacy of slavery, it was content to refine the terminology.

Let us leave fashionable morality and proverbs and go on to real thinkers. Plato and Aristotle know perfectly well that slaves are human beings, but Aristotle (we will confine our remarks to him) adds immediately that they are men of a second order. Aristotle's doctrine merits a detailed examination because Stoicism adopts a more or less opposite view. Under an outward show of rhetorical exhortation, *Letter* 47 rests on very firm conceptual foundations.

1. For Aristotle, a slave is a man, but one destined by nature to fulfill manual tasks. To assure oneself of this, it is only necessary to look at one. His body is thick and muscle-bound, while that of a free man is slim and elegant. The slave's mind would be incapable of liberal studies. Certainly, there are exceptions because nature operates wholesale. Free men have been known to have offspring worth no more than slaves; and, after the sack of a city, it sometimes happens that its free men are sold as slaves. For the Stoics, on the other hand, human nature is reducible to the soul, to reason, and takes no account of muscles or slow-wittedness.

2. For Aristotle, manual labor is unworthy of a free man, by nature. The Stoics show on the contrary that nature has passed no such decree because we see free men reduced to working with their hands during famine, when they must cultivate the earth, and during war, where they

carry their equipment themselves. Stoic nature has passed decrees only concerning the soul, in order to make it equal in all.

3. Finally, for Aristotle, the slave is the property of the master in the same way a piece of furniture or a tool is (except that the tool in question is endowed with speech). For the Stoics, it is counter to nature to suppose that it is possible to own a man because reason is free and sovereign. A slave can no more be possessed than his master can. The conclusion: we must change our terminology. If the slave works for his master, it is because the latter is sovereign over him or, to put it another way, by virtue of a contract, such as those who are equal under the law may execute between them. This is the source of Chrysippus's formula, which Seneca quotes: "The slave is actually a wage worker in perpetuity."[106]

The debate did not bear on the unity of the human race, which was a given since the beginning, but rather on what made man a man. For the Stoics, only reason mattered, and was in itself sufficient. Chrysippus granted reason its rights. In the same way, Saint Paul defined man by his immortal soul; because slavery prevented no one from attaining salvation, the apostle concluded: "Slaves, obey your masters." In the cosmic army of the Stoics, Fortune assigns the roles among the combatants. The emperor would conscientiously perform his role as a combatant, as Marcus Aurelius did, and the slave would conscientiously execute the free contract as wage worker in perpetuity that Fortune had implicitly signed for him. By the terms of this contract, the slave would work and the master would house and feed him.[107]

In practical terms, Stoicism wound up at the same status quo as Aristotle and Plato had. The status of perpetual hireling was assigned according to individual destiny, and to call it a contract was simply semantics: the slave could not annul it because it was in perpetuity. What would he do if his master did not uphold his promises, and, for instance, fed him poorly? The texts that have come down to us do not say, but it is easy to guess that the folly of the master who treated his slave as his property did not exempt a wise slave from respecting his own obligations: another's folly cannot be an excuse for a sage.

Having shifted the terminology, Chrysippus is able to reaffirm that slavery is unnatural, but the perpetual contract itself conforms to nature.[108] A contract is not a law mandated from on high; it is entered into between the sovereign contracting parties, who determine its content according to their liking. In it, they are free to respect nature, and the Stoics very much appreciated contracts; for them, it was only justice to respect them. To sum up: by redefining the terms of slavery, Chrysippus achieved a philosophical conception of it that was perfectly satisfactory in his eyes, not a concession to the society of his times. If the Stoics had been the masters of society and could have remodeled it to their liking, they would have retained slavery, albeit under another name.

In terms of real change, however, there are two small points to be noted. For Aristotle, slaves were too coarse to be able to study philosophy; for Plato, they simply did not exist for the purposes of self-cultivation, but rather to cultivate the earth in place of free men. They could learn (as an experiment, Socrates had a young slave perform a geometric exercise), but that was not the role to which they had been assigned. By contrast, for the Stoics, as for the Cynics and Epicureans, philosophy was accessible to both slaves and women. That is a milestone in the history of philosophy, but not in the general evolution of humanity. The other difference is that in laying claim to the virtue of humanity, so dear to the collective conscience of the ancients, Stoicism conferred on it the authority of philosophy. It was made a strict duty, not a matter of fashion and right thinking. How much practical difference this made is more uncertain: it follows the philosophy of accommodation, although it is not enough to be a humane master: to become one, it is necessary to see oneself from without. Seneca did not doubt that he bore himself as a great lord among the lower classes. In the final analysis, justice and benevolence, as the Stoics saw them, concerned individuals and had nothing to do with institutions and society as a whole. A slave would be well or badly treated according to his merits because Stoic justice was not weakness, and beneficence was not blind. The injustice of the institution of slavery, however, was not perceived. The doctrine took no account of institutions (and so slaves were treated as friends) because basically they did not matter (and so slaves remained slaves). Stoicism was a doctrine of personal ethics and sociology did not exist. They did not perceive anything called *society* intervening between natural law and the individual.

This attitude is both disconcerting and deceptive for us, but the fact is there. Our *rights of man* are no more a natural idea than any other.

The ancients were no more horrified by slavery than they suffered from the lack of electrical lighting or the steamship. Stoicism had no convictions; its only content was an impoverished notion of the self and an overgeneralized idea of the world. It lacked the means to think about politics or to take political positions. In Seneca's time, it furnished arguments (or excuses) to monarchists as well as to the enemies of Caesarism. We must not forget that "doing politics" (*politeuesthai* in Greek, *capessere rem publicam* in Latin) did not mean having principles and an opinion about politics or being an activist, as it does to us, but simply "take part in the public functions of the city, the duty of every free man." This was in contrast to living a life of leisure and ease, that is, not participating in public functions, preferring a life devoted to liberal study and philosophy.[109] From 63 on, this was Seneca's great dilemma. As for what political line to take, the Stoics never gave it a thought, never grew impassioned over it, and had no theoretical position on the matter. Marcus Aurelius was a Stoic, but privately; the sect as such was never either a doctrine of opposition or an official ideology like Confucianism.

Without any possibility of imagining a concrete politics, along with the reduction of every problem to a question of the morality of an individual whose capacity to exercise reason had been restored, one could justify—or contest—anything, from building a rational utopia to living reasonably and docilely according to the status quo. As far as individual liberty or national independence went, the Stoics had only one thing to say: true liberty is not being enslaved by one's passions.[110] This is in agreement with the main principle of all ancient political thought: only if you are able to control yourself are you fit to command others; conversely, obedience to a libertine, to a Nero, is unworthy of a free man. What is true of the leader is also true of the governed: an inability to obey—being a rebel—is the same as not being able to govern oneself. Political and social discipline are a reflection of internal discipline. With this precept as a starting point, it was entirely possible to enjoin slaves to obey their masters, and it was equally possible to justify Roman imperialism, as the Platonist Cicero did.[111] Whoever refused to submit to the Roman peace was morally undisciplined, a rebel by nature. Stoicism's strongest tendency was to reduce politics to a morality of self-discipline, but it never resolved the question of who, exactly, should dominate his passions. Should the master, the conqueror, or the emperor suppress their tyrannical impulses? Or should the slave, the non-Roman, and the subjects of Caesar restrain their disobedience? Every Stoic could decide for himself: doctrine had nothing to teach in this regard. However, another strong tendency was to take the side of good order—the established order; their morality never encouraged rebellion, utopias, or hope.

Let us take as an example the cosmopolitanism of the Stoics—those "citizens of the world." That world resembled human society so little that it had among its citizens "men and gods." It is, rather, the natural cosmos: the earth with its seasons and harvests, the heavens with their divine stars. The cosmos is the common city of men and gods because it was made for both of them as their comfortable dwelling. That they both live there is what makes them common citizens. Despite this, some contemporaries still see a political meaning in this universalism. To drive a stake through this misconception, let us consider an unambiguous passage from *Letter 95*:

> Public life is as mad as private; we restrain murderers, but what of wars, those slaughters of whole peoples? Greed and cruelty, exercised obscurely between isolated individuals, are, all in all, less serious. But it is by plebiscites and decrees of the senate that we are commanded to do what would be crimes if committed by private citizens. Men, whom nature made so gentle, have in these cases no remorse for butchering their own.

Here, Seneca is stigmatizing the cruelty of nations, so much worse than that of individuals. He neither declares nor excludes that this applies to the Roman nation as well. (The phrases "plebiscites" and "decrees of the senate" were used in Latin to denote the decisions of the assembly and council of every city, Roman or foreign.) The truth is that Seneca views these matters as a moralist and stigmatizes the cruelty of human cities in general. Is this done in the name of universalism? That is highly doubtful. To reproach the nations for the vice of cruelty is one thing, to dream of a politically unified humanity is quite another. It would be enough if every city were virtuous and gentle. Stoic reasoning is naturalist and ethical; it does not descend to the level of political institutions. The Stoics may have dreamed of a city of sages, without courts or money, (although we do not know, and probably neither did they, whether this city was to be humanity as a whole or the local subdivision of humanity comprised of sages). Or, no longer floating above reality, they may have dictated their duties to real men, and told them to perform their functions in their own cities—so much so that one of their disciples (Marcus Aurelius) would one day find himself in the process of waging a war of conquest in a foreign city. It is one thing to talk philosophy, to say that all men are brothers, and to deplore the atomic bomb (without excluding one's own country, obviously included in such general language), but it is another to come back down to earth and find out that a hostile nation has the bomb. The Stoics spoke as philosophers; for them, man was a reasonable animal, and also an animal made to "live in the city." They said no more on the subject, notwithstanding that "city" here is singular, not plural.

This was an empty universalism with no practical application. André Breton used to say that patriotism was the least philosophical of all ideas and, for a true believer in philosophy, it is impossible to contradict him. The Stoics would not have agreed with him, only because they had never considered the matter thoroughly. Indeed, they did not even suspect there was a difficulty—they sidestepped it. An ancient commentary on Plato incidentally demonstrating this has come down to us. Men naturally love those like themselves, and for Platonists, patriotism is mandatory because our compatriots are more similar to us than foreigners. The commentator approves of this wholeheartedly: he censures the Stoics who, with their habitual exaggeration, claim that "we feel as close to most distant barbarians of Asia as we do to ourselves" and our compatriots.[112] The information the commentator gives is certainly accurate. Stoicism functions entirely on the opposition between imperfection (*hexis* in Greek) and perfection (*diathesis*), for which everything is equal. Something is right or it is not. If you love men perfectly, you love them all equally, not yielding to a weak partiality that loves some more than others; because all men are equally reasonable, they are all equally our brothers. That's all well and good, but if the question is translating these affirmations into acts, we shall soon see that Seneca found patriotic reasons for altering nothing in the status quo: the best way to love Asian barbarians is for Rome to maintain them under her hegemony, for their own good.

Seneca, after all, remains a man of the past. Stoicism has been credited, a little too readily, for the progress in political morality under the Roman Empire: the sense of community, care for the poor, equality of all under universal law. If any philosophy could have made Roman domination moral, it was this one, for no other was so noble. It is, however, necessary to acknowledge that a philosophy is not entirely contained in what it pronounces, but also in its silences and lacunae. Nothing in Seneca gives a glimpse of the political and moral progress that in fact occurred a century after him, with no hint of prophecy from him. The second century of our era would see the empire cease, bit by bit, being a colonial hegemony, in which Roman Italy was the metropolis and the provinces kinds of colonies. A century and a half after the *Letters to Lucilius*, in 212, a great emperor, Caracalla (vilified by senatorial tradition) transformed all the free men of his empire into Roman citizens with a stroke of his pen. This was the culmination of a long evolution that had begun in Seneca's time, and whose initiator was the emperor Claudius, of whom the senator Seneca had so much bad to say. We will return to this shortly. In the same way, the second century would see the Roman government showing greater solicitude for its subjects and for the common people. It watched over the well-being of impoverished cities, distributed fallow land to the poor,[113] and attempted to make the empire what Henri Marrou called a cooperative of happiness, minding the well-being of the indigent, or at least proclaiming that it had a duty to do so.[114] Not a line in Seneca would allow us to foresee these preoccupations.

Stoicism was equally incapable of rethinking international politics, boundaries, or the problem of the plurality of existing societies that shatter general human society. Either it took no notice of it, or it naïvely chalked ethnocentrism and patriotism up to its own account, without perceiving the contradiction or posing the questions of conscience arising from internationalism, unjust wars, or racial exclusion. Stoic cosmopolitanism was an ocean of abstraction in which the limits of the Roman Empire were drowned as surely as those of Athens. Politics was not Stoicism's main preoccupation. Bergson remarked that practically all moralists virtuously enumerate our duties to our native land, then those we bear to the rest of humanity, but that on the second point their instructions remain pious wishes, sufficiently vague so that we are never confronted with the necessity of betraying our country for the profit of humanity.

Because Stoicism reduces man to pure reason, it is unable to think

about politics. Every conquest is contrary to justice and inspired by
avarice, but one could say as much for any other page in world history.
A Stoic historian, Posidonius, contemporary with the Roman conquest
of the Greek world, explained world history according to human passions; reading him, it was impossible not to wonder, faced with the
spectacle of so much folly: "What is the point of it all?"[115]

In Seneca, next to principled condemnations of war and conquest
in general, we find a Roman patriotism untouched by doubt. We must
insist on this because as soon as we speak of Stoic cosmopolitanism, we
can hastily conclude, on false evidence, that cosmopolitanism must
have lead them to a generous attitude toward the vanquished, and
equally must have prepared the Romans to grant equality of rights
between the metropolis and the colonies, that is, the provinces. It
would be as false to conclude that Christianity and Saint Paul paved the
way for the disappearance of slavery. In a pamphlet, Seneca ironically
mocks the Gauls to whom the emperor Claudius had granted senatorial dignity. The Stoic Thrasea, during a trial brought by provincials
against a Roman governor who had lined his pockets by pillaging his
subjects, waxed indignant over the weakness of the sovereign people
and took the part of the thief. According to Seneca, the Roman Empire
was destined by providence to reach the ends of the earth. When
Romans mastered a city, the soldiery might get carried away and do a
little massacring, but that did not last and they quickly returned to the
authentic Roman attitude of humanity (*On Benefits*, III, 33, 3 and II, 23,
2). To legitimate Roman hegemony, Seneca adopted the traditional
argument: the Romans exercised their authority justly and respected
the rights of their provincial subjects (*On the Shortness of Life*, XVIII, 3).
He did not imagine that the question was whether this authority
existed at all. For him, it was enough to claim that Caesar's conquest of
Gaul was suited to the public good of Rome (*Consolation to Marcia*, XIV,
3), and that it was praiseworthy to extend the bounds of empire
(*Consolation to Helvia*, IX, 7). The only conquests Seneca condemns are
those of others—he has no words harsh enough for those of Alexander
the Great.[116]

There is, however, a passage in Seneca that is seemingly exceptional,
although it confirms the rule and curiously concerns Spain, our
philosopher's original homeland. In *Letter* 66 Seneca invokes an episode
of Roman conquest, the siege of Numantia by Scipio Aemilianus. This

stronghold, close to Soria in Castille, had been the Alesia of Spain, and its defenders, seeing all hope lost, killed themselves rather than be taken prisoner by the Romans. Seneca exalts the courage of besiegers and Spaniards alike, who died, he says, with liberty in their hands—by which we must understand Stoic liberty, which gives the means to end one's days when fortune proves irresistible.

Why this evenhandedness between conquerors and natives? Is it Spanish patriotism or, rather, a kind of noble pride in the local past?[117] This is not impossible. Or is it a Stoic—and Senecan—sympathy for the grandeur of suicide? Certainly it is, but it is no less certain that Seneca regards the conquest of Numantia as legitimate (*On Anger*, I, 11, 7). How, then, can he justify both sides? The answer is that man's knowledge does not extend as far as god's. The Spaniards could not know that the Roman conquest was in the direction of providence. They reasoned from the things they perceived—an act of aggression—and defended their country. Their decision was objectively false, but in itself it was also just. They escaped this contradiction by taking the great and noble way out, which is always available—suicide. Cato reasoned with equal justice and equally falsely by siding with a republic condemned by destiny, and he would likewise kill himself.

Might providence and the direction of history, matters of so much concern to the moderns, be the same thing? This was a bitter question for a subject of the Caesars, who had confiscated the republic for the profit of their monarchy. But we should not move ahead too quickly: our concerns are not those of the Stoics, and it is necessary to go one step at a time.[118]

1. Destiny starts to uncoil from the initial organization of the world, like a rope braided in advance and once for all time. The designs of the god of providence are too reasonable to change in the course of their unfolding. Stoic providence does not act blow by blow, and it performs neither miracles nor acts of grace. It lets the rope uncoil, and neither supplication nor prayer are effective.

This very philosophical version of providence has nothing in common with the providence or fortune believed in by the mass of humanity. Popular belief declared events in conformity with its wishes to be providential, but closed its eyes when faced with contrary developments as it did not want to doubt providence when political affairs or the lot of an individual went badly. People wanted to believe that their city or the empire was protected by the good fortune or providence of the gods, whose protection they implored in prayers and sacrifices. However, they had all too frequent occasion to wonder if blind chance or an absurd destiny were not the true master of history and of individual lives, and it happened that people cursed the gods and their anger and caprices. Stoic providence is diametrically opposed to such ideas. It assured the good condition of the cosmos and humanity in a global sense, but not the individual lot of each person, and still less, if that were possible, the history of cities, kingdoms, or empires. It would be presumptuous to imagine that the Roman Empire could have been planned by providence. Stoics might well have subscribed to these lines of Voltaire, from a letter written in 1762:

> Individual providence, between the two of us, is an absurd chimera. The chain of events is immense and eternal, and personal preferences, favors, and individual disgrace are not made on account of an infinite cause.[119] It would be too ridiculous if the eternal architect continually adjusted and readjusted minor events. He doesn't care about our mice, nor our cats, nor our Jesuits, nor our navies, nor our parliaments.

The destinies of individuals and of various collective groups, big or small, are the consequences of the necessities of conserving the cosmos and the human species as a whole. They are also the consequence of fated human decisions (or, if you prefer, known to the gods in advance), but free. God, Seneca says, watches over the All, but has not time to be busy with the particulars.

2. Providence, then, watches over humanity as a whole, not over individual lives. Moreover, it watches over humanity as a living, reasonable species, not as one engaged in a historic adventure. Its action is limited to two things: ensuring the survival of the species as a whole and giving each individual, as a representative of the species, the possibility of self-liberation thanks to reason. Providence resembles a liberal government, not a prescriptive one, that leaves freedom for individual action and limits itself to insuring those public services that facilitate the life of the nation, such as universal education, which gives each meritworthy citizen the chance to take advantage of it. Beyond that, the interlaced physical and psychological causal factors (what we call liberty) are woven in the course of time to create the destiny we call collective history.

As we have seen, providence organizes nature for the good of the human species. Other animals are at our service; the crops grow with the seasons; people instinctively protect their offspring and intuitively understand justice within the species. Having so equipped the theater of the world, providence gives each representative of the species the same innate potential to survive and to attain happiness, thanks to individual reason, which is able to develop the intuitions of virtue and happiness. It comes down to each person's freedom to actually develop them and, through merit, to become his own liberator. Alas, most individuals are bad students, and their lives and world history form that immense history of folly we know all too well. This, however, is not the fault of providence, which carries its program of instruction to great lengths. At this point we should note again that it is by virtue of its pedagogical function that nature created fleas, who teach us to bear insomnia, and hid gold beneath the earth, according to Seneca, to remove it from our covetous eyes.

3. Providence does not meddle with the results. We read Stoic texts in vain for allusions to history, except one revealing instance confirming the rule: the Trojan War.

The Trojan War was an event willed by providence to eliminate a surfeit of human population the earth could no longer support. Chrysippus had read this explanation in two of Euripides's tragedies and believed it immediately because poets were the mouthpieces for "common notions." Thus, when providence intervenes in history, it is in favor of the biological equilibrium of the human race as such.

Other interventions do not promote the survival of the species, but have pedagogical aims. God sometimes sends famine or plague as a punishment for evil and instruction for all. Providence does not chastise them out of any love of immanent justice—that is only a popular wish; besides, the Stoics made no mystery of punishment. Its only aim was educational. Providence sends plagues only to provide an instructive example. This was a somewhat apologetic argument, and it was pushed farther: when minor misfortunes, such as disease, death, torture, and ruin happen to good people it teaches all of us that these are not, in fact, misfortunes—otherwise, providence would not send them against the just. Reciprocally, the happiness of the wicked, according to Seneca, teaches us to despise false goods such as prosperity or wealth. It is still possible to strip the apologetic character from such claims and simply to say that providence knew in advance that by the ramifications of destiny, there would be misery for some of the just and happiness for some of the wicked because of secondary effects within an organization that is sound overall. Providence, we are to assume, considered that these eventualities would serve as instructive examples.

4. It is, however, more pious to attribute the events providence allowed to occur to an express intention on its part. To be sure, in his dialogue *On Providence*, Seneca affirms that the gods watch over only the economy of the universe as a whole and that the global safety of mankind matters more to them than the fate of a single person. In *Letter* 110 he postpones the question of whether the gods have time to occupy themselves with each individual in a tone of marked skepticism, but in *Letter* 95 he writes (citing Chrysippus) that they "sometimes" take care of individuals.[120] Eventually, he seems to believe (if only in the manner of Freudian denial) that this is so from time to time. "It *seems* to me that nature had the Cynic Demetrius born in our times to serve as an example for us. I *cannot doubt* that we owe him to providence." Epictetus believed that Socrates, Diogenes, and Zeno received divine counsel to teach mankind. This is just about all the Stoic texts furnish us, and it was acknowledged that providence's interventions are purely pedagogical. The historian Stoic Posidonius found no more providential interventions in the mass of historical events than the Stoic geographer Strabo found in the details of his maps. The Stoics never spoke of a providential leader or of a providential victory, and there was not a single word about the providential nature of Roman domination.

5. The spectacle of history is so dark that we might be inclined to think that the pedagogy of providence has sadly failed. The Stoics had two responses to justify god. First, what Leibniz would call "conflicts": the designs of providence conflict with each other. Larger fish must live; in order to do so, they eat smaller ones. The overall plan of nature includes disease—for excellent reasons, of course—which are contrary to my nature. Let us be sacrificed to the All. If I knew that I was destined to step into a patch of mud, my foot would plunge in of its own accord, Chrysippus says, in one of his frequent excesses of zeal.[121]

God is innocent of these physical evils; man alone is the author of moral evil. Plutarch was wrong to scold Stoic providence for the death of Socrates and the crematoria of Phalaris: the blame lies with Phalaris and Socrates's accuser.

They are blameworthy because man is a free agent. For ancient philosophy, liberty was not the problem it is for us today. It is apparent and calls for no comment. What the Stoics call liberty is the progressive liberation of the self attained by the sage, thanks to his "liberty" in the modern sense. Rather than entering into details,[122] let us simply say that Seneca, faithful to his masters, distinguishes between antecedent cause—temptation, fear, or the opportunity that makes a thief—and efficient or active cause. The beauty of Helen tempted Paris who, unable to convince himself that such beauty amounted to nothing, acted and carried Helen away. One might object that Paris did not choose to have a lustful character. This may be true, but in the end it was he who was lustful, not another, and it was he who passed into action. The individual is not predetermined; he determines. God, having foreseen his conduct, has woven him into an enormous chain of destinies to come, and so planned the Trojan War. Every agent is free in the modern sense, and, reciprocally, he alone is free. Seneca explains that there is no such thing as a legion, only legionnaires. As happiness goes no farther than the skin of a single person, so causation goes from individual to individual one by one. Every soldier who followed Paris to the ramparts of Troy was personally responsible for what he did.

We must confess that, contrary to Chrysippus, we are troubled by a difficulty in the Trojan War; fundamentally it is the same as in the siege of Numantia. There is a discordance—despite the Stoic's claims—between blind destiny and our individual reason; between our nature and Nature, our impartial reason and our egocentricity, between the ideal good and those "preferred neutrals" so dear to our well-being. Providence inserted the Trojan War into its plan for the best possible destiny. But what should the sage do if he surmised that god wished to limit overpopulation? March in the front ranks deliberately in order to be killed? Let another be killed in his place because the identity of the victims could scarcely concern god? One thinks of Carneades, chuckling off to one side. He would be even more amused to see, as we shall in a moment, that truth (divine truth) and human reason can be two distinct things.

6. In spite of the isolated case of the Trojan War, the Stoics speak much less of history than of individual destinies; their plan was to encourage each person to accept his own. Without doubt, the theory of destiny and of providence applied to the grand march of history as well

as to individuals, but a philosophy's sense is not entirely self-contained. To characterize it, what it discusses is as important as what it affirms. Is it justifiable to attribute to Stoicism an implied theory of history that it never considered?

To think about this, Stoicism would have to forget its cynical utopia of a reformed republic, and above all it would be necessary for the course of history, unified under Rome, to take on the unity of a majestic drama, one which obsessed Seneca: Caesarism as victor over liberty. Prior to the Roman conquest, there were innumerable histories. The world of the successors to Alexander the Great, in which Stoicism spread, was a mosaic of hostile kingdoms and ever more numerous cities which, independent or autonomous, remained rivals, each conserving a fierce local patriotism.[123] There was no room to philosophize on this chaos, except to say that history itself was chaos.

Everything changed after the Roman conquest, once liberty—that is, senatorial oligarchy—was forced to bow before Caesarism. Some senators, dabbling in Stoicism, wondered why providence had not granted victory to the right side. "The gods sided with the winning party; Cato sided for vanquished liberty," the poet Lucan, Seneca's nephew, wrote.

Two explanations were proffered. One was a providential rebalancing of great forces; the other, the fated senility of the cosmos. The annual change of the seasons answers to a natural necessity, even if winter is not to our liking. Now is the winter of our discontent; our nature loathes it, but nature can do no better. The rivalry between magnates and civil war, from which Caesarism emerged, were the symptoms of an inevitable aging. In the world's winter, the monarchy of the emperors is a staff appropriate to old age, and Seneca was a convinced monarchist.

The other explanation was akin to that given by Chrysippus for the Trojan War. Seneca himself had written that unlimited power crumbles under its own weight, and that such a fall was providential. "What seems to harm us tends to the preservation of the All, permitting it to maintain itself and insuring its functions."[124] Echoing his nephew, Lucan, he adds, "Let men opt for everything god has opted for." His nephew was certainly of this opinion, supposing that the gods had wished for civil war in order to rebalance the world by arresting the abusive growth of Roman grandeur.

So, was Cato right or wrong to choose liberty when the gods

(although he had not guessed this) approved the opposite party? Yes, he was right because right reason and truth are two different things.

7. Events, great and small, do not all appear to be providential. Many are the fruit of our sins, and others, like the civil wars, were at the same time the fated counterpart of a general good. There is no question of the reality of providence, and there are providential events, but which ones? We can identify none with certainty: even a sin like the civil wars may also be part of the plan of the All, meant to avoid an even worse misfortune, but only the gods know this, presciently seeing the whole development of the chain they have wrought. Cato thought that Caesarism was a sin of ambition, and he combated it. He was wrong, and the issue of the war only proved it. Nonetheless, Cato was and remains a sage. Providential causation is not on the same level with human agents: it encompasses their faults and decisions in its overall plan. Man's rationality is limited to those things of which he is aware. Ignorant of the future as we are, according to the treatise *On Benefits*, "we must decide according to reason, and not according to truth," which only god knows.[125]

The consequence of all this is that we should act "formulating an exception, with reservation"; this is one of Stoicism's great maxims. It is easy to apply, because it amounts to saying, when undertaking something: "If god thinks best," *si dis placet*. As candidate for a magistracy, one will say, "I want to be elected, but only if destiny allows." Let there be no confusion about the sense of this verbal precaution. It is not an attempt to charm away bad luck, nor is it a pious formula of submission to the will of god. Rather, it makes manifest the perfection of a philosophically lucid soul, permitting it to train itself, yet again, to accept defeat and the decisions of destiny in advance.[126]

To be defeated, like Cato, or to wreck one's ship, like more than one excellent pilot caught in a hurricane, is only a technical defeat.[127] What matters, for anyone, is to succeed in being a sage. For that, no technical success is necessary. It is enough to have a clear philosophical view of the connection between human reason and that of providence, and to be ready to serenely accept that providence, which, more far-sighted than we, substitutes its own rationality for our own. All this is less evident than paradoxical. It is no surprise when a Christian says, "If God please." Christians, after all, do not compare themselves to an infinite being. The sage, however, is the mortal equal of god, and god does not

possess reason distinct from that of man. Therefore, whatever the consequences, every reasonable action ought to be crowned with success
because the sage is "in the direction of providence," if I may be permitted the expression. When you are "in the direction of history," your
future is guaranteed. The Stoics, though, are far from sure of this, and
we have just seen why: man's reason is the same as god's, but it does not
perceive the complete unfolding of history.

8. Seneca is abundantly aware of history, or rather politics. This
sensitivity is both bitter and tense. We are living through a decline of
the cosmic cycle in which nature lets only aged actors onto the stage of
the world, or those who do not want to learn their true role. We are too
old for liberty. True enough, in whatever era, the level of evil rises above
that of virtue. Evolution is like a murky tide that has risen up to our
necks. We must try to keep our heads above water, not lose hope, take
our part of the sorry reality that is eternal, and not decry decadence.

9. Lastly, in Seneca we find a less expected idea, that of the distinction between ends and means. Providence, as we have seen, does not
bring its full excellence to bear at every instant, as an irresponsible
spirit, all conviction, might, crying "Let the cosmos perish rather than
a principle!" Instead it includes time in its calculations and uses evils,
such as the Trojan War, as a means to a future end that will be good. In
this sense, Stoicism is not a philosophy of the moment. What god does
in such cases, man is destined to imitate. Seneca writes unabashedly:

> The sage even does things of which he does not approve, in order to open
> the way for yet greater goods. He will not mourn the death of morals, but
> will grant that they adapt to the age. Not that he, like so many, will make
> this fact serve his own glory or pleasure; he will do so to reach his own
> ends. The sage will do the same things as the lustful and the ignorant,
> but not in their manner, nor according to the same plan.[128]

These surprising phrases are worth a whole book coming from the
pen of the mentor and friend of Nero, a lustful prince and novice who
justified the highest hopes during the first five, and even ten, years of
his reign.

A monarchist is faithful to his prince as long as possible. He will be
no less faithful to the principle of monarchy, even to the point of supporting an evil prince out of regard for a legitimate dynasty. Seneca

extends this same fidelity to providence. In a disturbing passage in *On Benefits* he wonders how providence could have allowed the monster Caligula to mount the throne. He replies with this speculation: perhaps providence owed a debt to the dynasty. It needed to reimburse the son, Caligula, for the exceptional virtue of his father, Germanicus, who had died before being able to rule, to the despair of all the empire's inhabitants.

And Nero? Through his mother Agrippina, he was Germanicus's grandson.

CHAPTER 3

Epilogue: Final Witness and Death of the Liberator (63–65 C.E.)

From the year 62 or 63 until his death in 65, Seneca was absorbed in his writing and in meditation. He dictated the *Letters to Lucilius* to his secretaries (as was the custom then) and, in all probability, published the first volumes of them. His last years were those of a writer fully occupied with writing, and a meditator fully occupied by his interior life, of a subject of Nero knowing his days were numbered, and of a citizen confronted by a political drama that demanded he take a stand. Seneca shut himself up in solitude and lettered leisure in order to continue his political activity through other means of action—the spread of wisdom and the testimony he bore as a thinker to wisdom, by his attitude and by his conspicuous silence. Seneca realized that with the *Letters to Lucilius*, he had his life's work in hand. Like a poet who promises immortality to the beauty he sings, Seneca announced to Lucilius that he was making their two names immortal. With the help of old age, he was aware that his progress toward wisdom was considerable, and that he was in the process of self-transformation. Moreover, he knew that he was ready to face death unafraid, and could wager all on the final scene. As for what his attitude toward Nero should be, he sought counsel from his philosophy. The political problem of those days was not simple. It bears an external resemblance to those we have lived through in this century, and the same ethical options and collective reactions can, in a vague form, be found in it, but the givens and the stakes were different.

Where does the politically intolerable begin? Soon enough in a regime that allows political programs, an opposition, and transfers of power; sooner yet under a regime considered congenitally illegitimate, such as a dictatorship. Caesarism was intolerant of opposition, and confined itself to the management of events. In place of a program it involved struggles between cliques over the division of offices and influence. Still, in Seneca's eyes, Caesarism was not illegitimate *per se*. To the contrary, our author repeats in *On Benefits*, written under Nero, what he had affirmed at the beginning of his reign in *On Clemency*: in the present circumstances of the winter of the world, "The best regime is living under a just king."[1] The Cordoban parvenu might have preferred to live in the times of republican liberty, but he did not harbor nostalgia for that republic, a relic of a bygone age. He did not resemble Tacitus, playing the nostalgic anti-Caesarian just as Saint Simon, the newly coined duke exulted all the more in the ancient liberty of the nobility before Richelieu. Although he held the senate in high esteem, Seneca never belonged to the Stoic opposition, hiding their noble arrogance, nostalgia for the republic, and secret anti-Caesarism under the cloak of philosophy. Seneca expressly separated himself from this attitude and this political program, as we shall see, but nevertheless remained attached to members of the group by common opposition to Nero and an equal impotence. Even in 63, four years after the assassination of Agrippina and in the midst of utter tyranny, the bravest member of the Stoic opposition, Thrasea, asked no more than to be reconciled to Nero through Seneca's mediation.[2] And rightly so: despite the deceptive expression, "the Stoic opposition," philosophers were, at this time, less in a position to act as resisters than they were virtual objects of persecution to be preserved from the thunderbolts of Nero, enemy of anyone who thought differently than he, and well aware of what philosophers thought of him.

If Seneca was not anti-Caesarian in principle, he had become anti-Neronian as a matter of conscience. When did things become intolerable for him? Not with the death of Agrippina, which he shrouded in silence, unlike Thrasea, and for which posterity would soon reproach him. Thrasea's role was as worthy senator, not a grand vizier like the praetorian prefect Burrus, nor a close advisor of the prince, like Seneca. They made their decisions on other bases: Nero's parricide was a private crime and a sinister indication of character, but one that left hope alive that it might be possible to influence the young criminal, and made that influence more necessary than ever. Such a choice amounted to a bet on the future. Seneca and Burrus put their lives and honor on the line over the success or failure of their political choice. Unfortunately, Seneca was also a philosopher, and one day he would be reproached for not having the expected attitude faced with a Nero, something no one would have dreamed of doing to Burrus. Face to face with the powerful, a sage would have borne witness fearlessly to the eminent dignity of his philosophical vocation. (The reference was to a kind of philosophical priesthood rather than to the dignity of conscience in general: philosophers were presumed to have duties peculiar to their vocation.) Seneca paid the price for his multiform personality: from a philosopher, a morality based on conviction was expected; but as counselor to the prince, he applied a morality of responsibility.[3]

A principle of ancient politics was that a ruler respected the conscience of the ruled only if he respected himself. By abandoning himself to his murderous hatred of his mother, Nero sullied the consciences of his subjects. The tyranny that subsequently ensued was an attack on their consciences and their lives. At first, Nero aspired to impose his person and his glory on his subjects on the grounds of their subjection; to do this, he displayed a munificence that drained the treasury. He passed on to a rule of fiscal terror that gave strength to the opposition and imperiled his throne, leading him on to physical terror. His counselors had lost all hope of arresting this dynamic.

This, however, simplified Seneca's role. From that time on, he was a philosopher only. He withdrew from public life as fast as he could run, and closed his door to his clients. No longer would he go with them into the courts or the forum, renouncing any influence he may have had, so as not to seem the potential focus of opposition. He wrote that he left the senate and forum to consecrate himself to a far vaster task.[4] He played the role expected of a philosopher, that of witness.

As for politics, he pursued them in the only way still available, the recourse of so many opponents of Eastern bloc governments before 1989: keeping the torch of truth burning at least in thought. Seneca wrote as much in a text as anyone, Nero and his police included, could read: *Letter* 14. "Should a sage be involved in public affairs? Let us set this question aside for the moment. I will be satisfied to draw your attention to the attitude of present-day Stoics." (Under the cover of this modest plural, Seneca means himself.) "They exclude themselves from all public activity." (The Latin allows a willed ambiguity: it could equally well mean, "They are excluded.") "They cultivate their private lives and have withdrawn (*secesserunt*) to be the legislators of the human condition, while avoiding any provocation of those more powerful than they." Becoming, that is, prey of the despot and his police. This was the conduct Seneca himself attributed to Socrates in *On Tranquillity of the Soul*. Under the dictatorial oligarchy of The Thirty, with no remedy in sight and all trembling, Socrates went on preaching courage and virtue, offering "the great example of a citizen daring to walk in freedom under the eyes of the despots." Seneca's plan was to pretend not to see political reality, but to go on writing nonetheless, with a sincerity and ease that seemed oblivious to the tyrant and his threats; not to preach virtue in opposition to actual despotism, but also not to hide the light of truth or transgress against his principles.

This is the mystery—lying in plain sight—of the *Letters to Lucilius*; their character as oppositional writing in such circumstances has been insufficiently stressed. Indeed, there was no possible outlet other than mute protest. On the part of the governed, any independent opinion or speech amounted to insubordination. Active politics was the privilege of the six or seven hundred members of the ruling class, and even they did not have the right to a personal opinion, but were limited to carrying out the policies of the prince. The whole arrangement was equivalent to the single party dictatorships of this century. Allowing the government to govern was not enough: warm endorsement was required and silence held as disavowal.

We are now in a position to approach the key text of Seneca's last years—*Letter* 73, addressed to Lucilius—but in reality an open letter intended for Nero. On first reading it is deceptive, shocking, even scandalous. In it we read that Nero has brought about the rule of peace and liberty, and that philosophers, those lovers of literate leisure, are the most submissive of citizens. A Romanian historian was only too well situated to judge better: in a book published in Leiden in 1972, he wrote: "Seneca's hope was to convince Nero that his retirement was not to be assimilated to a form of opposition. Beneath the fawning and promises of submission and approval, we catch a whiff of statements giving us to understand that Seneca had no intention of becoming involved with the newly adopted policies of Nero's regime."[5] We must read between the lines of Seneca's letter.

As preface, let me offer an anecdote—one that seems authentic—to recreate the climate of those years. Two noble travelers from Greece arrived in Rome. "At the city gate, the guard asked them no questions, but was impressed and full of respect for their clothing, as they had the air of priests, nothing like that of vagabonds. They stayed at an inn close to the gate and were in the middle of dinner, when an individual entered in festive garb, with a beautiful voice. He went the rounds in Rome singing Nero's melodies, and so made his living. Since the travelers paid scant attention to his singing, he accused them of lèse-majesté and of being enemies of the divine voice of Nero."[6] Now let us return to *Letter 73*.

1. Head high, Seneca attacks: "In my opinion, it is wrong to think that those who are loyal devotees of philosophy are rebels or separatists, scorning magistrates, kings and, more generally, all legitimate authority. To the contrary, no one shows greater acknowledgment than they do of those authorities." Might denying in such terms that one was hostile to Nero amount to rallying to him? It might be if the choice depended on the philosophers, but in fact it depended solely on the police, who considered them suspect. Popular opinion had always held that a thinker was someone capable of defying the authorities—this aroused the admiration of some, while scandalizing others. Since 62, after the death of Burrus, the new prefect held the Stoic sect and its arrogance especially suspect. Was Seneca trying to distinguish himself from the arrogant Stoic opposition? No. Instead, he denies its existence, belying the thesis of the police and recognizing philosophy's right to exist. This amounted to refusing the ideological monopoly toward which Neronism tended.

2. As Nero was the real audience for this letter, it had necessarily to be written in wooden terms. Thrasea himself, did likewise when addressing the prince, even if it was to oppose him fundamentally. One day, tired of the game, he ceased doing so and Nero sentenced him to die.[7] All in all, to speak the wooden tongue of flattery was no more dishonorable than the clandestine speech of oppositional elements in our day, who elude the police rather than defying them in the glare of day.

We still have to decipher the language in question. Seneca praises the "peace and liberty" presently enjoyed by all citizens. This slogan, which has changed in meaning over the course of two millennia was, at that time, a sacramental way of invoking patriotism, the fundamental loyalty to the city and its ruler, beyond the reach of partisan dissension. The liberty in question was no less than the "public liberty of the Roman people," that is, national independence. "Peace" meant that independence was threatened by no enemy. Philosophers did not practice politics; they only acknowledged their native land. The reduction of all politics to the survival of a national group was so much a matter of convention that its applications became unreal in an immense empire defended on its frontiers by professional armies. Philosophers, Seneca writes, were faced with the dilemma of respecting the authorities and so living in peace or having to "stand watch, take up arms, and mount guard on the ramparts." Peace and liberty were an ancient form of blackmail inciting patriotism; a year after Seneca's suicide, they were used to have Thrasea condemned to death as an ingrate who formed a sectarian opposition to Nero, the guarantor of the country's independence free from external threat.[8] Thus private grievances were submerged in a general state of grievance.

3. Seneca did as much, submerging a seeming rally of support for Nero in his loyalty to public authority in general; he wielded only a blunted sword against Neronism. Seneca does not speak of what was dearest to Nero's heart—Nero himself—an emperor unlike any other. Seneca declares himself loyal to an anonymous sovereign, the defender of his country, even if he should lack the "divine voice" of the songster.

4. Philosophers were grateful to the sovereign, whatever he might be, because their only ambition was, thanks to a peaceful reign, to dedicate themselves to cultured leisure. This is not all: philosophers were even more grateful than the rest of the citizens, a distinction Seneca insists strongly on, and tells us why. Their leisure is more precious than that of other people because they consecrate it to the study of wisdom, the greatest of all goods. Such praise of philosophy was an attack on the artist Nero, the enemy of philosophy. Dying, Seneca stated that he had always addressed Nero with more frankness than flattery, and it was no idle boast.

5. Two years before this letter, Nero refused Seneca's request to retire from his status as friend of the prince, maintaining that whoever ceased to be with him became his adversary. *Letter* 73 claims that it is possible not to be anti-Nero while not automatically being pro-Nero. There is a third path, that of those philosophers who attend only to their own affairs.

6. What Seneca avoids saying is that philosophers, when they attend to their interior life, are simultaneously performing the work of the whole human race, and that their action is not limited to the ivory tower. All in all, *Letter* 73 undertakes (but with a dignity that made its success more than doubtful) to disarm Nero's hostility enough so that Seneca would have his hands free to sow the seeds of truth despite a climate of ideological despotism.

Not hiding his light under a bushel, while at the same time not provoking the tyrant, is what Seneca *does* in his published correspondence with Lucilius. More than that, he *states* that this is what he is doing, taking care to reveal his game so that no one could misunderstand.

This is what biographers of Seneca have failed to stress sufficiently: the *Letters* are an oppositional work—doubly so. It is a strange way to avoid provoking one's master to say that one is abstaining from provocation.

Instead, the most external aspects of the *Letters* have been studied—their allusions to Nero. These are very few, both in order to avoid provocation and so as not to degrade philosophy to the level of a pamphlet. The *Letters* are far removed from current events. There is not a word of the great fire in Rome; on the other hand, shortly after that disaster, Seneca writes pages of consolation about another fire that had just destroyed the city of Lyon and seriously affected a Lyonnaise friend. Must we assume allusion by silence? In Naples, where Seneca must have had to follow Nero, he remarked, as the reader will recall, on the passions aroused by the musical contests in the theater. What he does not say is that Nero participated in them himself! But what would the point of that have been? Nero is no more than an individual case, while society as a whole was perverted from the beginning.[9] By their very existence, the *Letters* are nothing but an immense allusion to universal error. To make it more precise by naming names would have been futile, and would also have run the risk of declining into mere satire. If anyone had asked Seneca what he thought of Nero, it would have been sufficient for him to refer his questioner to *Letter* 114, where he gives an analysis in general terms of the frequent phenomenon of proselytizing on behalf of vice. Souls whose internal government is that of a tyrant, not a good king, nurse the desires of others in order to fuel their imagination after their own desires have been surfeited.

As a timeless message of truth, the *Letters* form an epigram against their factual period, the reign of Nero, who had erected error as official ideology. Their only deliberate contact with daily life was to develop a strategy adapted to the reigning despotism, one whose justifications were themselves philosophical. This was to retire from public life and to serve humanity through writing, neither provoking nor fearing the tyrant—and saying so.

1. There is bearing witness and then there is bearing witness. The social-philosophical phenomenon of the so-called street-corner Cynics was well known in Rome. They harangued passersby on the vices of the age, of kings, and the rich. One of them, Isidorus, apostrophized Nero in public, reproaching him for singing well and acting badly. In later days, monks and dervishes publicly reprimanded czars and pashas. The Cynics often paid for their audacity with their lives. Seneca condemned their awkward zeal and their futile heroism—there were other ways to awaken consciences. It is just as natural "not to provoke the fury of the powerful as it is for a sailor not to hurl himself into the height of the tempest." Better still, "the sage will guard against the appearance of avoiding giving offense to the powerful, since avoiding offence is the same as blaming them."[10] Now, that is prudence. What was less prudent was to expressly say that one was guarding against appearances. Nonetheless, for a Stoic, prudence was not the same thing as fear; it was even its opposite.

Let us follow their reasoning. As we know, some things are preferable, among them life, which is better than death. No principle obliges us to throw ourselves into the lion's maw. Prudence or precaution is known as the subdivision of virtue that teaches us to foresee obstacles and avoid them. It is obviously different from fear because emotions are only parasitical phenomena. Still, we also know that preferable things are neutral. In the last analysis, only virtue can decide whether, considering the circumstances, life is truly better than a useful, heroic death. Useful, because virtue consists of fulfilling its own functions and thereby helping others to help themselves. True prudence, then, is the opposite of cowardice. It does not consist of hiding one's true colors. The poet Horace said: "A just and steady man has no fear of the menacing visage of a tyrant; he would remain unmoved even if the universe crumbled around him" at the end of a cosmic cycle. Virtuous prudence does not provoke tyrants, but it does not yield to them either. In the end, Seneca winds up being more in accordance than seemed likely with the Hollywood image of the philosopher. He exalts the example of Theodore of Cyrene who, for all that he was a theoretician of pleasure, defied the menaces of a dictator and his hangmen. Seneca's language at times borders on temerity: "Why keep coming back to Socrates, intrepid before thirty tyrants? Thirty or one, it comes to the same thing."[11] It is easy to imagine that under Nero, the very word "tyrant" was a bombshell. In the *Letters* it explodes eight other times.

2. Virtue is a doctrine of functionality in the service of others, but it is possible to serve others in more than one way. Better yet, every virtuous action, even if its function is not altruistic, renders a service to the rest of humankind. That is a Stoic theory which, if I am not mistaken, has yet to be noted. It is enounced in Epictetus: "God has so ordered the nature of the rational animal that he cannot seek his private good without contributing to universal utility."[12] Seneca agreed with this and he states its converse: if you do nothing for others, you do nothing at all. These notions are not late elaborations, but must go back to ancient Stoicism, because they give us the key for understanding an emphatic declaration of Chrysippus that has otherwise remained enigmatic. "It is enough for a single sage, wherever he is, to lift a finger, provided that he does so discerningly, for it to do good for all the sages over the whole earth." Chrysippus, as is well known, was not a man to shrink from taking things to their logical limits. Our conclusion shall be no less sweeping: whatever you do, you function for the good of humanity, provided that you function discerningly.

3. We know that the sage will or will not take part in public affairs according to whether or not he can act in them virtuously. If circumstances are such that he would waste his time involving himself in politics, or if he would compromise himself, he will shut himself up in a leisure devoted to progress in wisdom.

4. However, by virtue of Chrysippus's theorem, he will serve his fellow no less by the example his conduct provides if he does not write, and by his books if he does. The *Letters to Lucilius* say this again and again: there are better things to do than loiter in the senate or the forum. Politics must be abandoned in order to give instruction to the human race. The principle of living and dying in the midst of action is not violated if one stays shut up at home, according to *Letter* 8. At

home, Seneca adds, I work on my own account, but I also work for the good of posterity.

In acting thus, Seneca was taking considerable risks. Nero, who knew the convictions of his teacher and friend, was already suspicious of him, and simply by being a Stoic, he was equally suspect to the new praetorial prefect Tigellinus. He knew this so clearly that *Letter* 70 outlines his coming suicide and founds it in reason. To be convinced of this, it is enough to compare three texts.

People are most frightened of swords, hangmen, and the various tortures wielded, according to place and time, by the people, by a senate, or by a sovereign. Do not provoke such powers, says *Letter* 14. Moreover, physical suffering is among the "anti-preferables," and it is better not to suffer, if this is possible without a lack of virtue.

In order to suffer less, senators condemned to death or even simply accused, preferred to anticipate their punishment. In this period, execution was entrusted sometimes to the lictors, who began by thrashing their victim using the rods forming the fasces they carried over their shoulders. Later they decapitated him, using an axe. At other times an officer was charged with the execution, more or less skillfully decapitating the victim with his sword. Tacitus described the consequences: "Suicides were produced on demand by the fear of the executioner. Besides, since those condemned to die had their estates confiscated and were deprived of burial, while those who took justice into their own hands were buried, and their wills respected, quick action paid off."[13]

Such considerations were again common in the spring of 64, when Nero and Seneca were visiting Naples. The first senatorial suicide of the regime had just become known, that of "Silanus, on whom Claudius cast his eye / And who counted Augustus in ranks of his ancestors," as Racine writes in *Britannicus*. Such distinction made the senator a candidate to replace Nero, now unpopular, on the throne. Accused of conspiracy, Silanus opened his veins. He was at least the third member of his family in thirty years to whom the blood of Augustus proved fatal.

In the course of that same spring Seneca drafted *Letter* 70. In it he wonders at length whether anticipating his punishment amounted to yielding to a fearful anxiety instead of waiting for it tranquilly, and whether the condemned criminal should do the executioner's work. Socrates certainly waited for the executor of lowly offices to pour out the hemlock for him. Seneca's answer is that this is purely a question of personal taste, and that public opinion has no concern in it. Should we prefer the sword or poison? If a gentler death pleases, then it should be anticipated. The precise eventuality Seneca was contemplating is evident. The shadow of a probable and proximate punishment is clear in the *Letters*.[14]

There is more. The question of what people would say seems to have mattered a great deal to Seneca in this matter. He had visibly foreseen the posthumous echoes it would have in public opinion, and he knew perfectly well that there would always be critics, whatever exit he might choose—sword or poison, execution or suicide. Oddly, he seems to have supposed that his future censors would reproach him above all for weakness. "One will say that I lacked courage, another, that I acted precipitately, a third, that I might have chosen a more virile form of suicide."[15] It all seems as though Seneca, writing this letter, had already chosen a gentle death, and to anticipate the executioner. This was in fact the case—he already had the hemlock prepared, as we shall shortly see. In *Letter* 70 he was writing both the defense and the apologia for his suicide in advance.

Hemlock, then, or at least a less painful death than that at the hands of the executioner—*Letter* 77, written a little later, expressed a longing for suicide: "death little by little, in a steady weakening not without its pleasures, a peaceful annihilation I know well, having lost consciousness several times."

It would happen, and soon, but differently than he expected.

Nero was an atypical tyrant, too deprived of political sense to kill in a calculated manner. He did not persecute senators as such, and he loathed the Stoics long before massacring them. Even in 64 he was eliminating only a potential rival, not a professed adversary. After Britannicus and Silanus, yet another Silanus. The persecution of Christians was another thing altogether, and had nothing specifically Neronian about it. All his contemporaries approved of it, and Marcus Aurelius would do more or less as much. The murder of Agrippina was more a Freudian than a political crime. Until 65, Nero was a less bloody despot than most. His most numerous victims were probably crushed by the machinery of the treasury, which killed to confiscate, but then there was the Pisonian conspiracy; this brought Nero down out of the clouds and the torrents of blood were released. Seneca, who had nothing to do with it, died because of it.

The only alternative to Caesarism was regicide, and around the beginning of 65 a plot was formed to kill Nero and, because Augustus's last descendant was gone, to put an affable lord, Piso, on the throne. His modern ideas and taste for the arts would incline the mob of enthusiastic partisans of Nero in his favor. Neither Seneca nor Thrasea were involved in the conspiracy, which had nothing philosophical about it, uniting, for the most part, senators, nobles, officers of the imperial guard, and even one of the two commanders-in-chief. Obviously, this was a serious affair. Nero was to be stabbed in the middle of the circus during the chariot races on April 19, 65, but the conspirators wasted time and their secret emerged. Nero put Rome under a state of siege and launched a general repression, with faithful elements of his guard in the role of political police. Seneca's name was spoken in the course of the confessions. The conspirators tried to make contact with him, but he, shut up in his solitude, avoided them, whether aware or not of what was being plotted. Some even claimed that, in a conspiracy within the conspiracy, some of the plotters had planned to kill Piso himself, once Nero was gone, in order to raise Seneca to the throne. We do not know if this was an invention of the police or the kind of rumor common to every underground effort, but it is better not to take seriously the appealing historical dream of Seneca as emperor. Happiest of all was Nero, who had his pretext for another Freudian murder, that of his old preceptor. Thrasea, for his part, was not disquieted.

Why didn't either one of them have a hand in the plot? Perhaps they were not asked—a conspiracy does not always propose uniting all men of good will. Perhaps the two of them were too conspicuous; perhaps they were reproached for not being loyal to Piso; or perhaps they had refused. At any rate, Seneca did not share Tacitus's equally prudent and highly moral horror of regicide. He had in *On Benefits*, justified at length the right of the governed to rid themselves of a sovereign who did not respect the social contract. Collective duties, he wrote, took precedence over those owed to a single person. If there is no hope for the despot to improve, he should be killed. "For beings of this kind, death should be considered as a remedy. Since such a man will never return to mental health, let him be gone once and for all."[16]

Before recounting the dramatic days that followed, we must cover the details of the plan Seneca made for his death, because this plan was partly foiled in the event.

1. Voluntary death is both the guarantee of our liberty and its highest manifestation. Thus the Platonists were wrong to condemn suicide, according to *Letter* 70.

2. We must meditate on death all our lives long, not in order to convince ourselves that our bodies are mortal and prisons for our souls, but to prepare ourselves to pass over the bar, and to educate our powers of discernment and courage.

3. Our manner of dying, brave or cowardly, will be the measure of the progress we have made at that time on the path of virtue. It will be the test of truth, open to the eyes of all. If we die virtuously, we will also give a useful example to others, according to Chrysippus's theorem.

4. Since our powers of discernment forbid us to fear evils to come, because they are not here yet, we must not anticipate condemnation if it is still in doubt. That would be to kill oneself out of fear of death, (*Letter* 70). Seneca therefore must have imagined at least a pro forma trial before the senate, with several days of debate and only then, his sentence.[17]

5. On the other hand, we have the right to anticipate the sufferings of execution. He thus imagined the executioner's visit, coming to carry out the sentence with his own hands. On these last two points, Seneca's foresight proved faulty.

Roman penal law, or what goes by that name, was little concerned with actual laws. Its fundamental basis was the exercise of coercion, pure and simple, practiced by a magistrate with little care for form or the rights of the defense, imposing penalties not in accordance with the prescriptions of some code, but by custom or caprice. When the Pisonian conspiracy was uncovered, Nero, as the supreme magistrate,[18] did not leave the burden of trying the case of lèse-majesté to the senate, but took the fate of the guilty into his own hands. All there was by way of trial was an inquiry by the police and military repression. Nero sent an officer to decapitate the guilty or to bring them the order to put an end to their days.

Rome, crisscrossed by the guard and overrun with messengers on horseback, saw long ranks of prisoners in chains and was aware of the plot and the repression. One of the main guilty parties had sworn that he was charged with making contact with Seneca. He had gone to beg him not to close his door to Piso, but rather to tie the knot of friendship with him. Seneca refused, while adding courteously that Piso's health was as dear to him as his own. An insignificant conversation, but it was necessary to verify its authenticity. An officer of the guard was sent to ask Seneca if he acknowledged the tenor of the response he had given the conspirator.

Seneca had every interest in confirming a response that exculpated him. He was eating with his wife Paulina and two friends when the officer arrived at the door of his villa, three miles from the center of Rome. He did indeed confirm that he had closed his door to Piso, giving as an excuse his ill health and desire for retirement. He also told the officer that he saw no good reason that he should have had to sacrifice his quiet at another's caprice, that his nature was not so complacent as that, and that Nero knew this well, having always found him to be a free man, not a slave. The officer conveyed this mordant comment to Nero and his prefect, Tigellinus. Nero asked him if Seneca, after this ominous interrogation, seemed to be readying himself to end his life. The officer answered that Seneca had seemed to him to be perfectly calm, his features neither visibly fearful nor despairing. We see that, faithful to his plan, Seneca did not anticipate a death that remained in doubt. Nero ordered the officer to return to the villa and inform Seneca that he must kill himself. From this point we will let Tacitus tell the story, with a few remarks of our own.[19]

> Seneca, undisturbed, asked for his will. On the officer's refusal,[20] he turned to his friends and declared that, 'Since he had been prohibited to demonstrate his gratitude to them, he left them the only good remaining to him, and the most precious, the image of his life.[21] If they remembered it, the good reputation attaching to such noble study would be the reward for their faithful friendship.' His friends wept; he, now conversationally, now in a sterner tone of authority, recalled them to firmness of spirit, asking them insistently, 'What use were they making of those precepts of wisdom and of that meditation, carried on for so many years, on the reasons that defend us against inevitable fate. Did any one not know of Nero's ferocity? After the murders of his mother and brother, the only

thing left for him to add was the slaughter of the man who had raised and instructed him.'

After considerations of this kind, addressed equally to all, he took his wife in his arms and, softening slightly before the imminent catastrophe, he begged and implored her to moderate her grief, not to let it last forever, and to find honorable consolation for the loss of her spouse in contemplation of a life led virtuously. But she, in reply, assured him that she, too, had decided to die, and asked for someone to stab her.[22] Seneca did not want to object to her glory, while his love for her made him fear abandoning the woman he uniquely cherished to further outrages. 'I have just indicated to you,' he said, 'what might induce you to live on. You prefer the honor of dying, and I do not claim to reserve for myself the giving of such an example. So be it: with so courageous an end, your constancy equals mine, but your death will be more illustrious.' Then in the same instant, the steel opened the veins of their arms.

Seneca, whose body, weak with age and abstinence, bled too slowly, had the veins of his legs cut. Soon, crushed by the frightful pain, he feared that his suffering might break down his wife's courage, and that he himself, seeing the torments she was enduring, might allow himself to yield to weakness. He advised her to go into a neighboring room. Retaining his talents in his last moments, he called his secretaries and dictated a long text to them. Since it has been published, I will refrain from paraphrasing it.[23]

Nero, however, having no personal hatred for Paulina, and fearing he would make himself more unpopular by his cruelty, gave orders to prevent her dying. Urged by the soldiers, her slaves and freedmen bandaged her arms and stopped the bleeding. We do not know if she was aware of this or not since, such being the malignity of the mob, there were some who thought, inasmuch as she believed Nero was pitiless, she lusted after the fame of dying alongside her spouse,[24] while later, with hope of a gentler fate, she allowed herself to be conquered by the charms of life. She lived only a few more years, however, maintaining a laudable fidelity to the memory of her husband and displaying amply, by her pallor of face and body, how much of her vital force she had lost along with her blood.

As for Seneca, as his blood was flowing sluggishly and death was slow in coming, he begged Statius Annaeus, whom he knew by long experience to be a faithful friend and an able physician, to bring him the poison he had provided himself with long before. It was the same as was used at Athens on those whom a public tribunal had condemned to death.[25] It was brought to him, and he drank it, but in vain. His extremities were already cold and his body immune to the effects of the poison. Finally, he went into a warm bath, in the process splashing the closest of his slaves. This led him to remark that this was a libation he was offering to Jupiter the Liberator.[26] Then he had himself carried to the steam room in his house, where the vapors finally suffocated him. His body was burned unceremoniously, according to an express clause in his will, made at a time when, already very rich and influential, he had indicated his last wishes.

Tacitus's account ends here. Nero survived Seneca for another three years. Overturned by a revolt of the governors of central Gaul, Catalonia and Castille, and Tunisia and Constantinople, he had himself stabbed to death, miserably, by one of his freedmen in an isolated villa three miles from Rome. He was thirty years old.

Contrary to what is frequently repeated, Seneca's death, inspired as it was by Stoicism, was not an imitation of that of Socrates. Socrates died thanking Aesculapius for liberating his soul from his body. Seneca died thanking the god of the Stoics for having given him the intellectual means to die voluntarily. The only point in common is banal: both died in philosophical discussion with their friends. For ancient philosophy, teaching by example was a necessity, even at the brink.

The year 66 saw the blood continue to flow. Thrasea would give himself to death thanking, again, Jupiter the Liberator. As for Petronius, clever luxurious Petronius, the author of the Satyricon and Nero's ancient companion in pleasure and model of elegance, he too had to kill himself because of his ties to Piso's conspirators: Tigellinus, the praetorian prefect, was making a clean sweep of them and their friends. Petronius, we know, was close to the Epicurean sect, as many passages in his novel prove. He also died by opening his veins, but in the course of a last banquet with his friends, chatting and reciting light verse, refraining from the slightest mention of philosophy or speaking about the immortality of the soul. In fact, Petronius's suicide was a parodic reply to Seneca's Stoic suicide.[27] Death did not bring the quarrels of the philosophical sects to an end.

NOTES

PREFACE

1. On Foucault's ethics, which have been much misinterpreted in France, see Wilhelm Schmid's very accurate book *Auf der Suche nach einer neuen Lebenskunst: die Frage nach dem Grund und die Neubegründung der Ethik bei Foucault* (Frankfort: Suhrkamp, 1991).

2. Not taking Foucault for another Spengler, I would not presume to find the same *Zeitgeist* behind the neo-Stoic return of the *I* and immunological medicine, centered not on diseases and pathogens, but on the individual's defenses. Obviously, this is a simple coincidence, not a common underlying "discourse." It is a diverting coincidence nonetheless: see Anne-Marie Moulin's fine book *Le Dernier Langage de la médecine: histoire de l'immunologie, de Pasteur au sida* (Paris, 1991).

PROLOGUE

1. A. N. Sherwin White, *The Roman Citizenship* (Oxford, 1973), pp. 239–40. R. Syme, *Tacitus* (Oxford, 1958), pp. 589–90.

2. Tacitus, *Annals*, XIV, 53.

3. Seneca's ancesters on both sides were originally from the valley of the Guadalquivir. These Andalusian ancestors, natives of Corduba, the main city of the province of Southern Spain and of Urgavo (now Arjona, eighty kilometers east of Corduba and thirty from Bailen) may have been descendants of Roman or Italian veterans who settled in Spain; or natives who were made citizens at the same time as the veterans who settled as colonists in their village; or Italian immigrants, attracted by the mineral riches of the valley of the Guadalquivir (Arjona is not far from the mining center Castulo, now Linares); or native nobility who "collaborated" with their Roman masters and were granted citizenship as a reward; or products of mixed marriages between Italians and native women; or the offspring of freedmen of Romans and Italians who settled in Spain; or the (rare) Italian immigrants who went to Spain as planters (but Spain was not primarily a colony of agricultural settlement); or natives made citizens for fighting in the armies of Sertorius, Pompey, or Caesar. See Theodor Mommsen, *Histoire romaine*, ed. Claude Nicolet, (Paris, 1985), vol. 2, pp. 546–52; D. Nony in Cl. Nicolet, *Rome et la conquête du monde méditerranéen*, (Paris, 1978), pp. 664–77; J. M. Roldan in J. M. Blazquez, et al., *Historia de Espana antigua*, (Madrid, 1988), 197–223.

4. On CIL II, 2115, see A. Vassileiou, *Revue de philologie* 47 (1973): 299; J. M Gleason, *Classical Philology* 97 (1975): 278; H. G. Pflaum, *L'Année épigraphique*, 1977, n. 438.

Notes to Prologue *continued*

5. Cicero, *In Defense of Archias*, 26; Seneca the Elder, *Suasoriae* VI, 27. Cf. *Controversiae* I, pref.,
16. Let there be no mistake: this irony was directed toward "provincials" living far from the
capital and its graces; it was not the irony directed against "natives" who "aped" the civilized.
The same irony is found against the Italian Livy, born in distant Padua.

6. R. Syme, *Tacitus*, vol. 2, p. 536.

7. Seneca the Elder, *Controversiae*, II, pref. 3–4.

8. The internationalism of ancient culture makes Seneca's case banal. Zeno, the founder
of Stoicism, was a Hellenized Cypriot. The three oldest Roman authors came from peoples
conquered for less than a quarter century (Plautus, Ennius) or from an enemy race (the
Carthaginian Terence), and their mother tongue was not Latin.

9. *Controversiae* II, pref. 4. Another remark of Seneca the Elder reveals much about
Caesarism: he would be pleased if his sons were to have public careers, but only on the condition that they remain virtuous. Likewise under Stalin and Brezhnev, many Soviets, not all of
whom were young idealists, had the same scruples.

10. To understand the seriousness of this debate, one must understand that for the
Romans, declamation was as distinctive an art as haiku, ikebana, or calligraphy are among
other peoples, and that it occupied an important position in ancient cultural life. Rhetors and
philosophers vied for the soul of the younger generation; (see H. von Arnim, *Dio von Prusa*
(Berlin, 1898), pp. 4-114). Even the gestures of the declaimer were as rigorously codified as the
positions of classical ballet.

11. Seneca, *Letters to Lucilius* 108, 13–23 and 71, 19. Pythagorean dogma, with only partisans, could have as avowed adversaries only the impious or freethinkers: it was a consensual
doctrine, and therefore suitable for children. Seneca "as a child" (*Letters* 49, 2) listened to his
teacher preach Pythagorean precepts (Ibid. 108, 17–21). He was not the only one: cf. F.
Buecheler, *Carmina Latina Epigraphica* (Leipzig, 1895), n. 434.

12. Cf. G. Maurach, *Seneca, Leben und Werk* (Darmstadt, 1991), p. 23.

13. A. D Nock, *Conversion: the Old and the New in Religion from Alexander the Great to Augustine
of Hippo* (Oxford, 1933), pp. 168, 182.

14. P. Hadot, *Exercices spirituels et philosophie antique*, éd. 2. Paris (1987), p. 225. For the place
of philosophy in education, see I. Hadot, *Arts libéraux et philosophie dans la pensée antique*. Paris
(1984), pp. 215-261. On philosophy and society, see J. Hahn, *Der Philosoph und die Gesellschaft*.
Stuttgart (1989).

15. Syme, *Tacitus* (Oxford, 1958), vol. 2, pp. 571, 581. Prior to his entry into the Senate,
Seneca published at least one book, now lost, a treatise on earthquakes (*Natural Questions*, VI,
4, 2). He had written it as a "young man" (*iuvenis*), that is, "before having entered a public
career," even if one was fairly old. Seneca was interested in the sciences throughout his life.

16. Syme, op. cit., vol. 2, p. 356.

17. Books were indeed publicly displayed: see Martial, I, 117 (118), 10 and Buecheler,
Carmina Epigraphica n. 1111, 14. This part of the Argiletum came just after the Forum of
Domitian (or Nerva), where the booksellers were. Further up, the Argiletum corresponded to
the Via della Madonna de' Monti, roughly parallel to the Via Cavour.

18. *On the Brevity of Life*, 13, 2; *Letters* 69, 7; 82, 8; 113, 1; 33, 4.

19. The two nephews of Christ, peasants, lived parsimoniously with their families on a
plot valued at 9,000 denarii (Eusebius, *Ecclesiastical History*, III, 20, 2-3, 7).

20. Musonius, *Diatribes* XIX, 108 ed. Hense.

21. A. R. Hands, *Charities and Social Aid in Greece and Rome*, 30–1.

22. Thus he had introduced the Stoic Annaeus Cornutus, a provincial from Tripolitania
into Nero's entourage. Cornutus bore Seneca's family name, Annaeus; he was therefore either
a freedman of his or a "native" who had received Roman citizenship thanks to Seneca's protection.

23. Rescript of Octavian, cited by Joyce Reynolds, *Aphrodisias and Rome*, 102. For the religious skepticism that was the private doctrine of the senate, see C. Koch, *Religio* (Nuremberg, 1960).

24. J. Kaimio, *The Romans and the Greek Language* (Helsinki, 1979), p. 268.

25. A choice example is in R. Wittkower, *Art et Architecture en Italie, 1600–1750* (Paris, 1991), p. 64. But all in all, around 1905, to be in the avant-garde was to imitate Cézanne openly. Within the ancient system there was no question of eclecticism; rather, the question was to decide which model the artist's individual talent inclined to. He had to follow his talent, not fashion. See A. Blunt, *Théorie des arts en Italie* (Paris, 1966), p. 243.

26. Reciprocally, knowing how to obey was, for the governed, knowing how to keep an inborn disobedience in check and be master of one's self.

27. As B. Mortureux wrote ("Les idéaux stoïciens et les premiéres responsabilités politiques: le 'De Clementia,'" *Aufstieg und Niedergang der römischen Welt* [Berlin, 1989] XXXVI, no. 3, p. 1679), "The givens of reality are present only in a schematic form: Seneca reveals a unique virtue, clemency, to us; it acts as the nexus of a world simplified to the extreme, where men are organized into only two fundamentally opposed categories." In fact, an all-powerful prince faced with the mass of his subjects will act as a despot if he is not master of himself. It is revealing that Seneca wrote about both clemency and anger. At the same time, in a society governed by client-patron relations, *On Benefits* teaches patrons to act as benefactors.

28. *Life of Demetrius Poliorcetes*, III, 5.

29. As soon as he mounted the throne, Tiberius killed, or ordered the killing of, Agrippa Postumus. Caligula's first murder was Tiberius Gemellus, his cousin and heir apparent to the empire (Philo, *Embassy to Gaius*, 22, 31). Claudius had no one to kill: he was the last of the Claudians and his brother Germanicus was survived by only three women (among them Agrippina). The murder of Silanus is explained in the same way (Tacitus, *Annals*, XIII, 1): he was the son of the great-granddaughter of Augustus and a potential candidate for the throne. Some modern historians, however, believe that Britannicus really did die from disease—which, to be fair, might have a one-in-ten or one-in-one hundred chance of being true—and one of them has even published a letter from Britannicus's physician. When the faculty has spoken, one must submit. But my wife, herself a doctor, was willing to make out a certificate for me indicating that she would have refused permission to bury Britannicus.

30. The rich merchant of *Letter* 101 certainly belonged to the equestrian order. Seneca was unaware of the other half of the empire, namely a mosaic of almost autonomous cities governed by local oligarchies of the prominent and wealthy sitting astride a huge free peasantry. The central government charged them with assessing the taxes, with no interest in knowing whether they foisted the burden largely onto the mass of poor peasants.

31. M. T. Griffin, *Seneca: a Philosopher in Politics* (Oxford, Clarendon), 1976.

32. Syme, (1963), vol. 2, p. 591.

33. T. Mommsen, *Römisches Staatsrecht* (Berlin, 1887), vol. 2, pp. 1113–22.

34. Taking the criticisms of F. Bleicken [*Zum Regierungsstil des römischen Kaisers*, (Wiesbaden, 1982)] into account, the thesis of F. Millar (*The Emperor in the Roman World*, Cornell, 1977) seems to be close to the truth.

35. G. Maurach, *Seneca* (Darmstadt, 1975), p. 40. M. Griffin, *Seneca: a Philosopher in Politics* (Oxford, 1976), pp. 67–128. Syme, op. cit., pp. 262, 387, 552, 591.

36. On this comical episode, in which some have imagined Nero as an ancestor of economic liberalism, while others have ascribed the merit for the initiative to Seneca, see Syme, (1963), pp. 416–17.

37. Cf. P. Veyne, *La Société romaine* (Paris, 1991), pp. 85–6.

38. Seneca, fr. 19–20 ed. Haase. We shall return to this.

39. Griffin (1984), p. 190.

40. Ibid., pp. 215-20.

Notes to Prologue continued

41. The second of the Carmina Einsiedlensia, which, contrary to the latest editor (D. Korzeniewski, Hirtengedichte aus neronischer Zeit, Darmstadt 1971), I interpret as a spoof against the anti-Neronians; the poem, in fact, is neither unfinished nor mutilated: it ends by taking flight, in a climax. In it, we see a shepherd declaring to another that he has many worries, but does not want to say why. Then, pressed to explain himself, he has to confess, as though unwillingly, that civil peace and a golden age reign. (In line 33, the "triple tempest" seems to me to designate Pharsalus, Philippi, and Actium.)

42. Pliny the Younger, Letters, III, 5, 5.

43. For Lucan's original pro-Neronian stance, see, for example, Gordon Williams, Change and Decline: Roman Literature in the Early Empire, (Berkeley, 1978), p. 164; Annuaire du Collège de France, (Paris, 1985-86), pp. 734-37.

44. The only exception is an allusion (without a name) to the clemency of the person attending the spectacles in the arena, that is, the emperor (Letter 7, 5).

45. This is a decisive fact for a true understanding of Seneca's political evolution: it was of little use to ask to retire as a friend of the prince if you continued to be bound by the duties of the Senate. On this, see R. J. A. Talbert, The Senate of Imperial Rome (Princeton, 1984), p. 153; Griffin (1976), p. 36; Maurach (1991), p. 15.

46. Another decisive fact, one attested to by Pliny the Younger, Panegyric 86, 6; cf. Marcus Aurelius, Meditations I, 16.

47. Tacitus, Annals, XI, 4; Pliny the Younger, Letters, I, 5; III, 11. See K. Christ, Historia XXVII (1978): 455; P. A. Brunt, "Stoicism and the Principate" in Papers of the British School at Rome vol. 43, pp. 7-35 (Rome, 1975). K. Raaflaub, "Grundzüge, Ziele und Ideen der Opposition gegen die Kaiser" in Entretiens sur l'Antiquité classique vol. 33 (Geneva, 1986), pp. 1-63; and Squire, op. cit., pp. 24-25.

48. Tacitus, Agricola, 42, 5-6. But this may be only a verbal precaution: no prince, Tacitus says elsewhere, likes tyrannicide. The same verbal precaution appears in Epictetus, Dialogues, I, 29.

49. On the prestige of the senate in Seneca's eyes, see R. J. A. Talbert, op. cit., 25.

50. See especially Polybius, Histories, V, 9-12 and VII, 14 (on the destruction of the sanctuaries of Thermos in Aeolia during the War of the Allies).

51. Tacitus, Annals, XV, 45. On these pillages, cf. Pliny the Elder, Natural History, XVIII, 35: "Six landowners held half of Tunisia; Nero had them put to death." The confiscation Dio of Prusa speaks of (VII, 12) would also be ascribed to Nero, not Domitian.

52. Griffin (1976), p. 359. A "friend" should follow his prince on his travels according to Marcus Aurelius, Meditations, I, 16.

53. R. MacMullen, Corruption and the Decline of Rome (New Haven, 1988), p. 99. Under Tiberius, a praetorian prefect, Sejanus, seeking to oust the emperor, hesitated between two tactics: receive his clients, more numerous each day (but then Tiberius would realize that Sejanus's influence was growing); or close his doors to them (but then the same influence would decrease). (Tacitus, Annals, IV, 41, 1.)

54. On the chronology of these letters, see P. Grimal, Sénècque ou la conscience de l'Empire (Paris, 1978), 315 ff.

55. Letters, 64, 6; on god, 53, 11.

SENECA AS STOIC

1. Zeno of Kition on Cyprus is to be distinguished from Zeno of Elea.

2. On security in Seneca, see I. Hadot, Seneca und die griechisch-römische Tradition der Seelenleitung (Berlin, 1969), pp. 126-35; R. J. Newman, "Theory and Practice of Meditatio in Imperial Stoicism," in Aufstieg und Niedergang der römischen Welt, 1989, XXXVI, 3, p. 1495: "This state of security which Seneca identifies with virtue and wisdom."

3. Herodotus, *Histories*, I, 30. We may also cite Xenophon, *Life of Agesilaus*, 11: "Agesilaus was persuaded that those who lead a prosperous life are not yet happy, but that true felicity belongs only to those who die gloriously."

4. Plato, *Laws*, 840c, 733a, 661d, 662a.

5. W. Windelband, *Einführung in die Philosophie* (Berlin, 1914), 265–7.

6. To follow nature is to align oneself with one's natural needs and natural functions. We must eat to survive, not as gourmets. We must have sex to produce children. I should inform the curious reader that he will be disappointed on the latter point: Seneca speaks very little about love, and what might be called Stoic asceticism was in no way obsessed with sins of the flesh. Antiquity was the age of "venereal pleasures" (*aphrodisia* in Greek), not of the "flesh" of Christianity, the wiliest and most besetting of the temptations. No more was it the age of modern "sexuality," that uncrackable kernel of night, haunting because of its irrationality. "Venereal pleasures," on the contrary, were as simple as the appetite for food, and could be managed.

7. Sextus Empiricus, *Against the Schoolmasters*, [sic] V, 149; *Outlines of Pyrrhonism*, I, 29; III, 237; V, 156.

8. The idea that nature was kindly disposed to humanity and created for it would last a long time: the news of the terrible earthquake at Lisbon would still be a metaphysical scandal for Voltaire. This idea was overturned in the 1820s: in Shelley's *The Triumph of Life*, in Leopardi's *Zibaldone*, and in Schopenhauer, nature becomes a terrifying power, indifferent to man, murderous, and the cause of suffering. (*The Triumph of Life* is thought to have been written in 1822, but was not published until *Posthumous Poems of Percy Bysshe Shelley*, London, 1824. Leopardi composed the Zibaldone from 1817–1832. The manuscript remained unpublished until 1898, when it was issued in Florence under the title *Pensiere di varia filosofia e di bella letteratura*. It is cited according to the numbered pages of the manuscript.)

9. Cicero, *Academic Questions*, 38, 120; Porphyrius, *On Abstinence*, III, 20.

10. Leopardi, *Zibaldone*, pp. 4229, 4525.

11. J. Piaget, *La Représentation du monde chez l'enfant*, pp. 192, 302.

12. H. von Arnim, *Stoicorum veterum fragmenta*, (henceforth *SVF*) v. III, nn. 188 and 514.

13. Plotinus, *Enneads*, I, 4, 7.

14. Seneca and the other Stoics are not very clear on this point, and have given their commentators plenty of work to do. Curious readers may consult E. Bréhier, *Chrysippe* (Paris, 1950), pp. 247–8; I. Hadot (1969), p. 134, 150, 183, 132, n. 41; J. M. Rist in *Aufstieg und Niedergang der römischen Welt*, XXXVII, no. 3, p. 2000; B, Inwood, *Ethics and Human Action in Early Stoicism* (Oxford, 1985), pp. 175-81, 282, n. 193.

15. *SVF*, v. II, n. 278; v. III, n. 473 and 548.

16. This is a development of a suggestion of J. M. Rist, *Stoic Philosophy* (Cambridge, 1969), p. 88.

17. The key text is *Letter* 120, 4 ff., where the Greek word *analogia* is used. Unfortunately, this text was omitted in *SVF*, where it should have been cited in v. III, n. 229–36.

18. This is called *katekhesis* or *divulgatio famae* (*SVF*, III, n. 229). That is the reference for this sketch of sociological analysis.

19. The parallel between Seneca, *Letter* 115, 11, on "tender" children and Cicero, *Laws*, I, 47 "tender and naïve children" suggests that the implicit argument goes back to the founders of Stoicism.

20. This is the sense, simple as it is, of the words, "It is enough to want it." No reader would hesitate here, but Pohlenz thought he had to proclaim a "very Roman" doctrine of the will on Seneca's part. It is the fact that Pohlenz makes remarks on national characters, Seneca's "Roman genius" or the "Semitic character" of Zeno of Kition (see Rist (1969), p. 224.) The problem is that Zeno simply continued the work of Socrates, and that Seneca was a faithful disciple of Zeno. Forgetting that the Roman Empire's culture was Greek is to falsify it profoundly.

Notes to Seneca as Stoic *continued*

21. We have come back to the problem of which we were speaking above in n. 14. Seneca, in place of the "psychosomatic" conception of Chrysippus—judgment and body are two contemporaneous aspects of the same process—introduces a more "Aristotelian" description. The process is divided in time, with a first impulse being followed by a motion of restraint. In the more abstract parts of Stoic doctrine (ontology and logic), Seneca was but a gifted amateur, without the virtuosity of a professional—but psychology gained by it. See J. M. Rist in *Aufstieg und Niedergang der römischen Welt*, XXXVII, no. 3, p. 2000.

22. Inwood (1985), 190.

23. *SVF*, v. III, nn. 278 and 510.

24. Lucian, *Hermotimos*, 4-7.

25. I. Hadot (1969), pp. 156-7; Seneca, *On Constancy*, XIV, 1; *Consolation to Helvia*, XVI-XVII; *Consolation to Marcia*, I, XVI.

26. *SVF*, III, n. 657, 658, 662, 668.

27. Columella, *On Agriculture*, XI, 1, 11.

28. Diogenes of Babylon in *SVF*, III, 216, n. 32.

29. See also ibid., III, n. 539.

30. Musonius, fr. XVII ed. Hense.

31. In truth, the paradox may have had a different sense than what Seneca was thinking of: every vice put all the others into play, in same way that having one virtue completely was to have them all, because each implied the exercise of the other three (*SVF*, III, n. 255, 275, 280). It is not possible to be courageous without having prudence or discernment (which is what makes us understand that courage is a virtue); temperance (which distinguishes courage from bravado); and justice (which knows against whom it is necessary to manifest courage). In the same way, whoever has one vice has them all: an impious person lacks justice toward the gods (*SVF*, III, 660), but because justice implies the three other virtues, being impious is to lack all of them. Again, a mad person is ignorant of everything (ibid., III, 657 f.) Our conclusion: all or nothing.

32. If it were otherwise, Kant would not have been speaking of reality at all; he would only have formulated a pious wish, described a dream world, and preached moralizing sermons. Indeed, under the name of philosophy, a vapid literary genre flourishes that confounds reality with what it would be good for mankind to believe. Philosophy is often thought to be a kind of gospel, charged with bringing "the people of today the message they need," and to preach to them what they ought to bring themselves to believe.

33. P. Hadot *Exercises spirituels et philosphie antique.* ed. 2 (Paris, 1987).

34. Panaetius, fr. 116 ed. Van Straaten.

35. *SVF*, III, n. 501.

36. See n. 30.

37. Note deleted.

38. The premeditation of evils goes back to Chrysippus (von Arnim, op. cit., III, 482).

39. Cicero, *Tusculan Disputations*, IV, 5, 9.

40. Seneca, *Letter* 56, 6; cf. 100, 8: "a quiet, regulated tension." Cf. *SVF*, III, 111, "a well-regulated quiet," *eutaktos hesykhia* in Greek.

41. With the advent of phenomenology, this idea has been become banal. According to it, affectivity (*Gemüt*) is a form of intentionality. But G. Simmel had already made this the basis of his philosophy of love: "The person objectively regarded is completely different from the person loved." (*Das Individuum und die Freiheit*, Berlin, 1984, p. 137.) The same reasoning is used about death by René Char: "Death, in life, is immiscible, repugnant; death with death is approachable, it is nothing, even a queasy stomach creeps towards it without trembling." (*Retour amont*, Paris, 1966, p. 435.) To put it another way, to consider death as frightening or a woman as desirable, and then to see them more objectively (more comprehensively), is simply to pass from error to truth on the same object. It consists of looking in two different direc-

tions, and, consequently, seeing something else at the end of one's eyeglass. This change in direction is not a rectification in judgment, but a change of attitude, from love to indifference, or from death as one's individual future to death as the object of abstract speculation, of no concern to the body.

42. I paraphrase Hegel, *Phenomenolgy of Mind*, tr. Hyppolite, Aubier, 1941, I, 171.

43. *SVF*, I, n. 246 and IV, index *s.v. asteios*; III, n. 514: the sage washes and perfumes himself (that is, he goes to the baths; the custom of public bathing was traditional.)

44. *SVF*, III, 768.

45. The same objection applies to the case of wealth. Why doesn't the sage stoically endure poverty? Why does he accept gifts from a king? Chrysippus was not unaware of the objection (Diogenes Laertius, *Lives of the Philosophers*, VII, 189).

46. On the idea of a natural chain of beings over the course of the history of thought, see A. O. Lovejoy, *The Great Chain of Being: a Study of the History of an Idea* (Harvard, 1964).

47. [In the following, "honor" and "honorable" translate the French *honnêteté* and *honnête*, respectively. The French words and their Latin ancestors cover a considerably broader semantic field: probity, integrity, reputation; respectable, proper, worthy, virtuous. Trans.]

48. The architect Vitruvius recommends that his colleagues practice a little philosophy by not demanding excessive payment; Seneca himself says that a "religious and respectful" man will respect money deposited with him (*On the Tranquillity of the Soul*, XI, 2). In fact, temples and their attendants functioned as banks.

49. The parallel with economics is more than a game: cf. the word for value (*axia*) in *SVF*, III, 124-5 and the commentary of M. Forschner, "Das Gute und die Güter," in *Entretiens sur l'Antiquité classique* (Fondation Hardt), XXXII, 1985, pp. 325-50.

50. Cicero, *Tusculan Disputations*, V, 84.

51. *SVF*, III, 494, 496, 501; cf. I, 83, n. 361.

52. Here we must enter into a discussion of the history of philosophy because the curious reader runs the risk of finding in somewhat older books an erroneous version of the functions and of right action. To recapitulate: every living being must fulfill its functions, offices, or duties (in Greek, *kathekonta*). Every time one of them executes such an office correctly, it accomplishes a correct action or *katorthoma*. This much is clear: on the one hand, things that must be done; on the other, more or less correct execution of duties that must be fulfilled. This is found everywhere in Seneca, but in the first half of this century, a theory that was long in vogue changed all that. It was supposed that offices or *kathekonta* were middling duties, accessible to ordinary people, while *katorthomata* were more correct, more perfect duties, reserved for those aspiring to wisdom. In this account, Stoicism would have had two moralities, an elitist one involving *katorthomata* and a middling one, that of *kathekonta*. This theory responded to the desire of certain professors in German universities to inculcate in their student flocks a modest, devoted, rather conformist morality, and to rid Stoicism of its reputation as an aristocratic morality. The theory, however, is doubly false. A *katorthoma* is not a duty to be fulfilled, elitist or otherwise, but one of the innumerable actions that have fulfilled it correctly. Duty, or *kathekon*, is common to all men, whether they are simple or aspire to wisdom. There is only one morality. Simply put, most people execute their duties badly, or neglect to execute them at all, which is evidently a fault (*hamartema*), and not a right action, (*SVF* III, 500). Therefore, it can be said that every duty is the substance (*hyle*, III, 491) of right actions. Duty is a material subtance on which the corresponding actions are executed well or badly. It follows that duties are neutral goods; their substance allows for an unreservedly good action when the action is right. It even occurs (III, 559) that a madman may execute a duty correctly, purely by chance, just as a inept archer, by chance, sends his arrow to the bull's eye.

53. *SVF*, III, 500.

54. Ibid., III, 510.

55. Ibid., III, 513. For Kant, on the contrary, it is always imperative to return a deposit,

Notes to Seneca as Stoic *continued*

because if the practice of not returning it was universalized, the very idea of a deposit would be destroyed.

56. Cicero, *On Duties*, III, 90.

57. *SVF*, III, 499. Cf. Inwood (1985), p. 204.

58. *SVF*, III, 491. Seneca often speaks of *materia*, which means "matter for" or "occasion."

59. Ibid., III, 672 is an important passage for the expression "middling advantages" (*mesa*), which play a decisive role in the discussion of *kathekonta* as duties of an imagined middling wisdom. Cf. n. 107. For middling goods, see *SVF* III, 165.

60. Ibid., III, 500. For *tous arithmous* in the sense of "sum of the virtues," see *SVF* IV, Index, *s.v. arithmos*. The Latin translation can be found in Seneca, *Letter* 71, 16 (*habet numeros suos*). This apparently was a technical term in music meaning "the fullness of harmony." (Cf. A.A. Long and D. Sedley, *The Hellenistic Philosophers* (Cambridge 1987), v. II, p. 361.) See also *Letters* 71, 16, and 95, 5.

61. The scientific reason for not stealing is that one steals out of greed, greed is a passion, and every passion (even if it has achieved its ends) makes us unhappy because it is passionate, that is, a disturbance of the soul, and true happiness is the tranquillity of the soul. The scientific reason for not killing is that nature wills the survival of the human species, and one cannot be happy unless one sees everything from the point of view of nature, of god and the cosmos. Otherwise, one would rebel against death in a storm or an earthquake, rather than saying that nature could not have done otherwise.

62. H. Reiner, "Der Streit um die stoische Ethik," in *Zeitschrift für philosophische Forschung* no. XXI (1967): p. 261.

63. Seneca, *Letter* 75, 9, and compare *SVF* III, 539 *ad finem* and *Letter* 71, 4.

64. Plotinus, *Enneads*, I, 4, 10.

65. Aulus Gellius, *Attic Nights*, XIX, 1.

66. For what follows, cf. *SVF* III, 439 and 574; Epictetus, fr. 180 ed. Schweighäuser (from Aulus Gellius, XIX, 1).

67. I suspect these rather elliptic Latin words must be calques of some technical expression in Greek (e.g., *ta exothen dyskhrestemata*).

68. Cited by Plutarch, *Contradictions of the Stoics*, 26 (= *Moralia*, 10D) and *Common Notions* 8 (= *Moralia* 1062A). For an analysis of acts of judgment and the loss of tone and the pre-affects, see Bréhier (1910), pp. 247–54. When we succumb to avarice, what comes first—the pre-affect of greed or the weakening of tone? Neither one nor the other, but habit or "vice." We yield because we *are* avaricious people (that is our *habitus*), but we have become such because certain false judgments on the attractions of profit have become fixed in our soul and transformed into habit, disease, or vice, leading to a definitive loss of tone (except after long abstention from vice).

69. I. Hadot (1969), pp. 133–5, 183.

70. Ibid., 94.

71. Alas, a French resistance fighter of the years 1941 through 1944 reminisced, "Under torture, some talked without even knowing they had talked."

72. On this "transformation," see von Arnim, op. cit., III, 459. The event was recent, "sudden" when Seneca wrote this letter; it was an unexpected joy: he was close to port and everything had become easy.

73. Some have wished to connect this idea of transformation to the inescapable Posidonius: see E. Bickel, *Rheinisches Museum* 100 (1957), p. 98. But Seneca himself cites his source as Ariston. The idea of a change in form is congruent with Stoic physics and ontology.

74. In the treatise *On the Tranquillity of the Soul*, written before *Letter* 87, there is a very similar anecdote. A sense of disturbance, nausea, a feeling of having amounted to nothing when, after having renounced appearing in Rome followed by all his retinue, he felt a prick of regret crossing the train of another grandee.

75. A good man is a man "in progress," as he is portrayed by Chrysippus (*SVF* III, 510): "He who is progressing to the highest good accomplishes absolutely all his functions, neglecting none. But such a life cannot be called happy; he will not attain felicity until his middling actions (not perfect, by reason of his intention or state of soul) have in addition firmitude and the state of *hexis* [or *habitus*] and have acquired the kind of solidity proper to them." (Cf. *Letter* 71, 8: *ad summa procedens*, or 20, 6: *perduceris ad summum*.)

76. Or, better still, a modern attitude: "the transformation into consciousness of as large an experience as possible," as Malraux said. Cf. G. Simmel, *Einleitung in die Moralwissenschaft*, vol. I (Berlin, 1893) p. 357: "Opposed to eudaemonism is an attitude found in the noblest characters: an agitated existence, one that has known every joy and sorrow, to which nothing human—high or low—is alien. This seems to us of a higher value than stable, mediocre existences. It gives the feeling of having an ampler, more significant personality, a feeling that those who have tasted it once cannot do without, whatever the cost." A Goethean, Faustian ideal.

77. I. Hadot (1969), p. 119, n. 103. Seneca often speaks of glory. Some have seen something "very Roman" in this; that is to ignore the fact that the Greeks, far from being gentle esthetes, were a warrior people, enamored of glory, ambition, rivalry, and championship.

78. Rist (1969), pp. 231–55.

79. As R. Hirzel does in "Der Selbstmord," *Archiv für Religionswissenschaft* XI (1908).

80. The theater of Seneca is not comprised of "issue" plays. It reveals nonetheless a weighty, absurdist vision of the world and of man. This vision has been qualified as rhetorical, turgid, baroque, expressionist. Objects lose all usefulness within it, and have only a heavy density; the human body is so much meat to cut up, as in Caravaggio. Gross realities weigh down and preoccupy this world; their movements continue the often criminal logic of their own inertia. Murder is no more than the extension of a certain heaviness. Earth is seen from heaven or from the stars, but with nothing airy about it; on the contrary, telescoping astronomical grandeur with the human scale dehumanizes this uninhabitable earth. Thoughts stick to themselves like Sartre's "*en soi*"; they are the thoughts of a schizophrenic, of an insect, thoughts unthinkable in their density and their inevitability. Enmities have the persistence of matter. Face to face with this faceless world stands the repeated valor of Hercules, the Stoic hero, triumphant over everything that this earth, sea, and heaven contain of "the terrifying, the sinister, the infected, of the black and beastly." He triumphs, but only for a moment, until his voluntary death on the pyre, the only true triumph.

81. Simplicius, commenting on the Aristotelian *Categories* (*SVF* II, 456). The Greek words are *skhema* (form) and *tasis* (tension).

82. Obsession, ritualization, overcompensation, narcissism, defense mechanisms, political opposition, *contemptus mundi*, sense of duty, pantheistic fervor, escapism, ethical conformism, masochism, and so forth.

83. Cf. Nietzsche, *Umwertung aller Werte*, (March–December, 1884): "We have within us the potential and the elements of many personalities. Every character is a role. Most of our actions do not come from our depths, but are mere surface eruptions."

84. Malebranche, *Recherche de la vérité*, Book II, Part 3, Chapter IV.

85. Bréhier (1910), p. 198.

86. L. Wittgenstein, *Leçons et conversations*, Gallimard, collection "Idées," 154.

87. J.-B. Pontalis, *Après Freud*, (Paris, 1965), p. 266: in messianic hopes, what is important is not the future appearance of the messiah, but the present sense of hope, and this essential lasts only if the messiah's birth is always in the future. We might add that this hope will survive every disappointment. One sect in the United States was awaiting the end of the world and the salvation of the just, looking towards a fixed and very near date. They had taken precautions, storing water in vaults. On the destined evening, the sect gathered and waited. Nothing happened. Their hearts were little affected by this, an explanation for the disappointment was found, and the sect continued to prosper.

Notes to Seneca as Stoic *continued*

88. This is completely un-Platonic. For Plato, out of obedience to the gods, a person must not desert his position by committing suicide.

89. On Seneca's opinion about the immortality of the soul, see R. Hoven, *Stoïcisme et stoïciens face au problème de l'au-delà* (Liège and Paris, 1971). I am firm in my belief that the adroit and persuasive *Letter* 102 ends on a note of doubt, and a displacement of the problem. Seneca simply wanted to share his beautiful dream with his disciple in a useful way, and also to show him that greatness of soul is more important that immortality.

90. Hadot (1969), p. 56 n. 94 compares a passage of Seneca, *On Benefits* VII, 1, 6 with the Quadruple Remedy of Epicurus, p. 69, 17th ed. Usener. See also *Letter* 75, 17.

91. Platonic good itself is not a moral good or value, although this is sometimes claimed even today. "Such an interpretation takes us outside Greek thought." (Heidegger, *Questions* II, 148.)

92. M. Pohlenz, *Die Stoa: Geschichte einer geistigen Bewegung*, Göttingen (1947–1948), v. I, p. 134.

93. SVF III, 228 and 264 *ad finem*: instinct is right by nature, from which we conclude that it can be falsified by education, in the initial perversion; III, 311, 342–3; II, 1152; Cicero, *On Duties*, I, 22; Seneca, *Letters* 97, 15–16, and 108, 8, a key text, the only one to speak of "germs." God watches over the well-being of the species: Cicero, *On the Nature of the Gods*, II, 164.

94. SVF III, 689, 729 and I, 244; Epictetus, II, 4, 8 ed. Schenkl.

95. SVF III, 611; cf. I, 271; III, 494, 690, 694 ff.

96. Ibid., III, 314–26, 495.

97. Rist (1978), p. 263.

98. SVF I, 263.

99. Bréhier (1910), p. 219.

100. V. Goldschmidt *La Doctrine d'Epicuol* (Paris, 1977).

101. It is impossible to summarize in ten lines a debate that would require a volume; I can only give its general drift which, of course, is more false than general. Once a debate takes on the lines of a "great debate," we can be sure in advance that it has stepped outside the bounds of reality. I can at least give the antidote: *Letter* 109, on friendship, is not very far from Aristotle, according to whom god "has no need of friends. But the worst way for man to imitate god would be to do without friends. The true way is to have friends who, by their intercourse, supplement his finitude." See P. Aubenque, *Le Problème de l'être chez Aristote*, (Paris, 1972), 501, n. 1.

102. Rist (1978), p. 265.

103. On magnanimity, see U. Knoche, *Magnitudo animi, ein römischer Wertgedanke*, (Leipzig, 1935), and especially, R. A. Gauthier, *Magnanimité, l'idéal de la grandeur dans la philosophie païenne et la théologie chrétienne*, (Paris, 1951). See also P. Hadot (1987) 126 ff., I. Hadot, *Seneca und die Seelenleitung*, (Berlin, 1969), 128. One of the most beautiful pages of Thomas Aquinas is a transcendent encomium on greatness of soul: *Summa Theologica*, Secunda secundae, question 129, article 3, difficulty 5.

104. Besides, the problem of freedom, which is a modern one, is "a problem the Stoics did not set themselves." (J.-J. Duhot, *La Conception stoïcienne de la causalité*, Paris, 1989, p. 246.) Freedom is intuitively obvious and goes without saying.

105. On the virtue of humanity, cf. P. Veyne in *L'Homme romain*, ed. A. Giardina, Paris, 1991.

106. SVF III, 351. On manual labor by free men, III, 357. See also the previous note and Paul Veyne, "La Providence stoïcienne intervient-elle dans l'histoire?" Latomus 49 (1990), pp. 553–574.

107. Seneca, *On Benefits*, III, 20–21.

108. SVF III, 352; on contracts, I, 375.

109. These are the terms in which Seneca, along with the rest of Antiquity, poses the prob-

lem. The physician and philosopher Galen speaks in these terms of one of his teachers who had to renounce philosophy: "He had no free time any more, since his fellow-citizens had more or less compelled him to take part in the public functions of his city, seeing in him an just man, incorruptible, gentle, and approachable." (*Opera* ed. Kühn, v. 5, 41.)

110. *SVF* I, 208 and 222.

111. See J.-L. Ferrary in *Mélanges de l'École française de Rome*, (Rome, 1974), p. 763. When we inquire about the political ideas of an ancient author, it is difficult to pose the questions that were really his. We are tempted to pose the questions of our own day ("Was Juvenal on the right or the left?"), or questions on too grand a scale ("Were the Stoics for or against Roman imperialism?"). In fact, when the Stoic Posidonius attacked the "demagogue" who tried to deliver Athens from its Roman protectorate in 87 B.C.E., what he detested in this "demagogy" was its internal and external "disorder." He saw no further than the ends of his own morality. Similarly, when the Stoics surrounding Cleomenes or the Gracchi encouraged land redistribution at the expense of the big property holders, they were less "revolutionary" than they were striving after virtue; as good citizens, emulators of Sparta, they wanted to return to ancient simplicity.

112. Anonymous commentary on the *Theaetetus* on papyrus, cited in Long and Sedley (1987), v. I, p. 350 and II, p. 348.

113. H. Grassl, *Sozialökonomische Vorstellungen in der kaiserzeitlichen griechischen Literatur* (Wiesbaden, 1982).

114. K. H. Schwarte, "Salus Augusti publica" in *Bonner Festgabe für Johannes Straub* (Bonn, 1977), p. 229.

115. O. Gigon in *Entretiens sur l'Antiquité classique* (Fondation Hardt), XXXII, 1985. There has been much discussion about this Posidonius; Pohlenz's ideas about him are now discredited; the decisive turning point was the article by H. Strassburger, "Poseidonios on Problems of the Roman Empire," *Journal of Roman Studies* 55 (1965), pp. 40–53.

116. Only Carneades dared to wax ironic on this topic (Cicero, *The Republic*, III, 24): if the word justice has any meaning in this world, we would have to condemn conquests, yet we glorify them. Carneades is not casting blame in saying this: he is demonstrating the inanity of lofty words. See also J.-L. Ferrary, *Philhellélenisme et impérialisme*, (Rome, 1988), p. 359.

117. This historical pride should not be confused with nativist patriotism. Having destroyed Carthage and Corinth, the Romans established Italian colonies on the spot. Under the empire, the descendants of those Italian colonists would assume the glory of the old historic names of Greek Corinth and Phoenician Carthage, whose successors they considered themselves to be.

118. I have cited the sources in "La Providence stoïcienne: intervient-elle dans l'histoire?" in *Latomus* (1989).

119. The word infinite does not seem very Stoic. It does not seem to me that the Stoic god was infinite: the world is not, and he did not create the world. The world is his god-brain, god-organizer; they exist conjointly, eternally. The world is a huge living animal, suspended for eternity in the midst of a void that *is* infinite. From *Genesis* to the nonsense recounted by some current-day physicists about the big bang, the idea of god as creator is peculiar to Christianity; on the scale of the universe, it is a very "provincial" notion.

120. This passage, *Letter* 95, 50, should be compared with *SVF* II, 1176, where Chrysippus' *pote* corresponds to Seneca's *interim*. There was, therefore, no need to correct Seneca's text, and we have restored it.

121. *SVF* II, 937 and III, 191. Cf. I. Hadot (1969), 100.

122. Duhot (1989), especially p. 262 ff.

123. The claim is often made that Stoicism was the reaction of "the individual lost in a world grown too large" after the conquests of Alexander. That is a historically false vision of a very compartmentalized world, not to mention an oversimplified notion of psychosociological causation. Moreover, "individualism" can mean anything or nothing at all. Finally, this

Notes to Seneca as Stoic *continued*
reasoning would be easy to invert: the stifling system of the narrowly circumscribed Greek city-states ought to have caused the birth of a movement of individual escapism.

124. Here Seneca is speaking of the fall of overgrown empires, but he is also thinking of a Stoic physical theory: the equilibrium between the four elements, guaranteed by Providence, is constantly menaced. One day, fire, the most powerful, will win out (already there are volcanos) and overthrow the other three, in other words, the cosmos. That will mark the end of one cosmic cycle. But the indestructible god (he is made of a "subtle" fire, that is, finer and harder to grasp than our fire) will reestablish a new cosmos beginning with the elements, for a new cycle of the eternal return. He will reestablish it according to a plan identical to the preceding one because it would be ill-advised to modify a plan that was as perfect as it could be.

The reader will wonder what connection there could possibly be between this physics of equilibrium and a politics of equilibrium among human nations. From our point of view, evidently none, except by analogy and metaphor. But precisely the rigor of Stoic thought is often only verbal. Its monolithism "a unique, but fluid conception," in the words of Duhot (1989), pp. 130–3, is assured by tightening down bolts that are often mere metaphors.

125. The truth in question is opposed to our reason and our capacity to judge, limited by our knowledge, extending no farther than the present. This truth is the one that bears on the future, when the design of providence will appear. This kind of equivalence between "truth" and "future" derives, I imagine, from the Aristotelian problem of "future contingents." Can a proposition relating to a reality yet to come already be true, if the future is contingent?

126. Therefore the sage, having made his reservations, will never be disappointed, whether he fails or succeeds. See Inwood (1985), p. 214.

127. The pilot fails because certain evils (the storm, for instance) are the flip side of a good (their winds cleanse the atmosphere in order to drive out epidemics). Cato fails because it was providential to secure for humanity that prop of old age, the Caesarian monarchy.

128. Seneca, fr. 19–20 ed. Haase.

EPILOGUE

1. A few words on Stoic politics. The sect, as such, had no affirmed preference for a given regime. Long before, three centuries before Seneca, before the Roman conquest of Greece, in the time of the Hellenistic cities and a still-living dream of ancient Sparta, Chrysippus and his followers preferred the Spartan constitution because it was austere, close to natural simplicity, and because it blended harmoniously, in their opinion, monarchy, aristocracy, and democracy. (See *SVF* III, 700.) This was the basis for the support given by the Stoics Sphairos and Blossios to the reforms of Cleomenes at Sparta and, in Rome, those of the Gracchi, who were attempting to return to ancient simplicity by reconstructing a civic body founded on agriculture and the redistribution of land among citizen farmers. But all that was past. In the meantime, prior to the victory of Caesarism, the ideal of the good king had been developed, furnishing themes of thought, if not a properly political doctrine, to almost all the sects. We should, however, not reconstruct history mechanically, taking as theses what were merely the themes of daydreams or of speculation. Nor should we make mechanical and lazy use of the word "ideology." Philosophy began to have political influence and made its apology for Caesarism only after Caesarism had been established, leaving room for no alternative. (See K. Brugmann in *Entretiens sur l'Antiquité classique* (Fondation Hardt), v. XXXII, p. 280.) As for the Stoic senatorial opposition, it was not so much applying some political philosophy as it was wrapping its nostalgia for an age of noble ascendancy, heightened by a blaze of imagination and the warmth of conviction, in the banner of philosophy. See Brunt (1975) and Raaflaub (1986).

2. Tacitus, *Annals*, XV, 23.

3. He was also reproached for accepting gifts in the redistribution Nero made of the estate

of Britannicus, who was thought to have died from disease (Tacitus, *Annals* XIII, 18; it will be recalled that sharing legacies among one's friends was common conduct in Rome). Seneca seems to want to justify his acceptance of these gifts in *On Benefits* I, 15, 6; II, 18, 6-7; II, 20-21. The admirable Demetrius, however, refused Caligula's gifts (ibid., VII, 11, 1).

4. *Letter* 73, 4; on the Forum and defending his friends, *Letters* 8, 6, and 28, 6. He withdrew from all social life (Tacitus, XIV, 56 and XV, 45), while Thrasea continued to aid his clients (XVI, 22). In 62, Nero had two exiles put to death to insure the security of his throne—they were likely to become focuses for rebellion because one was an arrogant Stoic, and the other could conceal his plotting beneath apparent leisure (XIV, 57).

5. E. Cizek, *L'Époque de Néron et ses controverses idéologiques*, (Leiden, 1972), p. 155. *Letter* 73 dates from the second trimester of the year 64, a little before the great fire of Rome. See Grimal (1978), pp. 223, 453.

6. Philostratus, *Life of Apollonius*, IV, 39. The events took place during the consulate of Luccius Telesinus in 66. The words "in festive garb" mean, ironically, that he was wearing a crown, as drinkers, as well as musicians did.

7. Tacitus, *Annals*, XIV, 48 and XVI, 24. Under a "good" prince (and even, in the case of Trajan, the "best of princes," as he was officially proclaimed), the flattery was the same. Pliny's panegyric on Trajan is an "extraordinary masterpiece of hypocritical adulation, such as we hear today in totalitarian countries." (G. C. Picard, *La gloire des Sedatii* [Paris, 1990], p. 100).

8. Tacitus, *Annals*, XVI, 28. The same praise for Nero as the guarantor of national independence occurs in the *Carmina Einsiedlensia*. One or two centuries later, Celsus would call on Christians to help the emperor defend the empire (one wonders how Christians could have set about doing this), instead of being separatists. The origin of the phrase "peace and liberty" is religious: the public priests asked the gods for these favors for Rome. Seneca's use of a demonstrative (*Letter* 73, 5: "the benefit of *this* peace," meaning the present state of peace) is equally sacramental, in this phraseology, as the English demonstrative in "this country," (i.e., England). In clichéd French we say "notre beau pays." One spoke thus of the "felicity of this reign," meaning the present regime.

9. For prominent people to perform on stage, in the Circus or in the arena, was considered a scandal in Rome, but it was nonetheless in the process of becoming usual; examples multiply from the time of Sulla on, that is for a century and a half before. Lawgivers tried in vain (e.g., a decree of the Senate in 19) to forbid or limit the practice. In reality, this was less a matter of some abuses of the norm than of combat between the old norm and a more modern practice, which took its example from Greece, where prominent people appeared in athletic and musical contests (Cornelius Nepos, *Lives*, pref. 5). One fact proves that the scandal was not scandalous any more: among the nobles who appeared, like Nero, on the stage was no other than Thrasea, head of the Stoic oppostion (Tacitus, *Annals*, XVI, 21). To conclude: what seems a great oddity to us moderns, namely, an emperor singing on stage, was no longer strange in Rome, and was no longer deemed scandalous by at least one faction of public opinion. The problem lay elsewhere: for a noble to sacrifice his standing in public was democratic; for an emperor to do so was a fatal act of tyranny because he forced himself on the public.

10. *Letters* 14, 7-8; 29, 1; 103, 5. For Isidorus, see Suetonius, *Nero*, 39, 3. For the streetcorner Cynics, see M. Rostovtseff, *Histoire économique et sociale de l'Empire romain* (Collection "Bouquins"), 1988, 97-9; *Cambridge Ancient History* vol. XI (1954), p. 10 n.1; Alciphron, *Letter* II, 38 (In the Loeb edition, p. 144); Herodian, *History*, vol. 25; D. R. Dudley, *A History of Cynicism* (London, 1937), p. 143; Johannes Hahn, *Der Philosoph und die Gesellschaft: Selbstverständis öffentliches Auftreten und populäre Erwartungen in der höhen Kaiserzeit*. Stuttgart (1989), 25 and 172.

11. On the virtue of precaution (*cautio, eulabeia*), *Letters* 22, 7-8; 28, 7; 29, 8; 85, 26; Horace, *Odes* III, 3; *On the Tranquillity of the Soul*, XIV, 3.

12. Epictetus I, 19, 3. *On the Tranquillity of the Soul*, IV, 7-8; Chrysippus in *SVF* III, 627. Cf.

Letters 55, 5 and 85, 38, and the reciprocal idea in 94, 67. The principle is that it is impossible to withdraw from the cosmos (*Letter* 68, 2).

13. Tacitus, *Annals*, VI, 29; cf. Mommsen (1899), pp. 924, 934, 987, 1009.

14. Killing oneself in order to escape a tyrant was a justifiable motive for suicide in the eyes of the Stoics (*SVF* III, 768 *ad finem*).

15. Always the same realism: sometimes the accused would kill himself without even waiting for a sentence of death that was probable but not certain. The prince would then say the accused, whom he was going to pardon, had acted too precipitously. Furthermore, people decided whether a suicide was courageous or cowardly according to the method of death chosen—the sword was courageous, jumping out a window, cowardly.

16. *On Benefits*, VII, 20. The case of the murder of Caesar is not comparable (ibid., II, 19–20). Cf. *Hercules Furens*, 923; *On Benefits*, VII, 15, 2.

17. Practically speaking, the senate was the high court for crimes committed by senators. Cf. Mommsen (1899), p. 252.

18. Ibid., 260–9.

19. Tacitus, *Annals*, XV, 62–4. Veyne adopts the French translation by Burnouf.

20. Seneca wanted to bestow legacies on his friends according to custom, but the officer feared he might annul the legacy always made to the emperor or that he might add maledictions against Nero that would become known after the public reading of the will.

21. A philosopher instructs his disciples by his teaching and his own way of living. This was a current and respected view, and Seneca's words were in no way pompous.

22. Paulina was asking for one of her husband's freedmen to kill her.

23. This text has not survived.

24. There were illustrious precedents. After Brutus's suicide, his wife, the daughter of the Stoic Cato, killed herself by swallowing burning coals. Under Tiberius, the wives of two senators accused of lèse-majesté joined their husbands in voluntary death (Tacitus, *Annals*, VI, 29). In 42, the famous Arria made her suicide an example to her husband (Pliny the Younger, *Letters* III, 16); after Seneca's death, the daughter of that same Arria, none other than Thrasea's wife, wanted to kill herself with him (Tacitus, XVI, 34).

25. Hemlock; so Socrates died.

26. Jupiter the Liberator is the philosophical interpretation Seneca gives to one of the functions of the supreme Stoic god, whom the philosophers themselves often call Jupiter for convenience, bowing to popular usage. The god of the cosmos, having given men reason and the seeds of virtue, opens the path of liberation to them, and allows them to realize that because death is nothing, they make manifest and take possession of their liberty through rational suicide. There was, to be sure, a Jupiter the Liberator in Greece and Rome, the object of a public cult in certain cities, but he has nothing to do with our topic. That Jupiter had liberated a city from enemies wishing to enslave it. In any event, the Stoics were persuaded that the gods of the people and their names were an imperfect representation of the true gods, not entirely lacking in truth. For instance, they thought that Neptune was an imperfect image of one of the secondary divinities, the one charged with controlling water, one of the four elements; Hera (Juno to the Romans) was air (*aer* in Greek), as her name indicated! It is therefore probable that here Seneca is playing on the Jupiter the Liberator of common belief, by giving him his true nature: not the god who saved some city or other, but the true god, who gives to humanity as a whole the ability to liberate itself thanks to wisdom and to prove its liberty, should the case arise, by voluntary or heroic death.

27. A. D. Nock, *Conversion: the old and the new in religion from Alexander the Great to Augustine of Hippo* (Oxford, 1933), p. 297. Syme, op. cit., p. 538. Tacitus recounts Petronius's suicide (*Annals*, XVI, 18–19). On Petronius's Epicureanism, cf. *Revue des études anciennes*, LXVI (1964), p. 446.

CHRONOLOGY

I. STOICISM: FROM GREECE TO THE ROMAN EMPIRE
(All dates are B.C.E. Seneca was born around 1 C.E.)

Around 1400 — Hercules's (obviously legendary) lifetime. The Stoics wanted to believe in his existence and make him the first of their sages.

592–522 — An oriental potentate, Cambyses, King of the Persians, tries to conquer Africa. For Seneca, he typifies the insane conqueror.

Around 504 — Heraclitus of Ephesus founds the "materialist" physics of a universe in a perpetual state of transformation, with Fire-Reason as its intelligent artisan. The Stoics were Heracliteans in this sense.

490–480 — More madmen, the Persian kings Darius and Xerxes, try to conquer Greece.

458 — In *Agamemnon*, Aeschylus makes Zeus the sovereign deity and the master of justice.

399 — Socrates drinks the hemlock. The Stoics owed much to his thinking.

348 — Death of Plato; philosophy had become a rigorous technique.

334-323 — Alexander the Great's conquests. In the next three centuries, Greek culture would extend from Samarkand to Rome and Morocco, where Juba of Mauretania was both Berber king and Greek historian.

Stoicism was the creation of the Hellenistic period, running from the death of Alexander the Great (323) to the ever-greater conquests of Rome (197–30). This was no longer "classical" Greek civilization, but it was the opposite of a period of decadence. Hellenistic civilization (formerly called "Alexandrian") was the "universal" civilization of the time, resembling the French eighteenth century in its refinement. The *Venus of Melos* and the *Victory of Samothrace* are from this period.

322 — Death of Aristotle. The Stoics refined their own doctrines thanks to him, and in opposition to him.

312 — Zeno of Kition in Cyprus, the founder of Stoicism, arrives in Athens.

187

272   The Romans attain mastery of the entire Italian peninsula.

270   Death of Epicurus, whose sect would be the twin and rival of Stoicism.

262   Cleanthes succeeds Zeno as head of the Stoic sect.

260   Chrysippus of Soloi (in Sicily, across from Cyprus) arrives in Athens. He was the third founder of Stoicism and its most productive thinker.

Around 250   Eratosthenes estimates the circumference of the earth at twenty-five thousand miles. Archimedes accomplishes the quadrature of the parabola.

Around this period, a more or less apocryphal literature maintains the tradition (or embellishes the legend) of the doctrine of Pythagoras (dead around 500).

Around 220   The Roman Fabius Pictor writes the history of Rome in Greek.

197–189   Rome establishes its hegemony over Greece and the Greek East.

152   The Spanish city, Corduba, where Seneca will be born, becomes a Roman city.

The Roman West will become Hellenised, but in the Latin language.

146   Rome destroys Carthage and gains supremacy over the western Mediterranean.

144   The Greek Stoic Panaitios (or Panaetius) comes to live in Rome.

78   Cicero attends the lectures of the Greek Stoic Posidonius in Rhodes.

Despite their patriotism, the Romans experienced no particular discomfort in having as their culture that of another people, the Greeks; it *was* culture, pure and simple, and they perceived it as Greek only on points with which they disagreed, where they could comfort their inferiority complex toward Hellenism with a local disdain. Cato the Elder expressed his nationalism in a purely Greek literary form with perfect candor, and Seneca would be both Hellenized and, at times, xenophobic.

II. GOOD AND BAD EXAMPLES FROM ROME'S NATIONAL PAST (All dates are B.C.E.)

Around 507   Horatius Cocles defends Rome against its Etruscan neighbors; Mucius Scaevola stoically defies the Etruscan king.

269   Fabricius refuses the corrupting gifts of the Greek king Pyrrhus, the enemy of Rome.

250   Keeping his word given to the enemy, Regulus hands himself over to the Carthaginians, who torture him to death.

184   Scipio, having saved Rome from Hannibal's attacks, goes into voluntary exile in order not to endanger republican liberty. The censor Cato the Elder attempts to restore the austerity of ancient mores.

The beginnings of political and forensic eloquence. Development of a Latin theater abounding in the wise sayings Seneca loves to quote.

133   The Romans destroy Numantia, last stronghold of Spanish independence. According to Seneca, both sides were equally virtuous.

133–121   Agrarian conflicts. The Gracchi (demogogues or virtuous?) try to restore a civic body composed of small rural landholders.

106–100   The demogogue Marius, Rome's savior when it was menaced by an invasion of peoples from the north, is all-powerful.

94   Rutilius, unjustly accused of embezzlement, stoically refuses to defend himself and goes into self-imposed exile.

88   A crucial date—civil war breaks out between the demagogue Marius and the cruel oligarch Sulla. Six troubled decades of civil war followed with, conflicts of ambition, luxury, and decadence.

82–79   Dictatorship of Sulla and the first great atrocities, the proscriptions.

78–50   Pompey is the man on top, ambitious but good-natured. His prestigious conquests in Turkey and Syria are owed to his personal ambitions. He allows the forms of republican legality to continue to exist.

63   Cicero, as senator, has a reputation as a brilliant mind and great orator, but little influence. Nonetheless, he crushes a coup d'état attempted by Catilina and his clan.

61   The scandalous acquittal of the demagogue Clodius, a symbol of the epoch's immorality.

60   Caesar's powers grow; he agrees with Pompey to a secret sharing of influence.

58–52   Caesar conquers Gaul; Seneca will approve.

50   Civil war breaks out between Caesar and Pompey, who is vanquished and killed in 48.

48–44   The clement dictatorship of Caesar. Cicero writes his philosophical treatises, which are Platonic, with a strong influence from Stoicism. He is the greatest Roman orator and prose writer.

46   Partisans of Pompey continue the struggle against Caesar in Spain and Africa. They are beaten and one of them, Cato (a Stoic and great-grandson of the homonymous censor of 184), seeing the death of freedom and liberty, commits suicide. By a virtuous error, he had incorrectly understood that each side was equally faulty.

44   Caesar is murdered by Brutus. Seneca, as a monarchist, does not approve of this tyrannicide—the time for liberty had come and gone.

42   Mark Antony, Caesar's right-hand man, and Octavian (the future Emperor Augustus), Caesar's adopted son, form an alliance and set Italy awash in the blood of their proscriptions. They crush the Caesarians and divide the world: for Octavian, the Latin West; for Antony (allied with Cleopatra, the Greek queen of Egypt), the Greek East.

The literary apogee of Rome. The great Epicurean poet Lucretius had died, but Virgil reveals himself as the greatest Latin poet, along with Horace, and in the next generation, Ovid. Seneca often cites these classics.

31   War breaks out between Octavian and Antony; defeat, the deaths of Antony and Cleopatra, and reunification of the Roman Empire. The rule of the Caesars replaces the oligarchic "republic," putting an end to the fierce civil wars between competing magnates. Relieved, majority opinion becomes monarchist. Seneca, who had no roots in the old oligarchy, will also be a monarchist. Octavian becomes emperor, naming himself Augustus.

The Mediterranean had become a Roman lake. Augustus's nephews (by blood or adoption) bring the Alpine and Danubian regions into submission. The Rhine, the Danube, the Euphrates, and the Sahara are the frontiers of the bilingual Roman Empire. The Italian peninsula (whose inhabitants, if they are not slaves, are "Roman citizens") is its metropolis. The standard of living is close to that of the present-day Middle East.

III. SENECA AND HIS AGE
(All dates except as noted are c.e.)

31 B.C.E—14 c.e   Reign of Augustus, now a practitioner of clemency. His advisors are his son-in-law, the honest Agrippa (grandfather of Agrippina), and the effeminate Maecenas.

Under Augustus, Seneca the Elder of Corduba comes to cultivate eloquence in Rome.

Around 1   His son, Seneca, is born in Corduba.

4   Augustus adopts Tiberius, who adopts Germanicus, father of Agrippina, who will be Nero's mother.

14   Tiberius succeeds Augustus.

14–19   Seneca studies rhetoric and philosophy, and converts to philosophy, going through a Pythagorean period.

31   Tiberius savagely represses the ambitions of his prefect, Sejanus. His character changes and "purges" of the senate multiply.

37   Caligula, son of Germanicus, who died before taking the throne, and Agrippina's brother, succeeds Tiberius. Seneca publishes the *Consolation to Marcia* which, however, is not his first book. The reign quickly becomes bloody. Seneca will evoke the torture of Julius Canus, Julius Graecinus, and of Ptolemy of Mauretania, son of Juba. (N)

Around 39   Seneca, a knight, is elected quaestor and so enters the Senate.

41   Caligula is murdered; Claudius succeeds him. The emperor's freedmen are in control, among them Polybius. "Purges" in the senate and palace intrigues.

Claudius exiles Seneca to Corsica, where he writes the *Consolation to Helvia* and the *Consolation to Polybius*.

44   Claudius conquers southern England; one day, Seneca will draw part of his fortune from it.

48   Anticipating the major policy of the following century, Claudius proposes admitting Rome's provincial subjects to Roman citizenship, scandalizing Seneca.

Around 49   Seneca is named tutor to the young Nero, son of Agrippina and adopted son of Claudius. (N)

52   Saint Paul appears before the tribunal of Seneca's brother in Thessalonica.

54   Death of Claudius. Nero succeeds him because Britannicus, his son by birth, is younger than Nero, who is sixteen.

54–59   The "five good years" of Nero. Agrippina is quickly removed from power, which is exercized by the prefect Burrus and the prince's counsellors or friends, among whom is Seneca.

55   Britannicus is poisoned.

May–June, 55   Seneca is suffect consul. (N)

56   Seneca publishes *On Clemency*.

58   Condemnation and exile of Suillius, who had fiercely attacked Seneca's mores and wealth; Seneca will justify them in *On the Happy Life*.

59   Nero has Agrippina assassinated.

60   Nero establishes a Greek-style competition, the Neronian Games.

62   A senator, accused of lèse-majesté, is only exiled, not sentenced to death. Burrus dies; the prefect succeeding him will be Nero's evil spirit. Burrus' death causes Seneca to lose all influence. Already excused on account of age from his duty to sit in the senate, Seneca asks Nero to be relieved of his functions as a "friend of the prince." Nero refuses.

62–63   Nero's tyranny and "cult of personality" are unchained.

62 or 64   Opening of Nero's public baths and a Greek-style gymnasium.

64   Nero is a competitor and winner in a musical contest in the Greek city of Naples. He as yet does not dare to exhibit himself in public in Rome itself.

To replenish the treasury, emptied by his building program and his largesse to the plebeians of Rome, Nero has the riches of the temples pillaged. Seneca again asks Nero to let him retire; refused, he shuts himself up in solitude.

July 64   The Great Fire in Rome, caused accidentally. By this date, Seneca had already written about half of the *Letters*.

65   A conspiracy takes shape. Nero is to be assassinated in April as he exhibits himself as a singer and musician. Word of the plot leaks out. Seneca, who had nothing to do with it, is ordered by Nero to kill himself.

June 9, 68   Nero is removed from the throne and has himself killed.

89   The Emperor Domitian, another tyrant, expels the philosophers from Rome, among them the Stoic Epictetus.

180   Death of Marcus Aurelius, emperor and, privately, a Stoic.

After 260   Stoicism is extinct, but incorporated to an extent in Neoplatonist philosophers like Plotinus.